CW00828116

The Future Role and Structure of Local Government

Edited by

Guy Hollis, Gail Ham and Mark Ambler

Series editors: John Benington and Mike Geddes

LONGMAN

Published by Longman Industry and Public Service
Management, Longman Group UK Ltd, 6th Floor,
Westgate House, The High, Harlow, Essex CM20 1YR
Telephone: Harlow (0279) 442601; Fax: Harlow (0279) 444501;
Telex: 81491 Padlog

© Longman Group UK Ltd 1992

A catalogue record for this book is available from the British Library

ISBN 0-582-21285-5

Printed and bound in Great Britain by
Dotesios Ltd, Trowbridge, Wiltshire.

Longman Local Government Library

The Warwick Series on Local Economic and Social Strategies

This series is designed to contribute to the ability of policy makers and managers in local government to meet the challenges of the 1990s. The focus is on strategic questions of local economic and social change. The series deals with issues which confront local government (and local public services more widely) at the level of corporate or inter agency strategy (for example, industrial restructuring, Europeanisation, ageing, poverty, transport, the environment). These issues are challenging local government to move beyond its traditional and primary role as a distributor and deliverer of services and to explore the potential for influence in new economic roles (as a major employer, investor and purchaser within the local economy) and in its political and ideological roles (as a democratically elected body, with a mandate to represent the interests of the whole community).

The series will present the results of applied research and innovative policy initiatives in key areas of local government strategy, policy making, organisation and management. Its primary aim is to contribute to the development of good practice in local government policy making and corporate management, but it will also contribute to a better conceptual understanding of the role and functioning of the local state.

We hope this series will stimulate a lively and critical exchange of ideas and experience about policy making in the public sector. The editors welcome contributions to the debate from local policy makers, managers and academics.

John Benington and Mike Geddes

Contents

Introduction

Robin Wendt, Secretary, Association of County Councils

The structure of local government is, or should be, more than a simple administrative mechanism. Local government is in reality part of the system of government in the United Kingdom, sharing with central government the rights and responsibilities that go with elective democracy. If the UK had a written constitution it is inconceivable that the structure if not the duties of local government would not feature in it. A local authority needs to have and exercise 'authority' as well as being 'local'.

The present review of local government structure in England, Scotland and Wales will no doubt be seen by future historians as one of several attempts by twentieth century governments to get structure 'right' for the circumstances of the day. For that it is to be commended and supported. Not for the first time however structure is being considered without reference to role and function. There is no coherent attempt to fit 'form' to 'function', still less to relate structure to the wider issue of central–local relationships or the broader issue still of the place of UK local government in Europe.

The succeeding chapters of this book illustrate these points with great clarity. For over 1000 years local government has had a constitutional role. This role has changed enormously, as local government institutions have adapted to changing needs. Despite a decade of controversy about local government that role undeniably still exists.

Structure designers must ensure that the local government of the future will continue to have an active constitutional role. This will come through the contribution local government can make to pluralism and participation; through its ability to provide a focus for community identity (a key theme of the current review); and through its contribution to the diffusion of power in the political system. The high constitutional issues which underlie the review will not be adequately served unless the structure that emerges fully reflects these key principles.

The same point applies in the European dimension. UK local government must be able to take its place effectively in the European Community. Its voice must be heard when EC policies affecting local services are determined. It must be able to lobby effectively for EC funds. It must be able to stand alongside local governments in other EC states, and to command trust and respect from the EC and its institutions. The structure of local government is critical in enabling these requirements to be met. A structure which inhibited UK local government in its dealings with the EC would not be viable.

Linking structure to function, in terms of service responsibilities, should be a necessary part of any structural review. It has been strongly and widely argued that the present review should not proceed without an agreed definition of the functions which local government should perform, and an understanding that these will continue broadly unchanged throughout the review. That is an entirely sensible and logical position to adopt. Why then is it so difficult for this seemingly obvious point to be accepted?

The answer reflects a strand of thinking, common in governmental circles, that local government is to be seen not as a coherent whole with an integrated set of responsibilities, but as a series of parts each undertaking functions laid on it by different elements of central government and naturally subject to change over time. 'Local government is what we say it is and it does what we want it to do', the argument might be summarised. There is clearly some validity in this approach, not least the recognition that function cannot be static. It betrays however a view of local government as being little more than an agent of the centre, and as having no independent locus of its own. That argument therefore will not do.

It would come as no surprise if, before the current review has gone too far, issues of function came to assume greater prominence in the debate than they have to date. What do the growing responsibilities of local government for community care and the links with the housing service mean for local government structure? Of what relevance is the increasing emphasis on environmental protection? What do the continuing changes in education management mean for local government? Does the structure properly take account of the growing regulatory role of local authorities? What are the cumulative implications of these developments and others for local government structure? What further changes can be expected during the next decade?

To produce a coherent answer to these questions is itself a formidable task. Add to it the evaluation of the other key criteria for assessing structure — reflection of community identities and interests, assessment of the costs and benefits of change and the financial viability of authorities — and it becomes clear that the wisdom of Solomon will be needed to produce a structure that is not only right for its time but will be robust for the future.

The following chapters shed further light on all these key issues. They underline the constitutional importance of local government and the ways in which its role is changing. They address square-on the issue of function. They confirm that revising the structure of local government is no easy job. No structure fits perfectly to the criteria. A variety of outcomes is desirable and perhaps inevitable. Outcomes will however be more informed, and more likely to last, if they reflect the policy analysis in these chapters.

1 The constitutional role of local government

Central government is not God nor local government Adam
(Kingdom 1991)

Introduction

The British system of local government is recognised to be idiosyncratic, not based on any clear principles, and constantly thought to be in need of change (Birch 1990). But, as Burke observed, 'a state without the means of some change is without the means of its conservation'. True to this dictum, the Government has commissioned a review of the structure of local government, suggesting that there is a case for simplification so as to improve accountability and increase cost-effectiveness.

It is a well-accepted principle of organisation design that there is no one right way to structure organisations. The component elements of structure should be consistent with an organisation's internal and external position and provide for 'fit' with its purpose and its strategy (Galbraith and Kazanijan 1986, Mintzberg 1983). Local government today is a complex business, involving expenditure of some £60bn per annum on many diverse functions and activities which have a direct impact upon the lives of every citizen throughout the country. To identify optimal structural arrangements suiting this diversity of function and circumstance presents a considerable challenge, and requires significant issues of public policy to be fully aired during the course of the review.

Local government is more than the management of services. It is part of the country's system of government as a whole. Uniquely among institutions of government, it embodies local democracy. The task of designing the structure of local government thus has a fundamental constitutional significance. It concerns 'the location, conferment, distribution, exercise and limitation of authority and power among the organs of a state' (de Smith and Brazier 1990). The review of structure must therefore take as its starting point the constitutional role of local government and its democratic purpose.

This chapter surveys how the role of local government has evolved from earliest times to the present day, as the British constitution has itself evolved. It identifies the challenges facing local government in its constitutional role now and into the next century. Against this background, it suggests some fundamental design principles, implying a continuing and active role for local government in future constitutional development, which should guide the review's conclusions on structure. Chapter 2 considers how the traditional style of local government is changing, and needs to change, if it is to sustain such a role in the future.

Origins

England, from very early times, and after it the United Kingdom, has always been a unitary state, in which any local government has been constitutionally subordinate to the Crown in Parliament. This is sometimes taken to mean that local government is, has always been, and by extension should remain, entirely subservient to central government. In fact, as in so much in the British constitution, the true position is not so straightforward. The development of both institutions must be understood as manifestations of government.

In recent history, institutions of government have multiplied so that today it is usual to distinguish not only 'local' and 'central' government (much of which is in fact carried out away from the 'centre') but also government 'beyond the centre', in supranational institutions. This growth of government is a relatively modern phenomenon; for a very long time, government for most people was overwhelmingly local, carried out by local institutions and inherently very diverse. The term 'local government' was coined in the nineteenth century, when government as a whole began substantially to expand in scope and when many of the features of modern local government were laid down. Nonetheless, the Victorians' reforming zeal did not extend to wholesale abolition of old institutions, even though they had to deal with many new problems. Instead existing arrangements were gradually adapted to meet new needs. Thus the shires, for example, are very old institutions which continue to this day, so that by now their resilience is worthy of comment in itself.

The shires' origins lie in Anglo-Saxon arrangements established in the ninth and tenth centuries to meet fundamental needs: defence, revenue collection, and the establishment of royal influence and control over law and order. The boundaries of many of today's principal administrative areas were formalised during this period. The shire structure (and its now abandoned sub-division, the hundred) were superimposed on local and (it is assumed) ancient arrangements among formerly tribal or family communities for settling disputes and maintaining peace. The shire assemblies were simultaneously the recipients of royal writs containing the king's command, and the bodies competent to transact local business. The king appointed an official in each shire (the 'shire-reeve' or sheriff) to act as his agent in the locality and supervise the conduct of local affairs.

This early administrative system was retained by the Norman kings (as the parallel French name 'county' implies) who found it readily adaptable to the requirements of the feudal system and the assertion of the Crown's place as the unique source of all temporal authority. Norman control over Saxon shires was achieved by the building of castles in the centre of every shire and in other strategic sites, and through the practice of sending a body of itinerant judges to sit in local courts as the king's representative. This served a dual purpose of raising revenue (since justice was a profitable business) and ensuring that the king's justice was firmly established as superior to, and subsuming, local laws and customs.

Shire arrangements proved remarkably robust over the centuries. They were sufficiently flexible to support both 'centralising' Tudor and Stuart monarchs, as well as Hanoverian administrations largely uninterested in domestic affairs. Probably the most significant development in this respect was the emergence within the administrative framework of the Justices of the Peace. The administrative side of justice continued to be handled by sheriffs as paid officials of the Crown, but during the thirteenth century, medieval kings increasingly brought local landowners into the decision-making processes of law, order and local administration, as the cheapest and most satisfactory way of organising effective government locally. To entrust it to great lords would have been to invite civil war and a weakening of the monarchy. To commit it entirely to local officials dependent upon local fees for their livelihood would have opened the door to an unacceptable degree of corruption and potential oppression. To give it to salaried officials was not affordable. The Crown could not have sustained the cost on private income, and taxation would have required the consent to precisely those whose cooperation was instead more effectively secured through collaboration.

As the principle of representation to grant taxation gradually emerged, burgesses from corporate towns and 'knights from the shires' together matched importance in local matters with increasing importance in wider affairs through the growth of Parliament, where together they formed an essential part of the 'community of the realm'. The first requests from towns desiring freedom to pay dues directly to the

Crown (and hence not to the sheriff) had appeared in 1130. Gradually more and more towns sued for extra-feudal privileges, or 'liberties', from penurious medieval kings ready to grant them for a fee. These rights never extended in England to full political independence, unlike Continental towns, since English kings were too strong; but internally they were largely autonomous. They had the right to establish their own administration (or 'corporation'), to determine themselves how to raise money due to the king, to buy and sell property, enter into contracts, sue and be sued, and to run their own courts. Schemes of government differed widely; some had elected mayors and councillors, other self-appointed members of town oligarchies. As such they also came over the centuries to represent an elective tradition of self-government.

However, it would be wrong to conclude from these separate administrative arrangements that there was social division between town and shire communities. With the growth of trade and the steady decline of the social rigidities which had prompted the bid for release from feudal obligations, merchants in towns bought land in the country, and country gentry traded in the towns. Both were members of the governing class from which JPs were drawn and who, representing towns and counties, filled the House of Commons. Under the Tudors, JPs were established as the most essential of the Crown's agents in town and country. In addition to their judicial and law enforcement functions, they also administered Acts of Parliament, royal proclamations and Privy Council instructions.

The office of the JP thereby represented a highly effective balancing mechanism between the interests of the Crown at the centre, and the interests of the locality. They accepted a degree of supervision, but also enjoyed considerable autonomy in the enforcement of the Crown's orders and decrees. By the eighteenth century, after the upheaval of civil war and the purges of local government in towns and counties by Charles II and James II in their attempts to sustain royal authority against a hostile Parliament, it was recognised that stable government depended upon a working relationship between Crown and Commons and hence on a working relationship with those responsible for government locally.

There was social reform and economic development, and some of it was the subject of legislation. But most of this was private, local and facilitative, setting up local agencies where such things were desired by preponderant local interests. In the latter part of the eighteenth century, it was as common for MPs to initiate legislation for their localities in Parliament as it was for the Crown's Ministers. More than half Parliament's bills were private members' bills and a very high proportion of these were local bills meant to promote local interests.

Notwithstanding the workings of the patronage system (and because of the social cohesion among the governing class sustained by it) the de facto independence of local authorities was considerable.

In both town and country there was a subsidiary level of government in the form of the parish, which gradually absorbed the functions provided by the older feudal and pre-feudal courts. By the sixteenth century it was the accepted unit of government at the lowest level, when in the face of social and economic pressures, new local responsibilities in the area of poor relief were added to traditional law and order functions (memorably personified in Shakespeare's Dogberry and Verges). The main concern of central administration in Elizabethan legislation was to establish firmly the responsibility of individual parishes to look after their own poor and to restrict the growing problem of vagrancy, under JPs' supervision. How local communities met their own needs was for them to decide. For example, the problem was more severe in urban parishes than in rural areas and many towns adopted more far-reaching schemes than required by law, including work schemes for the able-bodied, relief pay for the infirm and disabled, and education and compulsory apprenticeships for paupers' children. The famous Speenhamland system, much scorned by Victorian reformers (see below) was the decision of a local legislature, the Berkshire magistrates, which was copied by other quarter sessions until it came to have wide application.

> Centralisation. No. Never with my consent. Not English
> (Mr Podsnap, *Our Mutual Friend*, Dickens)

Challenge and renewal

The old institutions collapsed in the nineteenth century, along with their independence, under the pressures of industrialisation and urbanisation. In 1780 government employees numbered only about 16,000. They were recruited overwhelmingly via patronage, and their most important administrative function was the collection of customs and excise duties. By 1870, patronage was in retreat; the number of government employees had increased to about 54,000 and their range of duties was far more diverse. Government was now, through the agency of inspectors and commissioners, a regulator, coordinator, and even director of local business of virtually every kind.

Government intervention seemed a necessary response to the problems of an industrialising society, in order to eliminate abuse which would otherwise prevent the free market from achieving its potential for growth to society's benefit. The Benthamite doctrine of the greatest happiness of the greatest number provided a justification for increase in the concern of government about social problems which was compatible with 'laissez faire' economics, and provided new mechanisms for achieving intervention with due concern for economy. As Mill put it: 'laissez faire . . . should be the general practice: every departure from it, unless required by some great good, is a certain evil'. New regulatory institutions were established to check on local performance within a compulsory national framework, creating a tension between central and local perspectives still in evidence today. Increasingly, in pursuit of 'great good', diversity was perceived as a weakness rather than a strength, and yet there was equally a great resistance to 'centralisation'.

Two examples provide an illustration of the new conflict between growing central authority and local responsibility. The Poor Law Commission is seen as one of the most assertive and obvious examples of the growth of government. The operation of the old Poor Law became a key concern as poor rates had increased rapidly from the end of the eighteenth century. The ad hoc schemes of parochial relief were held to exacerbate the very problems they were meant to alleviate, and to encourage idleness and improvidence. The Benthamite solution was to sweep away the myriad of local customs and instead to define a central standard for workhouse conditions which would give the able-bodied poor no incentive to claim poor relief. Only those genuinely incapable of providing for themselves would receive necessary support. The Poor Law Amendment Act of 1834 set up a central Poor Law Commission to lay down principles governing poverty relief throughout the country and supervise the implementation of the act by Poor Law Guardians, elected by parishes grouped into Poor Law 'Unions'.

In practice the act proved rather less of a centralisation force than had been intended, and diversity was just as pronounced as before. In many cases, JPs became Guardians and continued to make local decisions as they had before. In many areas Commissioners had a conspicuous lack of success in persuading local unions to adopt centrally favoured practice, especially where this meant expenditure on new facilities. In the north, where the act was perceived as wholly inappropriate to local industrial conditions, there was very considerable public opposition. Outright refusal to implement the Commission's policies led it to retreat and allow authorities to continue with their previous practice.

Conflict was even more pronounced in the area of public health. In the 1830s and 1840s the links between dirt and disease were conclusively established. It became clear that the most important factors affecting longevity were an individual's social class and place of residence. There was a clear need for reform, but responsibility for improving functions and services key to public health was seen very much as a local matter. The Public Health Act of 1848 was therefore an uneasy compromise between those who favoured central compulsion to improve health, and those who believed that disease was a local responsibility. It established a central Board of Health to supervise voluntary local boards. Compulsory local boards were required only in areas where the death-rate was higher than the national average.

The Board's high-handed way of operating produced a severe reaction. *The Times* wrote in 1854 that '. . . these gentlemen have contrived to overwhelm a good object with obloquy and hatred and to make the cholera itself scarcely a less dreaded visitation than their own'. It was wound up in 1858, in a triumph of localism. But the very considerable variation in progress locally continued to raise concern. In some areas different functions were provided by different authorities and there was continued argument over responsibilities. In some areas local boards stimulated the provision of better facilities, in others they merely added another tier of administration. Some towns in particular cut through the complexity of coordination by obtaining private acts to give councils necessary powers to take action.

Gradually more authorities took action under national statute and a greater degree of uniformity of provision began to appear. Under Gladstone's Local Government Board Act of 1871 and the Public Health Act of 1872, a general pattern of local sanitation authorities was created over the whole country, absorbing existing boroughs, local boards of health, and setting up new boards where there were none. Authorities were supervised by the Local Government Board, a central department with a general remit to supervise local functions. But the prevailing attitude remained one of scepticism about 'the State' and a presumption that, if individuals knew their own affairs best, so local communities must cater more knowledgeably for local needs than central authorities.

Reflecting this, during the nineteenth century local authorities gained a new legitimacy from the introduction of democracy. Alongside substantial social reform there was wholesale reform of the institutions of government locally and at the centre. Though the British constitution had been much admired by foreign observers, it was in no sense democratic. The House of Commons had remained essentially medieval in its form and was elected on a very narrow franchise. Until the 1832 Reform Act less than 5 per cent of the adult population enjoyed the right to vote. The franchise was based on varying property qualifications and constituencies were very unequal in size and number of electors. Seats took no account of population movement. Some major towns had no representation, while some 'rotten boroughs' had only a handful of electors. Gradually during the nineteenth century the franchise was extended and made uniform (though not universal); old borough constituencies disappeared and new constituencies were created in the new industrial areas; and electoral districts were equalised.

National changes threw into sharper perspective the forms and powers of local authorities. In the earlier part of the century, concern of those interested in parliamentary reform about the old boroughs made the condition of the old chartered corporations a matter of national interest. The 1835 Royal Commission on Municipal Corporations found wide diversity in the state of the old local authorities. Some were excellent and active in the interests of their community; others were little more than sociable clubs for the few which 'frequently expended (the corporate funds) in feasting and paying the salaries of incompetent officers'. The subsequent Municipal Corporations Act was significant in a way which had probably not been intended at the time.

Before it, corporations (like persons) had the power to do whatever the common law did not expressly disallow, subject only to the terms of their charters. Because of the concern about corruption and inefficiency, the Act restricted activities to a specific scope. Combined with the emergence of the 'ultra vires' principle, that Parliamentary corporations could do nothing which was not expressly provided for in a stature, this fundamentally altered the nature of their authority. But it also consolidated the elective and democratic principle. It gave corporations a standardised constitution, consisting of a mayor, aldermen, and councillors (the number depending upon the size of the borough), and required them to be elected by ratepayers, to hold council meetings open to the public and to have their accounts regularly audited.

All new boroughs created subsequently adopted this form of local government. As parliamentary and social reform progressed, pressure gradually increased to extend representative democratic government to the old shire authorities and to create a more uniform structure out of what was seen as 'chaos of areas, a chaos of authorities and a chaos of rates'. The public health authorities created in 1872 had established a precedent for a comprehensive and integrated pattern of authorities and in 1888 elected County Councils, on the same constitution as the boroughs, but based essentially on the old counties, replaced the magistrates in Quarter Sessions. Large towns (then defined as those with populations over 50,000) were established as 'county borough councils' with equivalent powers to the counties. This rationalisation of structure was completed by the 1894 Local Government Act, which created urban and rural district councils within the counties, based on consolidated sanitary districts. In rural areas, parishes were revived through the creation of elected parish councils.

The complete and consistent coverage thereby achieved enabled the gradual assimilation of special purpose authorities. By the early twentieth century, following a period of intense social, economic and political change, the place of local government in the wider constitution (and indeed, that constitution itself) had been both consolidated and confirmed. Local government had a clear conceptual and institutional identity. It was founded on openly democratic lines, paralleling the growth of the national franchise (indeed, in the case of female suffrage, anticipating it). It had come through significant social upheaval and institutional reform to achieve new prestige in the public eye and a tangible sense of confidence.

As the corollary, however, the formal status and powers of local government were more tightly defined through specific legislation and the operation of the ultra vires principle. And, in contrast to pre-industrial society, local authorities were increasingly divorced from the national political process and its leading institutions of Parliament, Ministers and a growing national civil service, producing a separation about which today there may be cause for regret. But after the great debates of centralisation and localism, a consensus had emerged about the need for central initiative in policy, combined with local discretion in implementation and execution The rationalised structure presented a large measure of uniformity across town and country, newly able to sustain significant responsibilities as the scope of government continued to increase.

During the first half of the present century local government took on more and more functions. To the administrative functions of the Justices of the Peace were gradually added the functions of the special purpose authorities set up to achieve social reform. Public health and highways were transferred from local boards in 1894. In 1902 the local School Boards which had been set up under the 1870 Education Act were abolished, and in their place local authorities set up committees (known as 'local education authorities') to provide schools and other educational services, such as meals and medical inspection.

New responsibilities were also acquired as the state's concern for the welfare of its citizens developed under the pressures of universal suffrage. In 1890 authorities were permitted to build low-cost houses, and in 1919 they were given central government subsidies to encourage them to do so. They acquired new powers to control the use and development of land, were able to set up local labour bureaux to help the unemployed to find work and were able also to spend money on public works to create jobs. During this period, they were also providing employment opportunities directly as a result of expanded trading activities.

There was considerable development of public transport, water, electricity and gas supply. Other enterprises included a racecourse (Doncaster), a bank (Birmingham), a telephone system (Hull), a theatre (Manchester) and numerous other amenities. Responsibilities in the health field were also gradually extended to include the provision of hospitals, sanatoria, and community care services for the mentally sub-normal and the mentally ill. By the early 1930s, when the 1933 Local Government Act consolidated the powers, functions and structure of local government, it had far more day to day influence in the lives of ordinary citizens than central government.

> We love independent 'local authorities' . . . The degree of local free-dom desirable in a country varies according to many circumstances, and a Parliamentary government may consist with any degree of it
> (Walter Bagehot)

Decline and dependency

It is a commonplace of commentaries on the history and development of local government that the latter half of the twentieth century has seen a steady decline from a 'golden age'. The decline is seen princi-pally in terms of loss of functions and a diminution in local discretion; loss of financial independence; and failure to maintain the public's interest in local government. Even as local government had reached its apotheosis, the move away had begun. The economic forces of the Great Depression saw central government wanting to implement a means-tested benefit scheme for the unemployed, to supplement poor-law relief operated by local authorities.

Since resources and also political attitudes differed, differences in provision intensified. While some authorities provided much more gen-erously than others, there were objections because ratepayers in poor areas, with high unemployment, both had to pay more in rates, and were less able to do so, than those in prosperous areas where there tended to be low unemployment anyway. The government therefore set up the Unemployment Assistance Board at 'arms length' from Ministers, to take the administration of discretionary relief away from local authorities and, as far as possible, out of politics altogether. Once again local diversity conflicted with national priorities.

The Second World War produced a revolution in attitudes toward the role of government and put welfare provision at the heart of nation-al policy. The creation of the Welfare State after the war prompted the entry of central government on a major scale as a direct service provider and served increasingly to present local responsibilities in terms of a role as central government's agent. Emphasis on universal provision to guarantee uniform and equal treatment in social security, health, housing and education led to a new emphasis on central control and on central funding. The administration and provision of social security and health were unified and centralised, and the activities of local government in education, remaining personal welfare services and housing were subjected to much greater central government supervision.

The move away from local government was not just for redistributive reasons, however. First, a national government had been returned with a very large majority on a clear mandate for change. Imposing such change from the top, rather than proceeding by negotiation or persuasion, had clear attractions. Second, rates were reckoned to be less able than national taxation to support the increases in spending required to support substantial levels of welfare provision. Third, without direct action and control by central government, new Keynesian policies on counter-cyclical spending to counter unemployment were potentially likely to be frustrated.

There were also strong producer forces whose interest lay not in diverse, small scale, local provision but in national conglomerates affording them a larger canvas. In less politically sensitive areas, the arguments against local provision therefore often turned on the achievement of economies of scale and the benefits of thereby achieving uniformly high standards. In the case of electricity, for example, the Central Electricity Board had been set up in 1926 to establish an electricity grid, to concentrate generation in the most efficient stations, and to standardise the industry. Pre-war, there had also been criticism of the inefficiency inherent in the small scale of local distribution, and the diversity and complexity of governing statutes. Post-war, the greater confidence in national planning and national public ownership, together with the success of the CEB in rationalising generation and producer interests in the industry, led to the removal of the function from local government in 1947 through the setting up of a public corporation. Similar arguments were used in the case of gas, set up as a public corporation in 1948.

Despite the considerable impact of these changes, however, it would be wrong to attribute them to any new interpretation of local government's constitutional position. And though local government lost functions, it also acquired new roles, for example in development planning in the Town and Country Planning Act 1947. The changes were not seen as 'centralisation', despite the increase in central government control and indeed, in the scope and scale of its activities. There was in general a high degree of political consensus about the introduction of the Welfare State, though other measures introduced by the post-war Labour Government, involving the nationalisation of private enterprises, were major issues between the two main parties. The feeling was not so much any anti-local bias, but perhaps, as Arthur Marwick has suggested, a new professional and managerialist confidence cutting across party politics: 'Conservative leaders . . . could join with Labour leaders . . . in supporting the large unit. Labour preferred the state, the

Conservatives . . . preferred large scale private industry. Both showed little interest in the small businessman' (Marwick 1945). And both regarded the structure of local government inherited from the previous century as offering units too small to be efficient.

Against the background of post-war consensus, welfarism and the new affluence, local authorities came to be seen, and to see themselves, principally as responsible for the delivery of services specified in national legislation, increasingly funded by central government grants, and guided and managed by central government circulars, inspectors and administrators. The prevailing assertion during this period was one of 'partnership', though admittedly with not much clarity about the partners' roles. For example, in the Labour Government's response to the 1976 Layfield Report on Local Government Finance (see below), the Government saw 'the duties and responsibilities involved in the provision of local public services as being shared on a partnership basis between central and local government. Within this framework, the balance of responsibility (would) vary over time as circumstances change'. The response concluded that changing emphasis in the relative responsibilities of central and local government remained compatible with 'a well understood and accepted constitutional relationship'.

Indeed, lack of clarity about respective roles allowed governments of both complexions to adopt different positions on local 'freedom' when it suited them to do so for policy purposes. For example, the new Labour Government in 1965 required local authorities to submit proposals for establishing comprehensive schools. The new Conservative Government in 1970 stressed that the reorganisation of secondary education was entirely a matter for local authorities. The same Conservative Government, in 1972, required local authorities to abandon subsidised rents and charge 'fair' (generally higher) rents under the Housing Finance Act. When Clay Cross councillors refused to do so, they were displaced by housing commissioners appointed by the Secretary of State.

But 'partnership' ensured that local government continued to be responsible for a very wide range of functions. Local discretion was not lost. Some authorities used their existing powers to develop new roles, especially in the area of economic development. There continued to be considerable variation in the way authorities used different powers. Reflecting this, there was (apart from cyclical variations) a steady growth in both local current and capital spending under both Conservative and Labour administrations, most significantly in education and housing, despite their different policies.

But as economic pressures forced constraint on public funding, growth in expenditure led increasingly to debate not about structure, or functions, but about financing. This was coupled with the long-term recognition that the method of raising local income through the rating system provided an unsatisfactory basis for local accountability and was in need of reform. While growth in the economy, and political consensus, allowed rising local government expenditure to be financed by national taxation, ratepayers could be largely shielded from the impact of the rising cost of local services. Over the century, central government grants to local government increased substantially, from 15 per cent of local government income in 1913, to 34 per cent in 1950 and 50 per cent in 1980. For a very long period, domestic rates in general remained only a very small proportion of household disposable income (around 2–3 per cent) though business rates rose substantially.

Since the report of the Layfield Committee, the system of financing has been seen as fundamental to the relationship with central government. It is still at the centre of current political controversy about local government's role. Layfield drew attention to the disadvantage of increasing dependence by local authorities on central government, associated with an inflexible and politically sensitive local tax. The Committee's report suggested that local accountability required both the removal of local government expenditure from the central government public expenditure planning process, thus lessening central involvement in the detail of local spending plans, and the introduction of a new source of revenue in addition to the rates, in the form of a local income tax.

The Labour Government's response displayed a reluctance to confront the more fundamental implications of change. It denied that local discretion was undermined and argued that local freedom to vary local income tax rates would in fact involve greater constraint than the current system, if it was not to 'complicate central government economic and financial management'. The incoming Conservative Government in 1979 had previously considered local income tax as a plausible alternative to the rating system, but came to power committed to reducing direct taxation and cutting public spending. In the circumstances, it could not accommodate the idea of giving local authorities power to set income tax, or of any emancipation of local government from public expenditure planning.

On the contrary, the early 1980s saw progressively tighter financial controls imposed on local government spending through the introduction of spending targets and penalties; new controls on capital expenditure; abolition of powers to set supplementary rates; steady reductions in rate support grant; and rate-capping. The introduction of the Community Charge, together with the uniform national non-domestic rate and a new grant system intended to equalise spending needs around a standard level of service provision, has served only to inten-

sify argument about relationships between central and local government, especially when juxtaposed with other legislative changes affecting local government's functional responsibilities. The system of local
government finance today remains a matter of substantial political controversy, reflecting broader debate about the role of local government
(see next section).

From today's perspective, the long term consequences of 'partnership', while preserving local government's importance in a changing
political landscape, turned out to have substantially contributed to
weakening the de facto constitutional position of Bagehot's 'independent local authorities', though the outward structures and forms of
local democracy remained unchanged. Inevitably, as the policy initiative passed from local authorities to central government, as central
government institutions themselves expanded in size and scope and
developed local delivery arrangements, and as local services increasingly were shaped by a political agenda set nationally, local authorities
lost touch with their traditional culture of independence and with the
optimism and confidence of earlier years. Financial dependence further
compromised ability to assert independence, and weakened accountability to local electorates. Over the course of the changes of a century
or so, local independence lost its political appeal.

> Once upon a time man looked to God to order the world. Then he
> looked to the market. Now he looks to Government. And when
> things go wrong people blame not 'Him' or 'it' but 'them'
>
> (King 1990)

Doubt and conflict

Functional and financial decline in local government is frequently seen
today in a wider context of an alleged failure of public institutions generally to deliver the performance required of them. Local government
became 'them'; part of a wider picture of social alienation and loss of
confidence in governments' ability to provide the benefits people had
come to expect. By some commentators this is seen as betokening
a general decline in 'civic culture', which has produced distrust in
government, a fragmentation of political response, and a tendency to
sharper dissent, which in itself threatens traditional constitutional
arrangements (Beer 1982). Linked to this endemic political failure,
specific managerial failures are adduced, implicating local and central
government alike: inhuman public housing, inadequate transport planning, inner city decay, falling educational standards, corruption, poverty, homelessness.

Evidence on this is sketchy and inconclusive. Local government's
democratic role is seen to be undermined by low levels of turnout (at
least when compared to general elections), by lack of contested seats,

and most of all perhaps by the hijacking of local elections by national politics, so that electoral behaviour in local elections is seen not as a response to local issues, but as a mid-term barometer of public opinion on national policy. In a recent study, it was found that over 80 per cent of the electorate vote in accordance with national political preferences when they voted in local elections, around 10 per cent moved away from national preferences towards a 'less political' candidate, and 10 per cent had no national preference and were therefore more likely to respond to local issues (Miller 1986). It is also worth pointing out, against the general charge of failure, that the same study found that 75 per cent of respondents were very or fairly satisfied with the performance of their authorities. It has therefore been suggested that lack of public interest in local issues may paradoxically reflect confidence rather than alienation or apathy.

But latterly, conflict has arisen from a more fundamental challenge to the post-war consensus about the role and purpose of the public sector, inspired in the main by the present Government, affecting the institutions of central and local government alike. Commentators discern that, since the mid-1980s, local government has entered a new era. Old-style local government, with its collective welfare functions, its sizeable assets, and its professional and producer orientation has been at odds with the ideology of a government committed to 'rolling back the frontiers of the state' and challenging public producer monopolies. A concern with public expenditure restraint, privatisation and contracting out has broadened into a comprehensive programme of reform, covering other areas of social and economic policy (education, housing, community care, urban development, training, employment and enterprise) as well as the financing, structure and management of local authorities themselves.

Precisely because it has provided an alternative democratic vehicle for political opposition, local government has found itself in the cockpit of politics, fought over by the so-called New Right and New Left. A newly adversarial and ideological dimension has been added to the old Benthamite tensions between centralism and localism. Changes in finance, function and structure (in the metropolitan areas) have been sufficiently significant to challenge the conventional assumptions about the purpose of local government and the principal political values it should represent, on both left and right. For the left, the core issue is how to combine meaningful powers of local choice with a continuing commitment to reducing inequalities. For the right, the issue is how to combine the exercise of individual choice in local government taxes and services, and hence much reduced reliance on central government funding, with the abolition of current pre-conceptions that collective provision of services should be the norm rather than the exception.

Yet a third strand in current thinking emphasises the role of local government in empowering local communities to formulate community responses to community needs. Here the issue is the extent to which local policies may run counter to national priorities and principles.

There is now a key constitutional problem for all parties and interest groups to confront: how are powers to be distributed between national and local tiers of government, exercised within the framework of a unitary state, and limited in the interests of democracy? If, as in this century and before, a political community is committed to achieving equality through national objectives, standards and redistributive finance, then the scope for local autonomy will necessarily be constrained. If, on the other hand, priority is given to maximising scope for achieving efficiency in the levels of service to be provided for a given level of charge in accordance with local preference, this will constrain central government's role. If local participation and autonomy is key, this will be likely to lead to conflict between central and local authorities as policy choices differ among authorities and between the local and central tiers.

It may be argued, however, that the agenda set by the present Government presents local government with the worst of all worlds, since it combines the new right's ideas of maximising individual choice through contracting out and opting out, with an even tighter system than before of central financial and management controls. Critics allege that the emphasis is entirely upon consumerism without concern for democratisation. They argue that the core liberal democratic values of individual liberty and local participation have been diminished through excessive centralisation, while previously shared social democratic values of collective action to achieve redistribution and equity have now been decisively rejected. It seems that the government has a conception of the relationship between local and central government which has little or no room for 'partnership', nor even for the legitimate expression of local political diversity within the present constitutional framework. The superiority of the national over the local mandate has been asserted by current Ministers more overtly than at any time previously, and the philosophy of detailed central control has never been so clearly stated as now, notwithstanding rhetoric about 'giving local government back to local people'.

> A feast to which many contribute is better than a dinner provided out of a single purse
> (Aristotle)

Towards a new constitution

The term 'unconstitutional' is often used by the Government's critics to describe the move towards increasing central control, which, by convention, was previously seen as 'un-English', and thus unlikely to happen. But the development of the British constitution 'owes far more to political expedience than to principle or theory, although the balances once struck tend to be exported as theory' (Jennings 1952). Hence the Widdicombe Report's carefully drafted statement of the current position of local government offers no defence based on inalienable right or absolute principle: 'The position of local government in our political system is . . . governed by constitutional convention as well as by the simple fact that it derives its existence and its powers from Parliament. It would, however, be wrong to assume that such constitutional convention amounts to or derives from any natural right for local government to exist. It is a convention based on, and subject to, the contribution which local government can bring to good government'.

In recent years there has been increasing questioning of the 'shifting and complex web of relationships and powers that forms the British constitution' (Norton 1984) and a call to replace expediency by a formalised and written constitution that could more obviously proclaim and safeguard important principles. This has provided a wider agenda within which defenders of local government have sought to ensure its protection within the system of government as a whole. Instead of relying on past practice — or 'convention' — the framework of developing relationships with the European Community has been seen as a more reliable basis on which to build guarantees of local government's position.

Critics suggest first that the failings in the British system are highlighted by membership of the European Community, whose framework and working methods are derived from civil law countries with written constitutions, fundamental rights and comprehensive systems of public law (Lester 1989). Second, a new 'communautaire' defence for local government is provided by adherence in Europe to the principle of 'subsidiarity' (for example, in the European Charter of Local Government) which declares that responsibilities should generally be exercised by those authorities closest to the citizen, since it is at local level that right to participate in the conduct of public affairs is most directly exercised.

The constitutions of many European states recognise the right of local self-government as a fundamental principle of democracy. Reflecting this most local authorities are enabled to take action in the interests of their community unless specifically prohibited from doing so by a wider authority. Powers of this kind have long been argued for in this country by those who consider that the framework which evolved in the nineteenth century is now inappropriate, restrictive and too open to abuse, and who wish to revive local government's autonomy. It is now incorporated into the programmes of the Labour Party, the Liberal Democrats, and also into the proposals of the all-party group, Charter 88, for a new constitutional settlement.

Whether or not formal constitutional change takes place in the future, however, there will undoubtedly continue to be changes in practice in constitutional relationships under the pressure of events. Though theoretical blueprints have exercised sometimes powerful influence in the past, the regulation of the exercise and distribution of power has essentially evolved pragmatically (though not always gradually) to meet perceived needs as they arose, and institutions likewise. 'The conventions of the constitution have meaning only when they are looked at against a background of continuous political change . . . They cannot be understood with the politics left out' (LeMay 1979).

The history rehearsed above shows how resilient institutions can be, if they adapt to changing circumstance. Local government has accommodated feudalism and the growth of monarchy; oligarchy and the development of constitutional monarchy; and industrialisation, democracy, and the Welfare State. It has responded to national pressures and wider constitutional change, whilst enabling local communities to respond to the day-to-day needs of managing their own affairs. There is no reason to suppose that it will not continue to do so, whether within the current or a new constitutional framework.

Any significant structural change, such as is contemplated in the present review of local government, will itself influence that evolutionary process. If new structures are to 'fit' the future strategy and purpose of local government, and enable it to contribute actively to future constitutional development, the review of local government cannot ignore certain fundamental questions. Commentators tell us that we are entering upon a new, so-called 'post-Fordist' era, with new patterns of work and home life, new expectations of quality of life, new social pressures and tensions (Handy 1984, 1989, Stoker 1991). In this post-industrial society, what kind of government will be 'good government' (to use Widdicombe's term) and what contribution will local democracy make to ensuring good government? How will it relate to national and indeed supranational democracy? How will the inevitable tensions between local, national and supranational institutions be managed?

Some design principles

The structure review will need to be based upon some broadly agreed principles, or guidelines, to ensure that its conclusions produce a form of local government capable of playing an active constitutional role in the future. Notwithstanding the current political controversy about the

nature of local government's formal powers, local democracy contributes to a strong constitution in several ways:

- it is an important source of diversity and of pluralism in a complex
  policy environment;
- it promotes active participation by individuals and local communities in the day-to-day business of government;
- it provides a common focus for community identity and for the resolution of conflict in the interests of the local community as a
  whole;
- it prevents too great a concentration of power at any one level of
  government.

Each of these is discussed below. The future structure must provide for
all these roles if local government is successfully to meet the demands
likely to be placed upon it in the future.

Pluralism

The policy issues which will confront governments at all levels are
likely to be increasingly complex, interlinked, and long-term. They will
require inter-agency, inter-authority, and inter-government responses.
It is unlikely that any single authority, whether at local or national
level, will be able to present a comprehensive response to the challenge
of reconciling economic aspirations and environmental pressures. As
Europe develops a more closely integrated political and economic
framework, and as the Community expands to accommodate huge economic and social diversity, authorities at every level will need to act
together to ensure that universal economic security can be reconciled
with individual freedom of choice. Public and private agencies will
have to integrate their strategies across functional and geographical
boundaries and beyond narrow concerns about organisational and professional territory.

But communities vary in their needs, in their atmosphere, and in
their preferences. If the response in the future to complex issues is adequately to take account of local diversity and differing local needs,
increasing interdependence will require renewed emphasis on effective
representation of local interests within a wider national and supranational policy context. The value of democratic local government in a
complex and diverse policy environment lies in its legitimacy as a
focus for expression of a local response to wider issues. It provides for
different views to be heard and for diversity to be fully and democratically represented within a wider policy environment to inform policy
choice. No other level of government or combination of other agencies

can in the same way claim the right or responsibility to assert a vision for the future of a local community, or determine a response to significant issues which is based upon local circumstances and priorities. The structure must adequately support this function as an important source of pluralism in the political system.

Participation

As issues become more complex and individuals' lives are more and more influenced by the actions of government at any level, the importance of interest in, access to and active involvement in government at the local level increases. Participation is important for two reasons. First, Mill called participation in public affairs the 'invigorating effect of freedom upon the character'. This is as relevant in a well-established democracy as in any emerging one, though it tends to be taken for granted. Secondly, it promotes responsive and accountable government, not just every so often through the ballot box, but through myriad day-to-day links with the public. It involves the accommodation of varying local and individual needs through a flexible and pragmatic approach to service provision, decentralised and performance-oriented management, and open and participative styles of operating. No central government or other single-purpose agency, even when its remit is specifically local, has the same facility to promote access to and active participation by local communities in assessment of, or decision-making about, the policies and services which directly impact upon them. The structure must therefore encourage and facilitate active participation on an individual and collective basis.

A focus for community

But promotion of effective participation is an increasingly demanding task. Local communities today are diverse. Individual localities can no longer be assumed to be homogeneous, as social and economic mobility, changing lifestyles and the geographical spread of people's lives lead to dispersed social networks and complex patterns of interaction. So-called 'territorial communities' may both include, and be transcended by, many different 'communities of interest' (Willmott 1989). Yet there is increasing attachment to the ideal of 'community' as a focus for organisation, as the expression of shared purpose and experience, and as the basis for mobilisation of collective resources — for a return to Burke's 'little platoons', which constitute the fundamental ties binding society.

Through the breadth and depth of its functions and services, local government has a key role in providing a common focus for community identity; in providing the opportunity for the democratic expression of different interests in the community; and in the operation of political and management processes resolving conflict between them. This role constitutes an important practical strength in the system of government, since local issues can be dealt with locally without needing to involve the centre. But more fundamentally, it ensures that local decisions are taken by those who are directly accountable to local people, who are those most closely affected. The structure must therefore relate to different community identities and to the need to promote the resolution of local conflict in the interests of the wider community as a whole.

Polity

The best form of government, following Aristotle, is a mixed constitution, where there are checks and balances on the exercise of power. Each individual element has a role in ensuring that no single group can pursue its own interest at the expense of the common good. It is a source of strength in any constitution, whether formally federal, unitary, or somewhere in between, that practical power should not be monopolised, lest this lead to complacency, corruption, or yet more serious abuse. Local government is not of course the only check on autocracy in the constitutional structure. But it provides an essential source of checks and balances on power through its independent electoral base, uncomfortable though this may be for central governments, of whatever political complexion. The structure must therefore provide adequately for constraint on too great a concentration of power at any one level of government.

This final aspect of local government's constitutional role is the most problematic politically, because it requires recognition of the legitimacy of political difference between central and local government, and for the accommodation within national objectives of local diversity. History suggests, however, that far from the exercise of local discretion providing a fundamental challenge to the fabric of the state, there is inevitable inter-dependency between national and local dimensions of government and that good government requires effective relationships between the two. In the future it is likely to mean additionally creating effective relationships with a third tier of government, 'beyond the centre'. In a democratic system, this is highly likely to mean having to work together despite political disagreement, however challenging and uncomfortable this is. It is after all a sign of strength in any system of government that dissent can be accommodated without threat to stability.

A more tolerant relationship would not necessarily require the provision of new powers for local government to take whatever action it considered appropriate in the interest of the community it represented. Nor would it necessarily require a new financial settlement, providing for greater local discretion in the raising and spending of resources, though resolution of this key issue would undoubtedly help. But within the current constitutional framework it means an acceptance of inevitable tension between democratically elected organs of government as a necessary consequence of active democracy and a reflection of a politically diverse society. It requires greater understanding from each side of the perspective and concerns of the other, than is displayed in the current debate. It is a necessary ingredient of a proper review of local government structure.

Conclusion

Local government thus finds itself at an historic crossroads. Its institutions have over a thousand years adapted to changing needs. It has lived through major social, economic and political upheaval in the last century. In this, it has successfully demonstrated its ability to adapt to new roles and new circumstances. Now it faces on the one hand a continuing and aggressive challenge to its traditional responsibilities, functions and ways of operating, and on the other, the prospect of a new relationship with a more decentralised national government in a regional context, with broader taxing powers and wider competence.

But local government is not merely an onlooker, accepting an agenda which others dictate and decide. Local authorities continue to have significant social and economic impact. They intervene, as well as react. The 'design principles' set out above presume a continuing and active role for local government in the future, notwithstanding current political controversy. They imply robust institutions with the scope and credibility to contribute nationally and internationally to complex and difficult policy issues; with the capabilities and resources to respond flexibly and innovatively to changing local needs and to the wishes of diverse local communities; and with the ability to guarantee an efficient, impartial and above all humane approach in their dealings with individuals. If local government is to continue to command democratic support for an active role in future constitutional developments, it must take the initiative in demonstrating by its actions and performance that benefits will accrue other than to itself. It must prove itself able to sustain effective and rewarding relationships both with the institutions with which it works and with the people it serves.

References

Beer, S. H. (1982) *Britain Against Itself.*

Birch, A. H. (1990) *The British System of Government* 8th Edn, Unwin Hyman.

Galbraith, J. R. and Kazanijan, R. K. (1986) *Strategy Implementation: Structure, Systems and Process* West Publishing Co.

Hand, C. (1984) *The Future of Work* Blackwell.

Handy, C. (1989) *The Age of Unreason* Hutchinson.

Jennings, Sir Ivor (1952) *Law and the Constitution* 4th Edn, quoted in Grant, M. 1989 'Central–Local Relations', in Jowell, J. and Oliver, D. (eds) *The Changing Constitution* 2nd Edn Oxford University Press.

King, A. (1990) 'Overload: problems of governing in the 1970s' *Political Studies* **23**, quoted in Birch, ibid.

Kingdom, J. (1991) *Local Government and Politics in Britain* Philip Allan.

LeMay, G. (1979) *The Victorian Constitution* Duckworth, quoted in Norton, ibid.

Lester, A. (1989) 'The Constitution: Decline and Renewal', in Jowell and Oliver, ibid.

Marwick, A. (1984) *British Society since 1945* Penguin.

Miller, W. (1986) 'Local electoral behaviour' in 'The Local Government Elector', *The Conduct of Local Authority Business* (Widdicombe) *Research* **3**, HMSO, quoted in Byrne, T. 1990 *Local Government in Britain*, 5th Edn Penguin.

Mintzberg, H. (1983) *Structure in Fives: Designing Effective Organisations* Prentice-Hall International.

Norton, P. (1984) *The British Polity* Longman.

de Smith, S. and Brazier, R. (1990) *Constitutional and Administrative Law* Penguin.

Stoker, G. (1991) 'Creating a local government for a post-Fordist society, the Thatcherite project?' in Stewart, J. and Stoker, G. (eds) *The Future of Local Government* Macmillan.

Willmot, P. (1989) *Community Initiatives, Patterns and Prospects,* Policy Studies Institute.

General bibliography

Ball, T. and Dagger, R. (1991) *Political Ideologies and the Democratic Ideal* Harper Collins.

Davies, K. (1983) *Local Government Law* Butterworths.

Evans, E. J. (1989) *The Forging of the Modern State* Longman.

Foster, C. D., Jackman, R. and Perlman, M. (1980) *Local Government Finance in a Unitary State* Allen & Unwin.

Graves, M. A. R. and Silcock, R. H. (1987) *Revolution, Reaction and the Triumph of Conservatism* Longman Paul.

Hennessy, P. (1989) *Whitehall* Secker & Warburg.

Holmes, G. (1974) *The Later Middle Ages* Cardinal.

Hunter Blair, P. (1970) *Anglo-Saxon England* Cambridge University Press.

Lloyd, T. O. (1984) *Empire to Welfare State* Oxford University Press.

Pares, R. (1973) *King George III and the Politicians* Oxford University Press.

Postan, M. M. (1976) *The Medieval Economy and Society* Penguin.

Stenton, D. M. (1974) *English Society in the Early Middle Ages* Penguin.

Whitelock, D. (1972) *The Beginnings of English Society* Penguin.

2 The changing style of local government — enabling in practice

Introduction

Chapter 1 considers the historic development of the constitutional role of local government. It concludes that local government today finds itself at a crossroads. Its purpose, powers, functions, financing and relations with central government in general are all a matter of intense and continuing debate. The paper argues that, nonetheless, the review of structure cannot ignore the contribution that democratic local government can make in the future to a strong constitution. It sets out some design principles to be taken into account in the review, implying a continuing and active constitutional role for local government.

The challenges facing local government are also causing a re-examination of traditional assumptions and approaches to the organisation and management of local authority services. Against the background of continuing political debate, local government is taking the initiative in developing a new style, adapting to the changing external environment and reflecting new ideas about how to meet the needs of the people it serves. Chapter 2 builds on the conclusions of Chapter 1. It identifies the main features of local government's changing style, examines how these can support a continuing and active constitutional role, and considers the implications for future structure which should be taken into account in the review.

Enabling — the new orthodoxy?

Many local authorities have had cause to challenge the traditional assumptions underlying the way they operated in the past, and to reassess styles, structures and methods of management. Conventionally this process of challenge and reassessment is seen as a response to the extensive programme of government legislation affecting local authority services, particularly education, housing, social services, and to the introduction of compulsory competitive tendering.

But this is to take too centrist a view of the impetus for change in local government. Of course new legislation has had a significant impact, but authorities have, as always, initiated change in response to local circumstances and priorities, as well as to external pressures, including financial and other resource constraints. They have initiated different ways of offering services and of managing their activities, with an eye to best practice in other authorities and organisations elsewhere in the public and private sectors. Frequently legislative change has been influenced by innovative approaches developed by local authorities (as for example in local management of schools).

Recently, however, changes have taken place against the background of often highly charged debate about the concept of the 'enabling authority', and about its significance for the powers, status, functions and overall configuration of local government. 'Enabling' is by its nature an imprecise term, capable of a variety of interpretations. For some in local government it is synonymous simply with contracting services out. Some commentators see it as a more fundamental challenge to the idea of collective provision of goods and services, as the platform for privatisation and 'rolling back the State', and hence as a threat to the very existence and purpose of local government. Others, however, see it as an opportunity, sustaining a redefinition of the role of local government as 'community government', emancipated from preoccupation with service provision, with increased financial resources generated locally and with new and broader powers to act in the community interest.

Unfortunately, the rival definitions and interpretations, competing for attention in what is inevitably a highly politicised debate, have served to distract attention from what is actually happening in practice. They obscure a valuable concept which helps to define a new orientation for local government. A recent study undertaken by the Public Finance Foundation observed that, whatever their political control, most authorities now see themselves as 'enablers', but that what characterises this perception is essentially a pragmatic and flexible view of their methods of operating: 'the common thread is that . . . the authority seeks to meet the needs of the community in the most effective way'.

As such, this may involve working with and through others, as well as taking action directly through service provision. It may involve a stance based on facilitating, stimulating and influencing others, as well as providing direct support through contracts and grants. Authorities define their role less with reference exclusively to the direct provision of services, and are increasingly emphasising their strategic responsibilities. Nor is it assumed that whatever services are provided must necessarily be standard or uniform. More flexibility and diversity are encouraged, to match statutory obligations and varying local and individual needs.

As with other public and private sector organisations, it is no longer assumed that local authorities need to employ all the staff and own all the resources they need to carry out their functions. New contractual control processes are increasingly being substituted for direct hierarchical arrangements, both internally and externally. In practice this is less a matter of political dogma than of focusing on what arrangements will deliver the best service. However, services are provided, there is increasing emphasis on the need to 'get close to the customer', to find out more about what people think of current performance, and to concentrate management and staff effort on achieving consistently high quality of service. It is no longer assumed that elected councillors and professional officers necessarily have a monopoly of knowledge about what people need and want.

The extent and nature of change differs from place to place, as might be expected from authorities which operate in different areas and respond to different needs. But behind the jargon, and across different interpretations, some consistent signs of changing style are gradually emerging, as authorities exchange experience of good practice. 'Enabling' is coming to mean not adherence to any particular political orthodoxy, but the development of different and more flexible ways of operating which are both more suited to the many and varied demands now placed on local government, and most effective in meeting the needs of local communities.

This means that, in practice, 'enabling' may mean doing different things, in different ways, in different places. Leaving aside differences associated with political complexion, the requirements of a multi-ethnic and socially mixed urban authority are likely to be different from those of a predominantly rural area, more sparsely populated and probably culturally less diverse. Uniform prescriptions for change, whether emanating from Ministers, central authorities, or external commentators, are unlikely to provide solutions matching the problems each local authority has to face.

This chapter therefore takes an empirical approach to 'enabling' in an attempt to demystify and depolarise the current debate. What characterises the new style of local government is no single 'right answer' to questions of management structure or process, but instead the development of several interrelated organisational and management attributes. These are emerging as good management practice in the complex environment local authorities now face. Authorities will differ in their approach in each respect; but, taken together, these provide a practical set of guidelines for what it means to be 'enabling':

- a strategic sense of the key policy issues facing local communities and of changing needs;
- a focus on determining the most effective response to those needs;
- an emphasis on clear objectives and standards, and on monitoring performance against them;
- investment in building long-term relationships with other agencies and organisations;
- an innovative approach to influencing, interpreting and implementing the regulatory framework in the interests of local communities;
- closer contact with the public, encouraging improved access to facilities, and greater involvement at all levels of decision-making.

This chapter considers these points in detail.

Enabling in practice

A strategic orientation

Governments at all levels are confronting significant policy issues raised by demographic and social change, economic trends, and growing environmental pressures. Maximising economic opportunity, and preventing environmental damage, requires radical action locally, nationally and internationally. Major policy concerns such as the achievement of sustainable growth, or the care of the vulnerable and disadvantaged, require a strategic approach which identifies the needs and concerns of local communities and focuses on developing a clear and integrated response.

Local authorities are building on their regulatory and service responsibilities to address an agenda of concern which in effect defines a broader vision for the future of a local community. For example, responsibilities for land-use planning are increasingly used as the basis for an integrated strategic approach to key economic and environmental issues, in an effort to match local needs and aspirations for employment, transport, leisure, and quality of life in general, across both urban and rural areas. This comprehensive response to complex issues increasingly requires the integration of strategies across traditional functional and geographical boundaries. It also requires effective inter-agency working with other authorities, local businesses and voluntary groups, and many different national bodies.

A strategic approach ensures that activity by different agencies in the same policy area is not fragmented or worse, counter-productive. It also ensures that local views are fully taken into account within a wider policy context. It requires a well-developed policy process within the authority whereby opportunities can be identified, different approaches considered (including the role of external agencies) and finally a strategy agreed as the basis for action. It needs regular feedback from performance monitoring, and a commitment to systematic policy evaluation and review to ensure that chosen strategies remain appropriate.

Determining an effective response

The corollary of developing clearly defined strategies as the basis for action is that proper attention must be paid to selecting the way in which the authority can most usefully act to achieve its objectives. Many modes of action are available. These go beyond the issue of whether to source a service internally or externally, which, though important, is by no means the only question to be resolved. Other modes of action include, for example:

- providing a new service directly or extending existing services;
- acting in collaboration with other agencies to promote new ventures or coordinate service provision or some other activity;
- creating new bodies, with others or alone;
- providing grant support;
- providing services in kind to other bodies in support of their activities;
- using purchasing power to influence suppliers;
- publicising issues and providing information;
- bringing individuals or groups together to promote discussion and encourage participation;
- influencing other bodies and public opinion generally through involvement in wider advisory or policy-making groupings.

The key factor in selecting the most appropriate mode of action is a realistic perception of the authority's own strengths and weaknesses. This helps identify where it can 'add value' by taking action itself, and where it is more effective to work with or through others. Authorities have for a long time been used to working with contractors in conventional commercial relationships, and to working with other public sector authorities. But the range of potential partners is now becoming increasingly diverse, from major business concerns to small voluntary groups. This requires a more developed understanding of the diverse problems and perspectives of local communities, and of their resources and potential for action. This must then be matched with the right response in terms of financial and other support.

The legal restrictions on local authorities (for example, the types of company structure an authority can set up for 'arms length' operation) are constraining moves away from direct service provision. A freer and more coherent legal framework within which authorities operate is needed if the full potential for innovation in this area is to be achieved.

Setting standards and monitoring performance

At the heart of much of the change in local government recently, as in other public sector organisations, is new concern about setting explicit performance criteria for standards of service. The recently published 'Citizens Charters' reflect increasing political interest in improving the quality of public services.

Though an important aspect of recent developments, the introduction of competition for the supply of services is not a quality improvement panacea. While contracting out (or internal 'contracting' through service level agreements) provides an effective discipline on managers to specify the services they require and the standards to be achieved, effecting monitoring of contract compliance is essential in ensuring the achievement of promised value for money gains. In addition, both public and private sector organisations are learning that, where contracted-out services are central to strategic objectives, it is essential to build effective relationships with a range of suppliers so that they can develop a full understanding of their customers' requirements. They can then tailor the service they provide accordingly, as well as provide a competitive price.

Beyond day-to-day monitoring of standards at the operational level, effective policy monitoring is also required to ensure that broader objectives are achieved. There is a continuous need to review whether the chosen means are bringing about the desired outcome, or if not, to identify the reasons for failure, learn from it, and adapt future strategy. Systematic policy evaluation, including regular performance review and close attention to the effectiveness of relationships with other organisations, is an essential part of effective policy-making and a key component of the successful substitution of new ways of working for traditional, hierarchical arrangements.

Openness about standards and performance achieved also helps improve public accountability. New practice in this area includes not just the publication of formal annual reports, but also setting explicit standards of performance publicly, so that the public can judge success. This needs to be combined with effective channels for communication of user views and the handling of complaints. Some authorities are also involving the public directly in defining standards and the criteria by which performance can be assessed, thereby bringing users actively into the process of review.

Developing partnerships

As problems have become more complex and the impact of special interest groups has increased, local government has become used to operating with many public, private and voluntary agencies. But the new focus on working with or through others is broadening relations with external bodies beyond immediate operational matters to new partnerships addressing wider strategic issues and reflecting a shared view of community needs. An authority's position vis-à-vis external bodies is, however, unique within an area, since as a locally elected body it is the only organisation which can stake a legitimate claim to speak on behalf of all the people in its area, and define a vision for the future of its community as a whole. This frequently requires local government to lead a local response to wider events.

Authorities maintain many different kinds of relationship with external bodies. They increasingly need to manage these in different ways. The relationship with a contractor or voluntary body depending financially upon the authority will be rather different from that with another tier of government, or with another public body. Some relationships are voluntarily entered into in pursuit of specific policy objectives, others are a necessary consequence of statutory responsibilities. Not all relationships with external bodies turn into long-term partnerships. Very rarely will the parties be neutral; each will want to influence the other, and will be able to bring different incentives (and sanctions) to bear. Where the authority has leverage, an effective partnership can be readily developed; where it does not, more subtle powers of persuasion and influence may be needed if divergent aims are to be overcome.

Complex policy issues require long-term coordination of multi-agency responses on a regular basis. Effective collaboration in these circumstances requires not just the usual informal and personal social networks, but more formally constituted ways of working together, which are clearly understood and publicly accountable. In the community care field, for example, joint planning arrangements have been formed with health authorities, and relationships developed with private and voluntary sector providers to create a mixed economy of care. This creates new pressures for other organisations too. Recognition of mutual dependence may be equally difficult for both sides, especially where they have both been habitually self-sufficient and used to exerting direct control over events. It means a new readiness by government generally and by other agencies to abandon traditional concerns for 'turf' in order to work together. 'Enabling' requires learning by all partners, including central government.

Influencing, interpreting and implementing the regulatory framework

Local authorities have extensive and increasing regulatory functions in a wide range of areas. Their work has both a local and national dimension in that they work within the framework of national legislation to ensure that no local community is put at a disadvantage. A local focus is especially important in development planning and environmental protection, to control the environmental impact of individual decisions affecting particular localities (such as the location of landfill sites or new infrastructure development). As public concern about quality of life grows it is important to prevent a 'beggar my neighbour' attitude, and to take a sensitive regulatory approach which modifies individual behaviour in the interest of maximising collective well-being at minimum cost.

Though they work within a wider legislative framework, authorities can ensure that this is oriented towards local interests in several ways. They can influence the structure of regulation at the policy formulation stage. For example, the approach now taken to prevent the spread of BSE was prompted by local experience in dealing with the disease where it was first identified. This may require acting in concert with other authorities and agencies in order to lobby for specific change and influence policy-makers. Once policy has been agreed and the regulatory framework determined, they have a key role in communicating the purpose and effect of new regulatory requirements. This helps authorities to ensure that there is adequate opportunity for businesses and individuals (subject to regulation) to anticipate its effects and so minimise the burden of compliance.

In enforcing regulation, the principal concern is to ensure that regulatory standards are consistently applied and that in carrying out enforcement activities, such as inspections, performance commitments are maintained. Consistency is becoming increasingly important within a European context (for example, in trading standards) where regular contacts between local authorities and European counterparts ensure that the approach taken is compatible and therefore no hindrance to the operation of the European internal market.

Encouraging access and involvement

The increasing need for agencies to work together comes at a time when surveys suggest that confusion remains about which agencies are responsible for which functions, and about how they relate to one another. This is not limited to local government. Many people, for example, believe that hospitals are still run by local authorities. Recognition of the need to improve communication with the public, to provide information about what local government is doing, and about what services are available, has led to new ways of communicating. Information centres, greater public relations activity, and using services with high levels of public contact, such as libraries, as access points into other services and to the working of the authority in general, are examples. Authorities are encouraging better access to services and facilities by disadvantaged groups through specialised provision such as interpreters for ethnic minority communities. More is now being done to ensure that elderly and disabled people can share the same services used by the rest of the community.

There is also increasing emphasis on involving users of services in the decisions directly affecting them. For example, the new focus on individual needs in community care encourages users to determine their preferred form of care. There is a renewed preoccupation across both public and private sectors with effective customer service, though it is recognised that consumers of most local government services cannot fully conform to the private sector model of individual choice. In the public context, the 'customer' is a more complex concept, since individuals have varying degrees of control over, and choice about, the services they receive. Many services provide a collective rather than individual benefit.

Linked to this 'consumerist' strand is the introduction of decentralised forms of management and more devolved political structures. At its simplest, this can mean delegating management decision-making and budgetary control to lower levels in the existing management hierarchy. More radical forms of decentralisation may involve bringing together responsibilities for several different services through a local office in an individual neighbourhood. This can then be paralleled by the development of political processes encouraging representation and participation through parish or neighbourhood councils.

Internal change

The development of 'enabling' attributes is leading to change in the way authorities work internally. The current approach to change and organisational development is both gradualist and diverse, reflecting local needs and circumstances, and different political cultures. Most internal structural change so far has reflected the separation of client/contractor roles required by compulsory competitive tendering. Other changes do not follow any consistent pattern. Though most authorities describe themselves as 'enablers', most are still in transition. For many the direct delivery of services continues to

be a significant preoccupation and the most important factor determining member roles and interests and internal organisation structures and processes. But it is also recognised that 'enabling' has important implications for the skills and style of people who work
within local government, whether as elected members or officers, and
for their working relationships with one another and with the community.

As authorities emphasise their strategic responsibilities, there is a
need for change in the role of the councillor, through rediscovery of the
role of 'civic leadership', as the government's consultation paper on
Internal Management recognises. This means a new emphasis on community representation, and on creating a 'dynamic atmosphere' for
community action, rather than a focus on the detail of how services are
delivered by the authority. This must be accompanied by a move away
from the traditional service and functional orientation of committees to
new structures with a more strategic emphasis.

Linked to this, the roles of officers and members must be more
clearly defined to allow members to concentrate on policy-making and
to give officers greater freedom within a clear policy and management
framework. This is not to exclude members from consideration of service planning and service quality, nor from individual cases which
raise serious policy issues or an unresolved complaint. But clearer
delineation of roles, allowing for more decentralisation and for detailed
decision-taking at lower levels, needs to be accompanied by proper
policy guidance, clearly defined management objectives, clear specifi-
cation of delegated authority and rigorous performance review by
members. All these are needed to ensure proper accountability.

The changing external environment and the changes in style of
operation require not only new structures and management processes,
but also new skills and competencies. New specialist professional
skills are required to handle the increasing diversity and complexity
of policy issues. Effective environmental impact assessment is an
example. New personal competencies, in the areas of influencing,
negotiating and consensus-building, are required to manage the greater
number and variety of political and professional relationships with
many different kinds of organisation, from multi-national corporations
and international government agencies, to local voluntary organisations
and user groups.

A mixed economy of service provision requires experience of contract management, and, as the management of authorities becomes
more complex, there is a continuing need to improve general management skills. Emphasis on improved customer service performance and
accountable management requires both efficient administration and a
responsive and understanding approach in dealing with members of the

public. This adds a new dimension to the traditional obligations to act reasonably, fairly, and in good faith in dealing with individual cases.

'Enabling' and the constitutional role of local government

In much of the current debate about the future of local government, as with many other organisations facing change, the question of structure is too often regarded as an end in itself. Discussion tends to concentrate upon how responsibilities are divided and functions allocated. These are important issues for local government, but it is essential in discussing these points not to lose sight of what structure is for. Its purpose is to provide a framework within which local government, as part of the system of government as a whole, is itself 'enabled' to meet the needs of the people it serves. The significance of 'enabling' for local government structure must therefore first be understood in the context of local government's constitutional role.

In Chapter 1 it is argued that local government:

- provides an essential source of pluralism in an increasingly complex and diverse policy environment;
- promotes active participation by individuals and local communities in the day-to-day business of government;
- provides a common focus for community identity and for the resolution of conflict in the interests of the local community as a whole;
- prevents too great a concentration of power at any one level of government.

The principal significance of 'enabling', as it is developing in practice, is that it provides the foundation for a continuing and active role for local government in contributing to future constitutional development. 'Enabling' directly encourages a pluralistic approach, in the emphasis on working with others to develop a comprehensive strategic response to local needs, and more flexible and diverse ways of meeting those needs. It directly promotes participation through improving access and involvement and encouraging a higher standard of performance oriented towards the 'customer'.

It is inherently focused on identifying and responding to the diverse interests of local communities and on the representation of those interests in a wider policy environment. It sets a standard based on professional credibility, openness and humanity which allows local government to present an effective and accountable source of checks and balances in the system of government as a whole. A fundamental requirement for future structure is that it should facilitate the full achievement of the 'enabling' style and further encourage authorities in the changes they are already making.

Implications for local government structure

The Government has suggested that the changing style of local government towards 'enabling' itself provides a reason and opportunity to reconsider structure. It has declared a preference for unitary authorities, whilst recognising that in some areas there may be a case for two tiers. The rationale behind the review of 1974 has been called into question. Since it is no longer assumed that local authorities will always provide services themselves, it is argued that there is no need for a uniform two-tier structure, based on optimal size for service delivery. Structure may instead match the particular circumstances of each area.

Enabling undoubtedly both permits and encourages a less uniform and rigid structure for local government in the future. But in itself it provides no simple answer to the form future structure should take. The enabling attributes described in this paper not only demand attention to the particular circumstances of each area, but require several complex factors to be taken into account:

- economic considerations;
- the nature of community;
- differing types of need;
- a collaborative policy environment.

These are discussed below.

Economic considerations

'Enabling' requires no less attention to be paid to the economics of service delivery now than in the past. In practice, where services are provided through contract, current experience already suggests that the issue of minimum efficient size is just as relevant for effective purchasing as for direct provision. Cost structures of different services vary widely. This is one reason why no single optimum size of authority could ever be reliably identified. For example, in the case of waste management, there is pressure to combine small geographical areas to secure a cost-effective service, because the economics of the industry are pushing private contractors to operate their collection, separation, transportation, and disposal services in an integrated way over a wide area. At the other end of the spectrum, grounds maintenance favours the small local supplier, who has relatively low entry costs and is able to offer a service customised to meet specific local requirements.

Whatever the source of provision, economies of scale will occur at a different point for different services. Where the cost and competitive structure of private industry favours the larger provider, smaller authorities may well be at a purchasing disadvantage unless they combine with others who have similar objectives. Larger authorities, however, can exert maximum purchasing power for large-scale services. They also have the flexibility to vary contract size for other services, so as to optimise value for money and meet the particular requirements of different services. The key issue for effective purchasing is bargaining power, and the move to the 'enabling' style therefore requires the review to think in terms of economic leverage, rather than simply in terms of size.

The nature of community

'Enabling' throws into still sharper focus the longstanding debate about how best to reconcile the economics of service provision with the effective articulation of community need. As this chapter shows, 'enabling' authorities are focused above all on meeting the needs of local communities in the most effective way. Yet the population of a particular geographical area may be very diverse. 'Community' is a misused term, and it is important that the review recognises the complexity of this concept. There are real communities at many territorial levels — street, parish, town, city, county, region, nation. But there are also many other types of community which cut across territory — religious, ethnic, gender, occupational, political, cultural, leisure-based. People may belong to many different communities simultaneously; but they may not always feel a sense of attachment to their neighbours. With greater economic and personal mobility, changing patterns of work and leisure, and the growth of communications media, people increasingly interact with others with whom they do not share local residence.

The review must therefore recognise that, however territories are defined, in today's increasingly complex society local government will be required to serve many diverse communities of interest. Even quite small local communities are not necessarily homogeneous and able unanimously to articulate local needs. Decision-making on 'the community's' behalf has to consider both narrow and wider interests. It must be sensitive to individual and collective needs, and be able both to arbitrate and conciliate where these are in conflict. The ability to ensure impartiality and independence of specific interest groups, whilst nonetheless encouraging them to contribute to the decision-making process, is an important aspect of local government's role in resolving local conflict. The structure of local government must therefore have the flexibility both to allow views to be expressed, and manage the inevitable conflict arising from this.

Differing types of need

Furthermore, by no means all types of need are highly localised. A key issue is how to recognise and plan effectively for the special needs of some client groups, such as the disabled, who are a minority within a community and whose requirements will tend to vary more in relation to individual circumstance than geographical location. To do this economically at an appropriate standard, a relatively large catchment area may be required. Some needs may be more geographically concentrated (for example, for leisure facilities), and less specialised in nature, and therefore the key issue will be how to meet them in accordance with local preferences. Where needs are required to be met at a minimum level of provision for wider policy reasons, a key issue is how to ensure consistent achievement of agreed standards across different localities, whilst nonetheless responding to local differences.

Structure must therefore be sufficiently flexible to respond to differing types of need in a way which fits the economics of service delivery, and matches local and national policy requirements. A two-tier (or multi-tier) structure potentially has more flexibility than a unitary system to define and respond to different types of need, since it combines smaller and larger areas within one structure and allows for both a localised and a more aggregated approach as appropriate. It also provides for purchasing flexibility. Exploiting this potential fully, however, requires the two tiers to work together in a coordinated way to agree overall policy, to determine the most appropriate strategic response, and agree a framework for localised decision-making. A good example of an integrated approach in the current structure is the planning and development control system. Counties and districts also work together in many other policy areas to meet the needs of their communities in an integrated way, though more could be done to encourage cooperation.

In a unitary structure, other arrangements would have to be made to provide for plurality and diversity of need. The more diverse a territory, the more esssential this is. Within larger unitary authorities, it would be necessary specifically to secure effective local input to ensure that local needs and preferences were identified. The emphasis in the 'enabling' style on decentralised management structures and the encouragement of greater public access and involvement has much to contribute in this respect. Parallel political decision-making structures would also allow local views to be represented by elected and hence accountable representatives. Area committee structures could be set up to ensure that the interests of individual localities were fully represented in decision-making. Parish and town councils could be given a more extensive role in consultation on matters affecting their area, and take on additional responsibilities for meeting localised needs.

A collaborative policy environment

The 'enabling' approach emphasises the importance of ensuring that local needs are viewed within a wider policy context, and conversely, that policy-making within other agencies and at other levels of government is fully informed by local experience and local diversity. It stresses the importance of effective inter-agency working and of the key role local government can play in bringing together community interests and representing local views in a wider national and international framework.

Smaller unitary authorities would need to make special arrangements to coordinate their policy planning to ensure that wider strategic issues were adequately addressed, and that local views carried sufficient weight with other agencies. Experience with joint arrangements suggests that this would require a high level of political agreement between authorities, and that a strategic response to key policy issues at the local level is more readily achieved through combining a wide territorial remit with a wide policy remit, whether in the present structure or within a unitary system. Political leverage in wider consultation and representation is as important as economic leverage in purchasing. The 'enabling' style of operation can only be carried fully into effect when local government is recognised by those with whom it collaborates in policy-making as credible in the enabling role.

Credibility is less a matter of size, as such, than of resources and capability. Human assets such as experience and proven expertise are as relevant as financial and physical resources and formal legal powers. Less tangible are the status and esteem in which authorities are held both by the public and by the agencies with which local authorities work. The views of local government's 'enabling' partners on the merits of alternative structures from their perspective will require careful consideration by the review.

Conclusion

The 'enabling' style, as it is developing in practice in local government, provides the foundation for a continuing and active role for local government in contributing to a strong national constitution. A fundamental requirement for future structure is that it should facilitate the full achievement of the enabling style, and further encourage local authorities in the changes they are already making.

'Enabling' permits a less uniform and rigid structure for local government in the future. But it provides no simple answer to the form structure should take. It neither leads conclusively to a unitary structure, nor determines an optimum size for a local authority. This chapter has presented the following key factors to be taken into account in the structural review in determining the best fit for the circumstances of each area:

- securing effective economic leverage in purchasing, taking into account the different cost structures of different services;
- responsiveness to the complexity and diversity of local communities and the need both to encourage active participation and balance conflicting views;
- matching differing types of need to policy requirements, local preferences and the economics of service delivery;
- effective coordination of strategic issues and the need to ensure credibility with 'enabling' partners in a wider policy environment.

3 Housing: continuing challenges and new opportunities

Introduction

> It is not too much to say that an adequate solution to the housing question is the foundation of all social progress
>
> (King George V 1919)

State intervention in housing has been a significant feature of social policy for over a century, and public housing has been, and remains, an important aspect of local government's responsibilities. Local authorities, along with the remaining New Towns, own about one fifth of all dwellings in Britain, over 4 million homes (*Housing and Construction Statistics* 1990). When these responsibilities are taken together with statutory duties towards the homeless and wider issues of strategic planning and community care (ACC/Coopers & Lybrand, forthcoming), it is clear that issues of housing policy and management continue to be directly relevant to conclusions on future local government structure.

Housing in recent years has become an area of considerable controversy. Government concerns about the extension of home ownership and about treating tenants as 'customers' have replaced earlier preoccupations with numbers and new build. External commentators have questioned conventional professional wisdom in the design and management of public housing, and have criticised central and local government policies alike. Beyond this, housing has been a key part of the Government's broader programme of change and reform of public sector service provision. The Duke of Edinburgh's *Inquiry into British Housing* observed that:

> The housing aims and strategies chime with other, wider Government concerns with increasing competition and choice, enhancing the role of the free market and emphasising individual rather than collective choice. Similarly the desire to introduce more business-like organisation into the public sector, to substitute private capital and market risk for public subsidy and to keep local authori-

ties in check are recurring themes in fields of policy other than housing.

(Duke of Edinburgh's Inquiry into British Housing, Information
Note 1)

Since the mid-1980s there has been extensive legislation directly affecting housing (Housing and Planning Act 1986, Landlord and Tenant Act 1987, Housing Act 1988, Local Government and Housing Act 1989) whilst legislation in other fields of social policy and in the area of local government finance (Social Security Act 1986, Local Government Act 1988, Children Act 1989, NHS and Community Care Act 1990) has also critically affected the operating environment. The objectives embodied by all the legislation were summarised in the White Paper on *Housing: The Government's Proposals* (1987):

- to spread home ownership;
- to revive the private rented sector;
- to transform 'local authorities (so that they) see themselves as enablers who ensure that everyone in their area is adequately housed, but not necessarily by them';
- to ensure that local authorities manage their stock in a more business-like way.

The latest policy initiatives in the Government's Citizen's Charter on tenants' rights and compulsory competitive tendering of housing management follow this pattern. Yet, despite the progress of right to buy, involving the removal of nearly a million homes from the sector during the 1980s, and of other initiatives such as voluntary transfer of stock to housing associations, there is increasing recognition that local authorities will continue to own large numbers of homes. Consequently a fundamental aim for both central and local government, of whatever political complexion, is to ensure that direct service provision is economic, efficient and effective.

But beyond this, local authorities must also provide for pressing housing need as it affects the vulnerable in society, including the homeless and special needs groups such as the old, disabled and disadvantaged. Housing associations have increasingly displaced local government as the main providers of new social housing. This means a new, 'enabling' focus for local government's housing role, requiring a comprehensive and multidisciplinary approach at a strategic level to identifying housing need, and flexibility in finding the best way to meet need through new sources of provision.

This chapter therefore takes as its principal themes:

- current issues affecting local authorities' continuing role in the direct ownership and management of stock;

- trends in demand for social housing, and, in particular, the issue of homelessness;
- the development of the 'enabling role' in housing;

and from this, identifies the key factors in the housing field relevant to the review of local government structure.

The direct role

Local government's performance

Organising the delivery of the housing service is a major undertaking. District and Borough Councils continue to manage a large number of homes. In virtually every area they are the largest single landlord. The Appendix to this chapter sets out existing District and Borough Council stockholdings organised by county. Reflecting the complexity of housing management today, a series of research projects on local government's performance in this field have been prepared since the mid-1980s for the Audit Commission, DoE, Welsh Office and Joseph Rowntree Foundation. The findings are outlined in the Information Notes to the Duke of Edinburgh's Inquiry into British Housing of 1990, hereafter referred to as 'the Inquiry'. Their assessment of these reports falls into four categories:

- the tenants' perspective;
- local responsiveness;
- efficiency and effectiveness;
- comparisons within and between landlords.

The tenants' perspective

A recent study by INLOGOV sought to discover what services council tenants regarded as crucial. The rankings were as follows:

- good repairs service (58 per cent);
- keeping the area in a good state of repair (42 per cent);
- choice of where to live (24 per cent);
- improvements and modernisation (23 per cent);
- right to do own improvements (21 per cent);
- having member of household take over tenancy at death (20 per cent);
- housing suitable for elderly people (20 per cent);
- low level of rent (20 per cent).

The survey also asked tenants about what quality of service they wanted from housing departments. Tenants' priorities were:

- staff who understand your problems (50 per cent);
- staff who explain things well (46 per cent);
- privacy when talking about personal matters (43 per cent);
- same staff dealing with your problems (31 per cent);
- friendly staff (24 per cent);
- minimal waiting before being dealt with (23 per cent);
- accessible local office (17 per cent).

As the Inquiry notes 'this sort of information is invaluable to a land-lord seeking to improve the service to tenants, since an obvious priority would be to concentrate on aspects of the service thought most impor-tant by the recipient'. Clearly (Information Note) there are lessons here for housing services irrespective of whether they are run by commer-cial, voluntary or governmental bodies.

There have been a number of attempts to discern tenants' views of landlords' performance. The INLOGOV study found 2 out of 3 tenants of local authorities and housing associations were either very or fairly satisfied with their housing service. Similarly the DoE report on the *Nature and Effectiveness of Housing Management* found that a similar proportion of the district council tenants they surveyed rated their housing service as at least satisfactory.

In many ways this DoE research was a rebuttal of an earlier Audit Commission report which found a 'crisis' in local authority housing management. It also punctured the view held in some quarters that housing associations were inherently better managers than local authorities. The DoE's researchers concluded that '. . . a more informed debate on policies for social rental sector housing should drop the widespread assumption that there is a pervasive crisis in man-aging council housing and take as its starting point that there are good and bad managers among local authorities . . .' and that is the starting point for this chapter.

While much of the research of the mid to late 1980s presents local authority housing in a broadly favourable light, there were some con-cerns. The DoE's researchers found that, for instance:

- 67 per cent of council tenants wanted more influence over their landlords;
- 30 per cent of tenants in large councils believed they received poor value for money;
- 57 per cent of council tenants regarded the mix and level of service provision as inappropriate and wanted more or better services.

The challenge for housing authorities is to maintain current good and popular practices, while improving quality in less effective areas. This will become more difficult to achieve, as the financial regime introduced by the Local Government and Housing Act 1989 influences rents upwards.

Local responsiveness

One way in which housing authorities are striving to maintain tenant allegiance is by encouraging participation in management decisions. In common with many other public and private enterprises, the housing service has initiated measures designed to get 'closer to the customer' and involve them in the day-to-day running of their estate. To facilitate this, the Institute of Housing has published a guide to stimulating 'Tenant Participation in Housing Management'. It cites examples of positive practice to encourage their wider application. Although most local authority housing departments now have some type of mechanism in place to facilitate participation, these vary widely in approach and effect.

Research has shown that three quarters of tenants wanted more say over council decisions (Information Note 6). To help meet this wish, a number of authorities have introduced Estate Management Boards. 'Composed of tenants, councillors and co-optees, (these) control an estate budget — "a sum of money separately identified from the Housing Revenue Account for the management and maintenance of an estate, separately accounted for, and under the control of a local manager or committee". The extent of control given to the board, over matters such as rent collection and lettings, may be negotiated' (Institute of Housing 1989). The DoE's Priority Estates Project has played a key role in promoting Estates Management Boards and other related initiatives. It has also encouraged local authority landlords to decentralise.

Research on trends in this practice area for the Rowntree Trust found that authorities with stock sizes of over 6,000 were more likely to be decentralising. With smaller authorities the tendency was towards amalgamation (Information Note 6). These findings help counter simplistic notions that large authorities are somehow faceless and uncaring bureaucracies. On the contrary the evidence is that larger authorities can be at the fore of initiatives to get closer to the customer. Furthermore, it is not automatically the case that authorities with small stockholdings are de facto closer to the customer. In rural areas with small but disparate stock holdings it may be viewed as uneconomic to provide local offices, notwithstanding the problems of managing over widely spread geographical areas. This is important for the debate on reorganisation because unitary authorities based on counties would result in the emergence of very substantial landlords (see Appendix to this chapter). It appears that local responsiveness is more a function of management will and resources than simply a function of stock size.

In summarising the Rowntree work the Inquiry noted that:

> Objectives behind decentralisation concerned quality and image of the service rather than greater control by tenants over the provision of the service. However, most local politicians and chief officers thought that decentralisation had increased participation. Overall, decentralisation was thought to have improved housing management but at a higher cost. Chief Officers felt that tenants were more satisfied with decentralised services.
>
> (Information Note 6)

A key problem with assessing decentralisation is that some of the more ambitious initiatives occurred before the introduction of comprehensive and systematic performance measurement and monitoring. It is generally assumed that decentralisation is costly but produces a positive response from tenants. But there is little hard evidence about either costs or benefits. It is possible that fear of costs and uncertainty of output could lead to a diminishing of interest in decentralisation in the prevailing climate, where concerns over resources are increasingly prominent in influencing local authorities' management approach. Nonetheless, it remains an important development in housing management which should be taken into account in considering future structure.

Efficiency and effectiveness

Devising performance measures to test efficiency and effectiveness in housing management has not been straightforward. Balancing measures that judge whether a landlord delivers services economically, with others that reflect tenant perception, is far from easy. As the Inquiry notes 'an expensive service may be very popular with tenants, particularly if they are shielded from its full costs'.

When basic performance measures have been used, however, wide differences in results have emerged. For example, the Audit Commission found that rent arrears as a percentage of gross rent debit stood at 17 per cent at the end of September 1985 in 11 authorities and at 6.1 per cent in other large authorities (Information Note 6). But determining the extent to which this is driven by the tenants' social circumstances or landlord performance is always difficult. At the time the research projects were in progress, few landlords were measuring performance or costing provision systematically. The former defect has begun to be addressed, particularly as local authority housing services are now statutorily obliged to issue annual performance statements to tenants. If CCT is extended to housing management, local authorities will need to develop more sophisticated means of costing and quality measurement to assess their competitiveness against external bidders.

Comparisons within and between landlords

The DoE research on the 'Nature and Effectiveness of Housing Management' tried to assess the relative merits of councils and associations as housing managers. Their work is an antidote to more simplistic and partisan notions which assert the innate superiority of one over another. In the end their analysis was that both local authorities and associations varied so widely as groups that such generalisation was impossible. Their conclusions, as summarised in the Inquiry, were that 'housing associations may provide a service which is well regarded by tenants, but this is achieved at higher cost than the service provided by local authorities' (Information Notes 6). This may appear to substantiate local government's long-standing assertion that resources are needed to ensure performance. In the current operational environment, any increase in resources for local government to improve the housing service would probably be tied down to specific performance criteria.

The current operational regime

Although recent research on local authority housing management portrays a broadly positive view of performance, it is important also to take account of current changes in the operational regime which are likely to have a significant impact on the direct role. In particular, the Local Government and Housing Act 1989 recast the financial arrangements relating to local authority housing. It is important to consider the likely effects in respect of rents and resources for repairs, improvements and new build, and to look at new ways of delivering social housing being considered by local authorities in response to these pressures.

Rents

A central plank of the Government's housing policies is that rents for council houses should move towards those of the open market. This implies that local authority rents should differ between areas to reflect market variations. The principal changes to rent setting take effect through the housing revenue account (HRA) subsidy provisions of the Local Government and Housing Act 1989.

Local authorities are now statutorily disallowed from running their housing revenue accounts at a deficit. For many authorities their ability to comply hinges on eligibility for housing revenue account subsidy. Central government makes an annual determination of this based on a notional assessment of a particular local authority's housing-related income and expenditure. If this is inadequate and a local authority believes, say, that more repairs and improvements are required than the notional budget allows, additional resources may have to be funded through rent increases.

Furthermore HRA subsidy now includes council tenants' housing benefits (which were previously paid separately). Again, partly because this is based on a notional calculation it is frequently inadequate to meet the local authority's obligations. Since the duty to prevent a deficit applies, the shortfall must be met from out of the rents of those not receiving benefit. For many local authorities this acts as a severe pressure influencing rents upwards. Given that approximately two thirds of council tenants are likely to be in receipt of housing benefit, the full burden of the shortfall has to be met by a minority of tenants. Over time this may make remaining in the council sector a less attractive option for them.

The notional assessments used by Government assume a certain level of financial and management performance. Should a local authority fail to deliver on these targets their tenants' rents will rise as a consequence. This is meant as an incentive to ensure that councils perform in a business-like fashion — a fundamental aim of the 1987 White Paper. Tenants are made aware of deficiencies in management performance through the annual performance statement council landlords are now obliged to provide.

In an extension of this more competitive philosophy, the Government now proposes in the consultation paper on the Tenant's Charter that performance indicators from housing should be gathered into local authority performance league tables, alongside those from other services. Additionally, the housing indicators would be compared with similar data from housing associations. This should enable tenants to assess the performance of their local authority landlord relative to other local authorities, as well as housing associations.

Although each year the Government issues guideline rent increases, these are currently exceeded by many authorities, mainly because the notional figures used by central government do not reflect their true position. The largest District council rent increase for 1991/92 was of the order of 39 per cent. In cash terms this exceeded the DoE guideline increase by £7.55 per week. It is perhaps worth noting that even those authorities which have satisfied the relevant performance criteria have been bound to pass on increases beyond the guidelines. The average council rent increase in 1991/92 for all English local authorities was 13 per cent, well in excess of inflation, while the average actual increase was over 70 per cent higher than the DoE guideline. Average council rents now stand at £27.31 per week (*Roof*

July/August 1991). While the new financial regime might have been expected to introduce market and performance-related variations in Council rents, disparities between apparently similar districts are quite marked. Amalgamation of authorities would raise issues of equity, though larger authorities could provide increased opportunity for cross-subsidy.

Resources

As for all other council functions involving capital expenditure, the housing service is affected by Part IV of the Local Government and Housing Act 1989, which aims to control local authority borrowing and curb indebtedness. It impacts most severely on the housing service in relation to the use of capital receipts. Under the previous financial regime housing authorities were permitted to spend the receipts from right to buy sales through a set formula over a number of years. Since the 1989 Act was implemented, only 25 per cent of the receipts from housing sales may be devoted to capital expenditure. The remainder have to be set aside for debt redemption. Housing is treated particularly harshly under this regime; for most other categories of receipt, half may be spent on capital expenditure while the remaining half is devoted to debt redemption. However, while this measure very severely constrains a housing authority's ability to target resources onto the upkeep of its own stock, the Government has made some concessions to facilitate the enabling role, which are discussed below. This reduced ability to fund repairs and improvements from capital receipts means that works to stock often have to be funded directly from rents, acting as a further pressure towards higher rents or reduced standards.

In addition, over the last year the concept of local authorities competing against one another for housing resources has been formalised and expanded. Although for some years Estate Action funding was allocated partly in relation to the perceived quality of the scheme, most DoE approvals of local authority housing expenditures were founded on needs-based assessments. Recently, however, the City Challenge bids were judged on the quality of submissions and presentations made to Ministers by competing local authorities. Following this initiative, a greater proportion of local authorities' Housing Investment Programme submissions to the DoE has also been subject to competition between authorities.

Tenants' Choice

The operating constraints introduced by the Local Government and Housing Act 1989 have been instrumental in encouraging local authorities to consider new ways of delivering social housing. In the run up to the implementation of the Act, local authorities were concerned that these new pressures on rents and resources would pave the way for incursions from predatory landlords. Through the earlier Housing Act of 1988, non-council landlords were permitted to acquire local authority stock, if need be against the wishes of that authority, provided the alternative body was approved by the Housing Corporation for the purpose and that the transfer secured a positive vote from tenants. This is known as 'Tenants' Choice'.

So far the perceived threat to local authority ownership from Tenants' Choice has not materialised. Only one case has been put to the vote, involving a tenants' group in central London who have pursued a long standing dispute with their local authority landlord through this route. Although the result of this ballot was positive, it is not expected to spark a revival of interest elsewhere, owing to the particular circumstances underlying the transfer.

Tenants' groups are put off pursuing the route for themselves because of the time it takes to secure approval from the Housing Corporation, as well as the complexity of the process of making a bid to the local authority. Housing Associations have more to gain through positive relations with local authorities through the latter's enabling role, and so have tended not to pursue what are seen as hostile bids for local authority stock. Meanwhile, with only one exception, the few private landlords who have sought approved landlord status have been rebuffed by the Housing Corporation. So far, evidence suggests that it is doubtful whether tenants would vote in favour of a profit-orientated body to take over their homes, when not-for-profit alternatives were available.

Housing action trusts (HATs)

Until earlier this year, when tenants in Hull voted in favour of a HAT, this form of new landlord, introduced at Part III of the Housing Act 1988, seemed destined never to appear in practice. Broadly, the HAT is based on the model of Urban Development Corporations and is intended to be targeted on areas of greatest need. The lifespan of a HAT is determined by the programme needed to resolve the issues it sets out to tackle. Initially prospective HATs were to be identified by the Government but latterly local authorities and indeed tenants themselves have instigated moves towards HATs. The first wave of HATs was withdrawn following adverse tenant reaction. Revisions were made to the HAT model proposed for two estates in Southwark LB last year but these too were rejected by tenants in a formal ballot. They opted instead to remain with the local authority.

The HAT proposals which have succeeded in Hull had the full support of the local authority along with assurances on rent levels and, crucially, the option to return to the local authority at the end of the HAT. Similar proposals have secured a positive vote on several estates in Waltham Forest. In other urban areas, notably Liverpool and Tower Hamlets, proposals for further HATs are now emerging.

Voluntary transfer

In response to the new financial regime and the potential threat from predatory landlords, many local authorities have given consideration to transferring their housing stock voluntarily. 'Voluntary transfer' describes the disposal of all or part of a local authority's tenanted stock to an independent and autonomous housing body. The transfer is voluntary in that it is initiated and supported by the authority. The receiving body need not be a registered housing association, although the common practice to date has involved this format. All transfers so far completed have involved newly created local bodies, but existing organisations including extant registered housing associations are eligible.

Voluntary transfer is undertaken using powers conferred through the Housing Act 1985 along with the provisions of the Housing and Planning Act 1986. The Secretary of State for the Environment must give consent and a majority of those tenants voting in a ballot must vote in favour for this permission to be forthcoming. General guidance is provided in Circular 6/88 and in the DoE's publication *Large Scale Voluntary Transfer of Local Authority Housing to Private Bodies* (June 1988).

To date some 16 District Councils have voluntarily transferred their stock. Several more are at an advanced stage in the process. However, districts retain extensive stock holdings as the Appendix to this chapter shows. For example, districts in Cheshire have 67,411 council houses, Avon 66,738, Hampshire 100,850 and Nottinghamshire 96,661. A recent survey of District Council Housing Chairs by Shelter found that 73 per cent had considered voluntary transfer in the last year, 91 per cent of these rejected it completely as an option, but over two thirds would reconsider transfer if the prevailing view from Government continued to be against councils as providers of homes (*Roof* May/June 1991). This may mean that any local government restructuring in relation to the housing service would be attempting to accommodate continuous change as local authorities consider and pursue voluntary transfer. The prospect of reorganisation could itself influence authorities towards voluntary transfer. District Councils may prefer to transfer stock voluntarily to avoid amalgamation or breaking up of stock by a new authority. On the other hand, transfer may be restricted by the supply of private finance. Doubts are now being expressed about whether there are sufficient funds available for all the authorities who may wish to transfer their stock.

Perhaps the key issue in connection with voluntary transfer is that local authority tenants do not appear to welcome change. In their research on the 'Nature and Effectiveness of Housing Management', the DoE found that tenants saw the source of service improvements coming from their local authority rather than alternative landlords. All votes in favour of voluntary transfers have been for bodies composed predominantly of the former local authority housing department, with a continuation of its not-for-profit modus operandi. The few attempts to introduce non-local housing associations or private landlords have been unsuccessful.

Compulsory competitive tendering (CCT)

The details of the Government's proposed extension of CCT to 'white collar' services are now emerging. In the recent consultation paper on improvements to the Tenant's Charter, the commitment given in the Citizen's Charter White Paper to subject housing management to CCT is reiterated. The DoE are awaiting the output of a research project on this prior to presenting detailed proposals. Whatever the outcome of the research, detailed proposals would have to address the following:

- Should CCT apply on a geographic (e.g. estates, ward or parish) or service (e.g. rent collection or waiting list maintenance) basis?
- Will tenants be consulted and if so how?
- Will tenderers need to be validated, perhaps as the Housing Corporation does with prospective new landlords?
- In view of the complexity of the housing service, how far will the costs of the 'client' effectively monitoring the 'contractor' mitigate potential savings?

While a more mature view of the implications for CCT on the housing service will have to be developed as details emerge, experience from other forms of CCT suggests that the business discipline applying to the service is sharpened with the obligation to become competitive. Should CCT lead both to different housing management arrangements and a better service, tenants' perspectives of alternative landlords may broaden.

Notwithstanding concerns about the resource implications of monitoring contractors, CCT (in any service) implies fewer retained functions, with the concomitant need for fewer staff and less resources to be directly employed by an authority. This may facilitate wider structural change by enabling the housing management function to be more readily combined with other management functions.

Key points

The main features of the direct housing provision role which have a bearing on the debate about local government structure are as follows:

- The stock retained by District and Borough Councils remains large. The changes associated with CCT, alongside voluntary and involuntary transfer, could reduce the range of functions to be provided directly, as well as the numbers of houses to be managed. Nonetheless, reorganising this scale of service provision into a new structure would require very detailed planning.
- It is the larger housing authorities which generally have taken steps to decentralise to deliver effective services closer to the customer. Achieving quality of service relates to commitment and resources and not just, or necessarily, size.
- For the time being a clear majority of tenants are content with the service provided and there is evidence that they are resistant to change.
- Legislation implemented from the late 1980s is fundamentally altering the operating context of the direct housing role. Rents are increasing at beyond the rate of inflation and the capacity to deliver on repairs and improvements is constrained. This may diminish tenant satisfaction with current arrangements.
- CCT in housing management, together with the widening role of housing associations, may broaden tenant perspective on alternative landlords.

Stock transfer has so far been slow but may increase in the future, depending upon the availability of private finance and the impact of the reorganisation of local government itself.

The next section of the chapter turns from analysis of the services directly provided to Council tenants towards the question of demand for social housing.

Demand for social housing

Estimating housing demand of wider groups beyond that of the statutorily homeless is problematic. There are no official estimates of housing need, which perhaps in itself suggests the lack of importance attached to future housing supply as an issue. In contrast to the 1950s and 1960s, when local authority housebuilding figures were a major political battleground, housing seldom now appears as an issue influencing voting in parliamentary elections. This may be because, unlike other publicly provided services such as education or health, which are used by the great majority of the population, social housing is provided for a minority of households. The level of mortgage arrears (according to the Bank of England there are now 785,000 households in arrears of two months or more), may yet give new direct relevance to the housing service for a larger proportion of the electorate. If a proportion of those in arrears look to local authorities for assistance in the last resort, supply of social housing could be placed in sharper focus at the national level.

In the absence of official house production targets, some work has been done to estimate the volume of housebuilding required. The findings are summarised in the Inquiry. In 1989 the National Housing Forum, a body in which the ACC is an active participant, endeavoured to assess the need for all categories of new housebuilding. Their findings implied an annual building rate of between 228,000 to 290,000. As the Inquiry notes, this is not out of kilter with what was achieved during the early 1970s, when 280,000 units were achieved per annum. However it appears somewhat ambitious set against the 175,000 dwellings constructed in 1989.

The Institute of Housing argued in a report published in 1989 that there was a requirement for 100,000 new units of social housing to be completed each year in England. Again this appears optimistic. It would entail building at three times the annual rate of local authorities and housing associations combined. In rural areas, the Rural Development Commission have established a case for 166,000 rural houses to be built in a 5 year programme. The ACC has expressed support for this. Its rural housing report 'Homes We Can Afford' sets out a range of innovative ways to tackle the rural housing shortage.

One of the most recent targets set for social housing is contained in a report for the ADC. It is broadly in line with the Institute of Housing's work suggesting that housing provision should be two to three times current levels. Their proposed targets lie between 75,000 to 115,000 units per annum (ADC June 1991). By any measure, demand for social housing is outstripping supply.

Issues of housing need are increasingly significant at all levels of local government, as authorities move towards the 'enabling' style discussed in a previous paper in this series. Perspectives differ across functions and across tiers: as strategic planning authorities, for example, counties will consider need based on a balance between demographic projections and land-use policy. As social services authorities, working closely with health authorities, the counties will consider the housing needs of vulnerable individuals within their communities. As housing authorities, districts will tend to define need in relation to waiting list applications and the numbers of statutorily homeless (whom they have an obligation to house — see below). Housing also impacts on many other areas of social policy in which local government has significant responsibilities; for instance, educational achievement, environmental health, employment opportunity, crime prevention.

In some areas, counties and districts are already working together to consider future housing provision against the background of the wider needs of local communities and to prevent, or reduce, the problems tending to occur when responsibility for meeting the needs of key client groups is split between functions and tiers. But an already complex situation has become more problematic as local government moves out of direct housing provision and involves other providers, as discussed in the next section. What is becoming steadily more apparent, however, is that a so-called crisis of management has become a real crisis of need — local authorities have been described recently as 'not strategists . . . but scavengers for affordable housing'. Nowhere is the crisis more acutely felt than in relation to homelessness.

Homelessness

The main legislation dealing with Homelessness is the Homeless Persons Act 1977 as consolidated at Part III of the Housing Act 1985. Prior to the 1977 Act counties had a major role in homelessness provision through the National Assistance Act of 1948, which placed a duty on the counties to provide temporary accommodation for 'persons in urgent or unforeseen need'. A Ministry of Health circular stressed that the purpose was to assist people made homeless through an emergency such as fire or flood; it was not intended to deal with the 'inadequately housed' (*Roof* September/October 1991).

While this duty rested with counties, housing stock was held by another tier of local government. To comply with their duties counties often had to resort to inadequate hostels, many of which had been used under the pre-1948 Poor Law. Alone amongst the local authority associations the ACC approved of the proposals in the then Homelessness Bill which sought, inter alia, to unite the responsibilities for stock ownership and accommodating the homeless. Similar problems are now being met in implementing the Children Act.

As the law now stands, District and Borough Councils have the statutory duty to provide a service to the homeless. The duties include the following:

- An obligation to find accommodation for people who are homeless, or threatened with homelessness, through no fault of their own, provided they are in priority need, for example pregnant women, and anyone with whom a pregnant woman lives or might reasonably be expected to live.

- For those in priority need but deemed to be intentionally homeless the authority must provide temporary accommodation for a reasonable period and offer advice and assistance in finding accommodation.
- For people who are homeless but not in priority need authorities have a duty to provide appropriate advice and assistance in finding accommodation.

The process for deciding whether someone is homeless unintentionally and has priority need is complex. It is one of the most litigious areas of housing law, often because the local authority assessing eligibility is frequently the same authority that must house the homeless person. It may consequently have a less than impartial interest in the outcome, especially where resources are constrained.

Accommodating those households towards whom the authority accepts a duty is often not straightforward. Invariably, there is a considerable waiting list. In many areas there is such a shortage of permanent council houses that more expensive short-term measures have to be used, such as bed and breakfast, or leasing from private landlords. Coordination between authorities can also be difficult. If a local authority believes that an otherwise eligible person has a safe local connection elsewhere, he or she can be referred on for rehousing to the local authority for that area. To help resolve the inevitable disputes that surround decisions whereby one authority places a duty on another, there is a local authority assocations agreement as well as a statutory disputes procedure. The recent Government Review of Homelessness identified the problem that the difficulties and sensitivities of running this service contribute to a lack of consistency in approach between authorities.

The implementation of the Children Act 1989 introduced still further scope for disputes between local authorities. Outside London and the metropolitan areas, counties as social services authorities have a duty to provide accommodation to a child in 'need' aged 16 or over whose welfare is otherwise likely to be 'seriously prejudiced'. This has again raised the question of divided responsibilities for homelessness, in that one tier of local government has a duty to respond to need, while another tier holds the means of doing so, namely the housing stock. For this reason, under the Children Act the counties can call on districts to help provide the necessary accommodation, insofar as this is compatible with the districts' obligations to vulnerable people. But, as the most recent edition of the DoE's Code of Guidance on Homelessness acknowledges, there is no 'formal correlation' between the definition of vulnerability in the Housing Act 1985, to which the districts operate and the definition of 'serious prejudice' or 'need', to which the counties are obliged to operate under the Children Act. Partly in response to lobbying from counties through the ACC, the new Code of Guidance recognises the dangers of lack of coordination between tiers of local government, and draws housing authorities' attention to potential difficulties.

The potential increase of responsibility under the Children Act, on top of existing increasing demand, is coming at a difficult time for housing authorities. For example, The London Research Centre produce a regular 'Housing Update' incorporating information on homelessness. The edition from May/June 1991 found that:

> The latest homelessness statistics show that the upward trend in acceptances seen over the last decade is continuing. Across the country there has been a 15 per cent rise in homelessness over the previous year. The largest increases over the period 1988–90 were in the Midlands and in Yorkshire and Humberside. The continuing rise in the figures is all the more significant, because there are clear indications that local authorities are making efforts to tighten up on the criteria they use to decide whether or not an applicant is homeless.

During 1990 over 100,000 households were accepted as homeless by English authorities outside Greater London. Reflecting this increase in acceptances, more than 50,000 households are now placed in temporary accommodation by housing authorities. There is widespread concern that households being evicted due to mortgage arrears are swelling the ranks of those that local authorities are obliged to rehouse. In 1990–91 there were 48,000 repossessions for mortgage arrears. This translated into a 50 per cent increase in acceptances by local authorities of families citing mortgage arrears as the cause of homelessness. The figures for households either in temporary accommodation and/or having been repossessed stand in stark contrast to the 35,000 new homes built by Councils and Housing Associations together in 1990/91 (*Roof* September/October 1991).

The rise in homelessness is an unwelcome feature of the economic cycle. But it comes at a time when housing authorities' ability to respond is constrained by the current emphasis of Government policy upon housing associations as the primary source of new social housing. This is discussed in more detail in the next section. The key issue for the review, however, is that future local government structure must enable an effective strategic response to the emerging crisis of demand.

Key points

The important points in relation to homelessness, and demand more generally, which bear upon the debate on local government structure are as follows:

• Demand is comprehensively outstripping supply. This applies to permanent dwellings made available by councils and housing associations, and to those relatively limited groups that have a statutory call on the local authority.

• A full assessment of housing need must take account of strategic planning issues, community care needs, and wider issues of social policy, as well as questions of statutory entitlement. This requires closer coordination at a policy level across functions and tiers if the needs of local communities are to be met.

• Problems are particularly acute as they affect the homeless. First, inconsistencies in some housing authorities' interpretation of the homelessness legislation mean that a homeless household's prospects of securing a local authority home may vary, depending on the authority to which they apply. Second, inconsistencies in the legal framework governing districts' and counties' different responsibilities for homeless young people have the potential to create major problems of coordination. Unless there is meticulous planning and inter-tier cooperation, some vulnerable young people will slip through the net.

• A key issue for the review is to ensure that future structure enables an effective strategic response to the emerging crisis of demand.

The enabling role

In common with other areas of local authority service provision, current Government policy is to encourage housing need to be met through the 'enabling' role rather than directly provided. To assist housing authorities with this change of emphasis the Institute of Housing have recently published a comprehensive guide, *Working Together in the 1990s*, which sets out the ways in which local authorities can assist housing associations to create new homes. The following examples illustrate the range of ways in which authorities are acting as 'enablers' in the housing field.

Sale of local authority land to housing associations

Land costs typically comprise between 25 per cent to 50 per cent of the costs of social housing schemes. Clearly, the more cheaply housing associations are able to acquire and assemble building land, the more economic and effective they will be in providing social housing. Usually, when local authorities dispose of land at below market value they are compelled, under the terms of the Local Government and Housing Act 1989, to set aside the relevant proportion of the receipt they would have received at the imputed full market value. However, where the land is sold at a discount, or even passed on at nil value to a housing association in exchange for nomination rights, this restriction is eased. The imputed capital receipt is discounted by the value of the nomination rights, prior to the intervention of the set aside rules.

Financial assistance to housing associations

Provided the Housing Corporation is agreeable local authorities can make Local Authority Housing Association Grant (HAG) available to local housing associations. There are several advantages for the local authority. First, the priorities for local authority HAG are those of the Council, rather than those of the Housing Corporation. (It cannot be presumed that the two will necessarily coincide.) Second, it is an efficient use of council resources. Nomination rights are secured for significantly less than the full cost of the houses, while the ongoing management and maintenance costs rest with the association.

Voluntary stock transfer to housing associations

The mechanism by which this is undertaken was described earlier. Where local authorities transfer the whole of their stock to housing associations a substantial capital receipt will accrue. If this receipt is sufficient to clear all the authority's debt, it may be applied in its entirety to capital expenditure, including assistance to housing associations. This is subject only to a formula setting annual limits on the rate of spend related to the numbers of local authority tax payers. Essentially what voluntary transfer does is to release the asset value of existing local authority housing. Although the valuation methodology takes full cognisance of tenants' security of tenure and obligations to set affordable rents, the process by which future income (e.g. rents) is netted off against outgoings (e.g. repairs and management) and adjusted for inflation, tends to produce a substantial net positive value. The first 15 voluntary transfers involved a total of 70,802 homes and achieved a transfer price of £611.8 million (*Social Housing* March 1991).

The Chief Executive of North Housing Association, one of the largest in England, has argued that the refinancing opportunities afforded by voluntary transfer should not necessarily have to involve a change of ownership (*Roof* September/October 1991). On this basis local authorities could run directly substantial development programmes, paid for by private finance, raised against their stock as asset backing. Generally the larger the stock, the greater the asset backing, and thus the more favourable terms for private finance. This could represent a powerful argument for the amalgamation of local authority housing departments to achieve larger stocks for financing purposes. Indeed, under similar pressure to attract private finance, there has already been a tendency for small housing associations to merge.

Use of planning powers

The planning process can facilitate social housing in two main ways: first, by permitting development on sites not usually available for residential use. For example, affordable homes could be developed on land previously zoned for agriculture if a consideration is forthcoming in excess of normal agricultural values (typically £700 to £2,000 an acre), but below the open market value for housing land. Second, planning can also assist through the use of 'planning gain' agreements under s106 of the Town and Country Planning Act 1990. Under such agreements developers may agree to make available discounted land or homes for social housing in return for a planning decision which they find beneficial overall.

Urban renewal

For many years local government has had statutory powers to tackle private sector housing problems in urban areas targeted for special treatment. These were overhauled by the Local Government and Housing Act 1989. The Institute of Housing's guide to the enabling role comments adversely on some of the changes. In particular they draw attention to the increased complexity of declaring areas to be targeted, and the difficulties associated with the introduction of means testing for occupiers. Notwithstanding this criticism, the Institute of Housing suggest several positive measures that authorities can take to facilitate urban renewal. These include making grants available to housing associations for major repairs and also for the adaption of homes for disabled people, and the sale of compulsorily purchased properties to housing associations. Under the Capital Finance Regulations the capital receipt accruing may be offset by the cost of replacing the dwelling before the intervention of the set aside rules.

Nomination agreements

Local authorities are now cast in the role of enabling others, especially housing associations, to supply social housing. But their residual statutory duties in respect of the homeless, as well as the maintenance of a waiting list of those in housing need, means that they must take a strong interest in those whom associations house. There has been widespread concern that associations have not accepted a reasonable share of homeless people. The Housing Minister has argued strongly that associations should house more homeless people. At present 42 per cent of all new housing association lettings are made to local authority nominees, of which only 38 per cent are homeless cases (*Housing Association Weekly* 14 June 1991). Without improvements on these proportions, a strategy using others to meet the local authority's statutory duties runs the risk of failing to meet the needs of the most vulnerable.

The Housing Corporation has therefore stipulated that half of all lettings in schemes they fund should be made to local authority nominees. For schemes which the local authority has helped fund, or contributed land or other assistance, the proportion may legitimately be higher. To ensure cooperation the NFHA, AMA and ADC have a nationally applicable agreement. In London, the ALA, LBA and LHAC have produced a rigorous good practice guide on responsibilities for the homeless, which provides a useful model.

Impact of the enabling role

Perceptions of the 'enabling' role amongst housing authorities currently differ considerably. First, it is a major change in direction. For many the transition from the more direct 'providing' role to the strategic focus and influencing and facilitating style implied by 'enabling' is proving difficult. There is uncertainty over quite what is meant, and about what can be achieved. Secondly, there have been major problems for housing associations, due to the Housing Corporation's recent cash crisis. This came at a most unfortunate time, denting the credibility of associations to deliver just as the enabling role was being introduced.

The novelty, lack of clarity and uncertainty of output involved in the 'enabling' role was reflected in a recent Shelter survey of (Conservative) Chairs of Housing in District Councils. 77 per cent thought councils should be allowed to build directly for rent while 43 per cent reported that they had been affected by the Housing Corporation's financial difficulties (*Roof* May/June 1991). However, in the longer term, as the Housing Corporation's financial position improves, and as awareness and experience of the potential of the enabling role grows, helped by the work of the Institute of Housing, housing authorities are likely to develop more confidence.

Members and housing officers in those authorities which have voluntarily transferred their housing stock are to a degree pioneers. The direct role was foregone when the stock transferred, yet as a consequence they have money, and in some cases, land, available to enable development by other providers. A recent survey by Coopers and Lybrand Deloitte suggested that members had experienced difficulty coming to terms with the concept that homes developed with the council's money were not theirs, but rather belonged to housing associations (albeit with nomination agreements). However, both members and officers welcomed being liberated from dealing with individual tenancy problems, especially neighbour disputes. Remarkably, few savings in committee time were identified, principally because councils were instead engaged upon major development programmes (for the first time in some years). Methods of 'enabling', such as those described above, involve complex processes, which take time to set up and implement.

Beyond this, 'enabling' requires a broader and more complex view of need, which is able to encompass the interaction of a wide range of policy issues affecting the extent and manner of social housing provision. It requires new ways of working, a new approach to maximising value from available resources, and a wide spread of contacts with key professionals and agencies working within local communities.

The move to 'enabling' requires the review of local government structure to consider the perspective of 'providers'. Discussion with the Housing Corporation and House Builders' Federation suggests that there may be advantage from the provider viewpoint in dealing with fewer and larger authorities. For example, setting up the mechanisms for combining Housing Corporation funding with local authority assistance is technically demanding. The fewer interested parties involved in such negotiations, the easier it may be to deliver social housing. Concern was also expressed about lack of consistency between districts, and about their willingness or ability to work effectively with associations. Small scale local interests can hold back development of social housing, where this is in the wider strategic interests of a larger area.

Finally, the transformation to strategic 'enabler' carries risk. As direct functions are lost, public awareness may decrease. If housing authorities increasingly act in an enabling role, irrespective of their structure and scale, attention must be given to ensuring that the public knows about key local issues, what is being achieved, and that the contribution of both the provider and enabler to bringing about effective solutions is recognised.

Key points

In summary, the main points arising from local authorities' new style of operating are:

● Local authority housing departments are going through a major

transition of role from 'providers' to 'enablers', involving many
new ways of meeting housing need, and a new style of working.
- The enabling role is not without its problems. It is at least as complex as the direct role because of the range of options available, the
need to ensure objectives are met, and the number of participants in
any decision and transaction. The benefits of the enabling role must
also be communicated effectively to the public if they are to understand local government's new contribution to meeting need.
- The interests of housing 'providers' may lie in favour of larger
authorities able to take a more consistent and more strategic view of
objectives and relationships.

Conclusion

Notwithstanding the extensive legislative changes introduced by the
present Government, the stock of local authority housing remains
large. The reorganisation of service provision on this scale within any
new local government structure would require very careful planning to
ensure continuity with present housing management arrangements, so
that tenants' interests were protected.

However, a number of factors may affect the extent to which direct
provision is a consideration in the longer term. The development of
compulsory competitive tendering will reduce and change the range of
functions to be considered, and may encourage a focus on authorities
able to manage several housing management contracts of varying size.
Other factors (particularly continuing rent increases) could hasten the
currently slow progress with voluntary transfers. Both authorities' and
tenants' attitudes may yet shift more in favour of alternative landlords.

Where tenants continue to be reluctant to move away from local
authority landlords, however, a key issue for the review will be to
determine the structural framework most likely to provide an environment most conducive to better management. Current local authority
territories may not constitute either the optimal size or the best pattern
of distribution for cost-effective management. Experience suggests that
the structure must provide for:

- the ability to ensure consistent standards of housing management
performance (whether provided externally or in-house);
- the flexibility and scope for decentralisation at acceptable cost;
- the human and material resources to manage in a more demanding
operating environment and within increasingly constrained financial
arrangements.

From the 'enabling' perspective, there are two key issues for the
review. First, enabling is fundamentally about meeting the needs of the
community in the most effective way. There is a crisis in demand for

social housing and the review must establish a structure able to provide an adequate response. Existing difficulties in dealing with the homeless, particularly young people, and with other special housing needs, suggest that there may now be advantage in bringing strategic and policy responsibilities in different functions more closely together. This would allow a more consistent approach reflecting local needs and priorities, across functional areas. It would also help mitigate the worst effects of present inconsistencies within the legal framework. Second, such a clearly defined and consistently implemented view is also what new providers (or partners) seek. The technical complexity of present funding arrangements and partnership schemes is such that both Housing Associations and private developers are likely to see advantage in being able to deal with fewer, larger and more strategic authorities. Small-scale views may tend to discourage policies for social housing development framed in the wider interests of a larger area.

The extent and nature of change in housing management, and the wider policy issues associated with the requirement to take a more strategic approach to identifying and defining demand, suggest that the time may be right to consider change in the historic allocation of responsibilities in the housing field and bring together responsibilities for housing with other areas of social policy, and with strategic planning, with a unitary structure.

A structure based on larger-scale unitary authorities could provide significant advantages in the policy arena, and create new opportunities to work effectively with housing providers and with central government, in response to the emerging need for growth in social housing provision. Against the background of the other changes described in this paper affecting the direct role, large authorities could sustain a flexible approach to meeting tenants' needs, provided that there was sufficient commitment to decentralisation and to achieving high levels of performance on a consistent basis.

As in many other important policy areas, the review of local government structure comes at a time of considerable change and development in the housing field. It is important that the review recognises this rapidly changing environment, and provides for a flexible and pragmatic response which enables new and practical solutions to be developed to answer the 'housing question' of the nineties and beyond, to ensure continuing social progress.

Appendix

County	District	Total	County total
Avon	Bath	6,692	
	Bristol	37,594	

County	District	Total	County total
	Kingswood	4,663	
	Northavon	5,186	
	Wansdyke	4,530	
	Woodspring	8,073	66,738
Bedfordshire	Luton	15,458	
	Mid Beds	7,190	
	South Beds	7,596	30,244
Berkshire	Bracknell	8,709	
	Reading	9,277	
	Slough	10,924	
	Windsor	7,433	
	Wokingham	3,501	39,844
Buckinghamshire	Aylesbury Vale	10,240	
	Milton Keynes	6,533	
	Wycombe	8,875	25,648
Cambridgeshire	Cambridge	10,400	
	East Cambs	4,275	
	Fenland	4,706	
	Huntingdon	8,720	
	Peterborough	13,500	
	South Cambs	7,351	48,952
Cheshire	Chester	8,284	
	Congleton	4,600	
	Crewe and Nantwich	7,434	
	Ellesmere Port	7,964	
	Halton	9,010	
	Macclesfield	8,611	
	Vale Royal	8,999	
	Warrington	12,509	67,411
Cleveland	Hartlepool	11,221	
	Langbaurgh	17,247	
	Middlesbrough	16,500	
	Stockton on Tees	17,256	62,224
Cornwall	Caradon	4,504	
	Carrick	6,000	
	Kerrier	4,109	
	North Cornwall	4,150	
	Penwich	3,822	
	Restormel	4,057	26,642

County	District	Total	County total
Cumbria	Allerdale	6,714	
	Barrow-in-Furness	4,717	
	Carlisle	10,168	
	Copeland	5,650	
	Eden	2,433	
	South Lakeland	4,854	34,536
Derbyshire	Amber Valley	7,136	
	Bolsover	7,961	
	Chesterfield	13,290	
	Derby City	19,869	
	Derbyshire Dales	4,743	
	Erewash	9,496	
	High Peak	6,200	
	North East Derby	10,500	
	South Derbyshire	4,257	83,452
Devon	East Devon	5,230	
	Exeter	7,700	
	Mid Devon	4,586	
	North Devon	3,836*	
	Plymouth	21,952	
	South Hams	4,000	
	Teignbridge	4,669	
	Torbay	3,582	
	Torridge	2,132	
	West Devon	1,799	59,486
Dorset	Bournemouth	6,034	
	North Dorset	3,728	
	Poole	5,525	
	Purbeck	2,004	
	West Dorset	5,889	
	Weymouth	3,605	26,785
Durham	Chester-le-Street	7,436	
	Darlington	8,160	
	Derwentshire	11,987	
	Durham	10,142	
	Easington	16,658	
	Sedgefield	15,013	
	Teesdale	1,800	
	Wear Valley	7,325	78,521

County	District	Total	County total
East Sussex	Brighton	13,000	
	Eastbourne	5,177	
	Hastings	5,066	
	Hove	3,791	
	Lewes	4,172	
	Rother	3,838	
	Wealden	4,036	39,080
Essex	Basildon	5,915	
	Braintree	11,600	
	Brentwood	3,405	
	Castle Point	2,701	
	Chelmsford	8,919	
	Colchester	8,582	
	Epping Forest	9,090	
	Harlow	15,578	
	Maldon	2,967	
	Rochford	2,294	
	Southend	7,630	
	Tendring	4,348	
	Thurrock	1,400	
	Uttlesford	3,710	88,139
Gloucestershire	Cheltenham	7,054	
	Cotswold	4,991	
	Forest of Dean	5,141	
	Gloucester	6,343	
	Stroud	6,870	
	Tewkesbury	4,052	34,451
Hampshire	Basingstoke	10,381	
	East Hants	4,364	
	Eastleigh	5,303	
	Fareham	3,191	
	Gosport	5,412	
	Hart	2,570	
	Havant	3,697	
	New Forest	6,852	
	Portsmouth	19,471	
	Rushmoor	5,579	
	Southampton	20,961	
	Test Valley	6,950	
	Winchester	6,119	100,850

County	District	Total	County total
Hereford and Worcester	Bromsgrove	3,849	
	Hereford City	7,716	
	Leominster	2,124	
	Malvern Hills	5,269	
	Redditch	8,800	
	South Herefordshire	2,271	
	Worcester	5,500	
	Wychavon	8,179	
	Wyre Forest	7,316	51,024
Hertfordshire	Broxbourne	4,610	
	Dacorum	15,085	
	East Hertfordshire	7,700	
	Hertsmere	6,700	
	North Herts	11,061	
	St Albans	8,600	
	Stevenage	13,000	
	Three Rivers	5,508	
	Watford	6,479	
	Welwyn Hatfield	12,500	91,243
Humberside	Beverley	5,358	
	Boothferry	4,606	
	Cleethorpes	3,322	
	East Yorkshire	4,686	
	Glanford	3,525	
	Great Grimsby	7,773	
	Holderness	2,314	
	Hull	42,321	
	Scunthorpe	8,000	81,905
Kent	Ashford	7,774	
	Canterbury	6,815	
	Dartford	5,957	
	Dover	6,514	
	Gillingham	4,241	
	Gravesham	7,750	
	Maidstone	8,819	
	Stepway	4,150	
	Thanet	6,760	
	Tunbridge Wells	5,799	64,579

County	District	Total	County total
Lancashire	Blackburn	14,500	
	Blackpool	7,400	
	Burnley	6,666	
	Chorley	4,101	
	Fylde	2,919	
	Hyndburn	4,585	
	Lancaster	5,394	
	Pendle	4,691	
	Preston	12,000	
	Ribble Valley	2,208	
	Rossendale	5,800	
	South Ribble	3,941	
	West Lancashire	10,683	
	Wyre	3,309	88,197
Leicestershire	Blaby	2,901	
	Charnwood	7,500	
	Harborough	3,172	
	Hinkley and Bosworth	4,642	
	Leicester	33,491	
	Melton	2,735	
	North West Leicestershire	5,830	
	Oadby and Wigston	1,631	
	Rutland	1,802	63,704
Lincolnshire	Boston	5,000	
	East Lindsey	5,761	
	Lincoln	8,724	
	North Kesteven	4,863	
	South Holland	4,899	
	South Kesteven	8,465	
	West Lindsey	5,212	42,924
Norfolk	Breckland	7,573	
	Great Yarmouth	7,538	
	King's Lynn	8,872	
	North Norfolk	5,900	
	Norwich	23,378	
	South Norfolk	5,256	58,517
North Yorkshire	Craven	2,005	
	Hambleton	4,355	
	Harrogate	5,962	
	Richmondshire	2,414	

County	District	Total	County total
	Scarborough	7,232	
	Selby	5,000	
	York	10,475	37,443
Northamptonshire	Corby	9,143	
	Daventry	4,300	
	East Northants	4,865	
	Kettering	5,500	
	Northampton	16,744	
	South Northants	3,883	
	Wellingborough	6,195	50,630
Northumberland	Alnwick	3,143	
	Berwick-U-Tweed	3,466	
	Blyth	10,084	
	Castle Morpeth	3,800	
	Tynedale	4,840	
	Wansbeck	9,058	34,391
Nottinghamshire	Ashfield	10,000	
	Bassetlaw	9,318	
	Broxtowe	6,062	
	Gedling	5,360	
	Mansfield	10,342	
	Newark	7,991	
	Nottingham	43,400	
	Rushcliffe	4,188	96,661
Oxfordshire	Cherwell	7,365	
	Oxford City	9,900	
	South Oxfordshire	8,192	
	Vale of White Horse	5,874	
	West Oxfordshire	4,950	36,281
Shropshire	Bridgnorth	3,244	
	North Shropshire	3,100	
	Oswestry	2,796	
	Shrewsbury	6,459	
	South Shropshire	1,900	
	Wrekin	10,322	27,821
Somerset	Mendip	6,064	
	Sedgemoor	6,013	
	South Somerset	10,923	

County	District	Total	County total
	Taunton Deane	7,728	
	West Somerset	2,004	32,732
Staffordshire	Cannock	8,600	
	East Staffs	6,319	
	Lichfield	5,600	
	Newcastle-U-L	12,400	
	South Staffs	5,807	
	Stafford	7,540	
	Staffordshire Moorlands	4,264	
	Stoke-on-Trent City	32,359	
	Tamworth	6,500	78,229
Suffolk	Babergh	4,779	
	Forest Heath	3,812	
	Ipswich	12,400	
	Mid Suffolk	4,455	
	St Edmundsbury	7,917	
	Waveney	5,995	39,358
Surrey	Elmbridge	5,409	
	Epsom and Ewell	1,950	
	Guildford	7,427	
	Mole Valley	4,512	
	Reigate and Banstead	6,892	
	Runnymede	4,007	
	Spelthorne	4,200	
	Surrey Heath	3,005	
	Tandridge	4,850	
	Waverley	6,755	
	Woking	4,830	53,837
Warwickshire	North Warwickshire	4,288	
	Nuneaton and Bedworth	9,133	
	Rugby	5,558	
	Stratford on Avon	7,324	
	Warwick	7,187	33,490
West Sussex	Adur	3,620	
	Arun	5,142	
	Chichester	7,050	
	Crawley	10,780	
	Horsham	5,865	
	Worthing	3,069	35,526
Wiltshire	Kennet	5,356	

County	District	Total	County total
	North Wilts	6,678	
	Salisbury	8,938	
	Thamesdown	13,617	
	West Wiltshire	6,742	41,331

Source: Municipal Year Book 1991 and CIPFA Housing Statistics
*Direct from Council figures for 31/03/91
Note: Excludes the 16 District Councils which have voluntarily transferred their stock

References and bibliography

Housing & Construction Statistics December Quarter 1990.

ACC/Coopers and Lybrand paper *Caring for the Vulnerable* forthcoming.

Institute of Housing (1989) *Tenant Participation in Housing Management.*

'I'm a conservative but . . .' *Roof* May/June 1991.

'Fast Facts' *Roof* July/August 1991.

'A new sense of duty' *Roof* September/October 1991.

'No rest on arrears' *Roof* September/October 1991.

'Backdoor' *Roof* September/October 1991.

'Bridging the affordability gap in 1990' *ADC* June 1991.

Social Housing March 1991.

Housing Association Weekly 14 June 1991.

'Inquiry into British Housing Information Notes: 1990', Joseph Rowntree Foundation *Housing Year Book* 1991 Longman.

Ross Fraser, Institute of Housing (1991) *Working Together in the 1990s.*

Institute of Housing (1989) *Tenant Participation in Housing Management.*

James Driscoll 'Public housing after the Local Government and Housing Act 1989' *Modern Law Review* **54**.

Coopers & Lybrand Deloitte (June 1991) *Quality and Competition in Public Housing.*

The Nature and Effectiveness of Housing Management in England, HMSO 1989.

Partners in Meeting Housing Need ALA/LHAC/LBA 1989.

Homelessness: Code of Guidance for Local Authorities (third edition) HMSO 1991.

Foster, S. and Burrows, L. (1991) *Urgent Need for Homes,* Shelter.

Coopers & Lybrand Deloitte/CIPFA 1991. *Housing Finance.*

4 The future role of local education authorities

Education is what survives when what has been learnt has been forgotten

(B. F. Skinner)

Introduction

Education is a key area for the Government's review of local government structure. It is by far the largest local government service, and has perhaps the highest political profile. It is at, or near, the top of the political agenda for each of the three main political parties. There is a clear consensus that something needs to be done; much less on what that should be.

During the last decade, education has experienced great change. This has radically transformed both the traditional role of local education authorities, and also the traditional balance of responsibilities between central and local government. Further change may be still more radical: the current debate about the management of the education service could lead to local government losing a responsibility it has held for nearly a century.

The review of local government structure thus coincides with an intense debate about the changing nature of the education service, its local management and the shape of local education authorities in the 1990s and beyond. This chapter considers the future role for local education authorities and the implications of changes in this role for local government structure. The chapter presents a set of criteria which can be applied to determine how the review of the structure of local government can best address the future needs of the education service.

That future will in many respects be determined by political choice. But the review provides the opportunity to ensure that political choice is informed by broad and wide-ranging discussion about the implications of change for the management and delivery of an effective education service.

The education system: developments, trends and issues

The education system

The education system in England and Wales contains a large number of different players. Two aspects need to be highlighted at the outset:

- the system is already a mixed economy in the sense that the status, responsibilities and degrees of independence of different players vary widely;
- there is a major role at both national and local level for elected representatives and their supporting departments.

At the local level, education is by far the largest service provided by local authorities, accounting for some 60 per cent of total local authority expenditure. Within local government, education is the responsibility of a single tier of local authorities: counties, and metropolitan districts and London boroughs.

Under the Education Act 1944 the Secretary of State has 'the duty . . . to promote the education of the people . . . and to secure the effective execution by local authorities, under his control and direction, of the national policy . . .' (s.1). Local education authorities have 'the duty . . . to contribute towards the spiritual, moral, mental and physical development of the community by securing . . . efficient education' (s.7) and to ensure 'schools . . . sufficient in number, character and equipment to afford for all pupils . . . such variety of instruction and training as may be desirable in view of their different ages, abilities and aptitudes' (s.8). Though the precise boundaries of powers and duties has changed under subsequent legislation, this broad division of duties has not been challenged overtly at a fundamental level, notwithstanding intense long-running political and professional debate about the aims of education and who should determine them.

Developments and trends

The education system has gone through major change over the last twenty years — some externally imposed, much internally generated. Developments and trends which have emerged include the following:

Increasing centralisation

In a number of important respects powers have shifted from local education authorities and other bodies to the national level (central government and its agencies). Examples include:

- the legislation giving central government responsibility for the pre-scription of a national curriculum and its associated assessment arrangements;
- increasing restriction by the centre on what local education auth-orities can and cannot do, e.g. in the spending of capital receipts;
- the development of nationally determined education support grants and local education authority training grants, and their later consoli-dation into the national scheme for grants for education support and training;
- the requirement under local management that maintained schools and colleges be funded through a formula having prior government approval.

Narrowing of local education authority management responsibilities

The most significant and consistent trend in recent years has been the narrowing of local authorities' responsibilities for education. This has been particularly pronounced in higher education. Polytechnics and colleges with substantial higher education provision were given corpo-rate status under the Education Reform Act 1988, and the Polytechnics and Colleges Funding Council was established to distribute exchequer funding to individual polytechnics and colleges. There are now pro-posals (under the Further and Higher Education Bill 1992) to remove further education colleges and sixth-form colleges from the local edu-cation authority sector. In the schools sector, the introduction of city technology colleges has had relatively limited effect on the scale and scope of local education authority provision. The emergence of grant maintained schools, if the trend continues, will over time have a much greater impact. Current proposals in the Education (Schools) Bill 1992 will, if enacted, substantially reduce local education authority powers in the area of school inspection.

Increased delegation

Day-to-day management responsibilities have also been redistributed from local education authorities to individual schools and colleges and their governing bodies under schemes of local management of schools and colleges (LMS and LMC). Local management built substantially both on pioneering work being undertaken by a number of local educa-tion authorities before the Education Reform Act of 1988, and on the earlier extension of governors' responsibilities provided for under the Education (No 2) Act of 1986, and commands widespread support.

Increasing parental influence and involvement

Since the second half of the 1970s there has been a gradual and explicit extension of parental influence in the education system. Following the Taylor Report of 1977 (A New Partnership In Our Schools) the Education Act of 1980 required the appointment of parent governors and the public articulation by local education authorities of admission limits and procedures, including appeal arrangements. The Education (No 2) Act 1986 established a duty to hold parents' meetings. That Act and the Education Reform Act 1988 further extended parents' rights in school admission decisions (open enrolment). The 1988 Act also empowered parents to opt, by ballot, for grant maintained status for their children's school. Most recently, the Citizen's and Parent's Charters signalled the Government's intention to legislate for more published information for parents about schools and their performance. Provisions for this are included in the Education (Schools) Bill 1992.

Increasing employer influence

Successive governments over the last decade have sought to increase the extent of employers' influence over, and participation in, the education service. Greater employer participation in the work of schools has been encouraged nationally through the Technical and Vocational Education Initiative. Increased employer representation on the governing bodies of polytechnics and colleges has increased employer influence in higher and further education, particularly in vocational education and training. The creation of Training and Enterprise councils (TECs) as employer-led bodies with a significant role in funding part-time local vocational education and training is perhaps the most high profile example of the empowerment of employers. Other examples include the leading role of employers and industrialists on bodies such as the National Curriculum Council (NCC), the Schools Examinations and Assessment Council (SEAC), and the National Council for Vocational Qualifications (NCVQ).

Increasing lay influence

The influence of lay governors on the management of schools was enhanced following the Education No 2 Act of 1986, which increased the number of lay members on governing bodies. This has been matched by a reduction in the number of local education authority members. As was the case with polytechnics and colleges under the Education Reform Act 1988, the Further and Higher Education Bill 1992 makes no provision for further education and sixth-form college governors to be nominated by local education authorities. The Education (Schools) Bill 1992 proposes lay membership of school inspection teams.

Decreasing 'producer' influence

The increase in employer and lay influence on school management has been mirrored by a decrease in the influence of the teaching profession over policy for the education service. A generation ago the curriculum and its teaching and assessment were very largely determined by education professionals — teachers themselves, education staff in universities and colleges, Her Majesty's Inspectorate, and education officers and advisers/inspectors in local education authorities. James Callaghan's 1976 Ruskin College speech signalled the onset of change. Since then professional input into education policy-making has steadily reduced. The Schools Council was wound up and the Advisory Committee on the Supply and Education of Teachers adjourned indefinitely. Teachers' bargaining rights were removed, with the creation firstly of the Interim Advisory Council, then of the Teacher Review Body. Arguably such decreasing 'producer' influence can be seen as a general cultural change, with citizens more ready to challenge control by self-directing professional groups, whether in education, health or law and order.

Increasing financial pressure

Progressive erosion of local authority spending discretion, through the development and use of standard spending assessments to prescribe local authority spending at national level, and the introduction of ratecapping and chargecapping measures, has produced increasing pressure on local authority finances. The increasing focus of local authorities on value for money and on efficiency, effectiveness and economy in the delivery of services has also meant that local education authorities now operate under a much tighter financial regime.

Increasing differential funding

Central government has shown greater preparedness to fund educational provision differentially. Examples include capital and revenue grants made by central government to city technology colleges, funding for the assisted places scheme, and approaches to recurrent and capital funding for grant maintained schools.

Increasing emphasis on markets and competition

The past decade has seen a shift in the nature of local authority management towards a clearer business orientation, through the introduction of a clear purchaser/provider split and compulsory competitive tendering, and by the stimulation of greater customer orientation through local management and open enrolment.

Emergence of an enabling role

These factors have effected a major shift in the role of local education authorities. As their responsibilities for the direct provision and administration of education have been more tightly circumscribed, the concept of a new 'enabling' role has emerged. This shift to an enabling role has involved local education authorities developing new forms of partnerships with key players at the local level — particularly with polytechnics and higher education colleges, Training and Enterprise Councils, and individual grant-maintained schools. It has also led local education authorities to focus more on strategic planning, structural and funding issues, monitoring standards and school and college performance, and seeking to promote and improve performance with maximum delegation of management responsibilities to individual institutions. The enabling role thus has two key characteristics: partnership and strategic management.

Issues for the future

Education continues to have a high political profile: issues attracting particular attention are outlined below. The current review of local government structure provides an opportunity to ensure that key issues for the future are addressed effectively and that suitable arrangements for the governance and management of the education service are put in place.

Education and economic performance

There is substantial evidence that the UK under-invests in human capital compared with competitor countries, particularly in pre-school age and post-16 provision. The continued division between academic and vocational routes, and the associated narrowness of the post-16 academic curriculum, also disadvantage the UK against other major industrial countries.

National Curriculum

A consensus has emerged that a National Curriculum is desirable; how it should be structured and delivered at the local level, and how its achievement should be assessed, remain matters of debate.

Standards and quality

There is clear consensus that more rigorous monitoring and evaluation of the standards and quality of education is necessary, and that resources should be targeted more effectively to underpin quality. There is less agreement on how this should be undertaken. These trends are illustrated on the one hand, by the development of standard assessment tasks and the emergence of national attainment targets; and on the other, by the move away from a national model for records of achievement and the lack of consensus about the purpose and shape of teacher appraisal. The absence of robust output and added value measures (and some scepticism about the concept and application of more simplistic performance indicators) has meant that debate on standards and quality in the education area has often been based more on assertion than on proven experience. It is not clear that the present proposals in the Education (Schools) Bill 1992 on providing information on school performance in published form to parents and others will provide a sufficiently coherent and rigorous framework for promoting improvements in performance, and for identifying and addressing areas where performance should be improved.

Post-16 provision

There is professional, but not political, consensus on the need for change in the shape of post-16 provision. The issue remains high on the political agenda, but the response so far has been a variety of inconsistent intiatives. The development of training credits offers an interesting way towards increasing participation. Attempts to bridge the vocational/academic divide have until now foundered on the 'gold standard' of A-levels, and the success of general National Vocational Qualifications, or general National Qualifications, in this respect is not yet certain.

Local management

There is general commitment to maximum delegation of management responsibilities and budgets to institutions. But there is less agreement on how formula funding should work, particularly once the current transitional period has ended. The debate continues about the extent to which small schools (particularly in rural areas) need to be (and should be) given special protection under local management and formula funding.

Planning and the rationalisation of spare places

There is conflict between local planning and management in order to minimise surplus places, and open enrolment, opting out and interventions by the Secretary of State on specific reorganisation or closure proposals. Present arrangements make it difficult for local education authorities to meet both the wishes of parents and exhortations of bodies such as the Audit Commission. Planning in the 16–19 sector will become more problematic if further education and sixth form colleges are moved out of the local education authority maintained sector, while sixth forms in schools remain within it.

Role of governors

The existence of well-informed and committed governors and of effective governing bodies is central to the success of locally managed schools and colleges, of grant maintained schools, and of incorporated polytechnics and higher education colleges. It will also be essential to the success of incorporated further education and sixth form colleges (if the current Bill is enacted). But there is some evidence of increasing difficulty in recruiting and keeping sufficient numbers of governors of the right quality. Governors of grant maintained and locally managed schools are generally being asked to bear a range of responsibilities similar to those of independent school governors. It has been claimed that prospective governors are deterred by the scope and scale of the responsibilities and liabilities which they are asked to assume.

The developments and trends identified above raise a number of questions about the proper balance between central and local accountability and authority. Concerns have been voiced in particular about the extent of the move away from the traditional balance between central and local government, which has been to call into question the local government role in education policy and provision in a fundamental way.

There is also a continuing debate about how far market models can be applied to education. Choice for parents in many areas is constrained by geographical factors and by the physical capacity of schools. The present drive to promote and extend parental choice may raise expectations which cannot easily be met. The fear has also been expressed that, if a significant number of schools become grant maintained, parental choice will be affected by re-emerging selection by over-subscribed schools.

Many of the developments identified above are comparatively recent. It remains to be seen, for example, whether local education authorities and Training and Enterprise Councils will successfully forge strong and effective alliances in the long term to promote innovative and successful approaches to local economic development and the integration of post-16 academic and vocational education and training. But the pace of change overall looks set to continue. These issues represent a challenging agenda to be addressed at both the national and the local level.

The role of local education authorities into the 1990s

The implications of local management for the role of local education authorities were first discussed in the Coopers and Lybrand report to the Department of Education and Science on local management of schools, and reiterated by the Audit Commission in its occasional paper *Losing an Empire, Finding a Role*. The development of local management of schools leads to a fundamental shift in the role of local education authorities, from the detailed management of individual schools and colleges, to an increasingly strategic one of planning and quality assurance.

However, this new strategic or enabling role has developed against a background of an increasing number of grant maintained schools. In many ways the grant maintained concept represents simply an extension of the concept of local management to the extreme end of the spectrum, rather than a quantum leap beyond. From a school's point of view this is probably right. What is less clear are the implications for the local education authority in its new enabling role, particularly when grant maintained schools may not perceive themselves as still being part of the local authority education system.

This section therefore examines the new role of local education authorities under this extreme position, taking as the starting point the key functions for which local education authorities are responsible at present. This does not mean that a dramatic shift towards a grant maintained system should, or even will, necessarily come about. Overall policy direction and context may of course change significantly at national level, especially if there is a change of government.

The predominantly grant maintained scenario is illustrated for three reasons. First, present trends: more schools are achieving grant maintained status and, given the incentives presently offered, this trend is likely to continue, particularly for secondary schools. The second reason is that the enabling role of the local education authority would be most pronounced in this context. Thirdly and most importantly, the fully grant maintained scenario *is* an extreme: if a local role can be justified even in that scenario, then for anything less a stronger local role is likely to be needed. Such a scenario is not used in this paper in any predictive or normative sense.

The current local education authority functions used for this analysis of the enabling role are as follows:

- strategic policy and planning;
- information and advice on provision;
- services to pupils and students;
- services to schools and colleges;
- quality assurance;
- funding and resource allocation.

Strategic policy and planning

In a predominantly grant maintained education system, some aspects of the current role of local education authorities in setting the strategic direction and overall policy framework for the education service would pass to central agencies, such as the Department of Education and Science and the National Curriculum Council, and some to individual governing bodies. However, a local intermediate body would still have an important role in a number of areas.

Insofar as education provision consists of more than the aggregation of separate institutions, there is a strong case for a local body with the credibility and expertise to define, create and shape a vision of the sort of education service required to meet all the needs of local communities. Its role would include the promotion of values and approaches to education services which reflect local concerns and aspirations. In sparsely populated rural areas, a high priority might be accorded to outreach. In inner city areas, priority might be accorded to securing equality of educational opportunity through a focused programme of English (as a second language) tuition. Such a local body would also need to continue to build and strengthen partnerships with other local educational providers (in both the state and independent sectors) and with other influential bodies, so that the pattern of provision at the local level is developed in a coherent way to meet local needs.

The second important dimension of strategy concerns the overall planning of provision. The provision of school places cannot be left entirely to the market, partly because of the long lead time for change, and partly because those currently within the system cannot constantly revisit their decisions as others make later choices. The timely provision of sufficient places requires intervention in the market. Related to this is the management of large numbers of surplus places (both for pupils and staff) which cannot be left, both because this is unsatisfactory for those still in the schools and also because it is a waste of public resources. Decisions on forward provision need to take account of local circumstances and overall availability in the area, as well as local views.

While in theory this could be done nationally, there is clearly a good case for a local body to have this responsibility in order to respond to local sensitivities and circumstances, and facilitate public scrutiny of decisions affecting local communities. Responding to local views and priorities inevitably has a political dimension, and so there would be advantage in the strategic policy and planning role being undertaken by some form of locally elected and accountable authority, even with most schools grant maintained.

Information and advice on provision

Allied to the planning function is information and advice. To give real effect to parental choice (whether in the context of the more market-orientated grant maintained system or otherwise), parents must have adequate information on which to base choices about their children's schooling and so enable them to use their rights and entitlements. There is a further local role here too. To give real substance to the concept of parental choice under the Citizens' and Parents' Charters, there would need to be some independent regulation of the market for school admissions, including some form of appeals process. Both these functions need to be delivered by a local body. Taken in isolation, they would not of themselves require an elected body; but it would be perverse not to combine them with the strategic planning function.

Services to pupils and students

Certain services to pupils and students need a perspective wider than that of an individual institution, such as:

- home to school transport;
- regulatory duties such as health and safety and school attendance;
- assessing (and securing appropriate provision to meet) the special educational needs of individual children and young adults;
- providing support to individual pupils and students in the form of grants and awards;
- meeting some of the non-vocational educational, cultural and leisure demands of adults.

The wider aims of the youth service and of adult education more generally can also only be met by a body with a focus at a wider level than an individual centre or institute, and with the capacity to collaborate with, and coordinate the activities of, a wide range of voluntary bodies.

Some of these functions are statutory, some discretionary; all require locally arranged provision. The provider needs to be publicly accountable to the supplier of funds. Insofar as these functions are locally funded, this should be an elected local authority.

Services to schools and colleges

Even under a grant maintained system, schools (and colleges) would still need to secure some services from local sources. Examples include professional advice and services related to the curriculum and its teaching and assessment (e.g. in-service training, curriculum advice) and management services (e.g. finance, personnel and payroll). Both grant maintained and locally managed schools would have budgets to purchase such services. There is no intrinsic reason why such services cannot be provided by the market. However, relying only on external sources of curriculum advice could be problematic, given the need to ensure a consistent approach and maintain standards, particularly when schools are facing problems and are in need of help. Equally there is good reason for local authorities to provide these services, by agreement with individual schools.

Quality assurance

Quality assurance processes are needed to satisfy three main groups of clients:

- the governing body of an institution — so that it has independent advice on quality to inform the discharge of its responsibilities;
- a central or local authority/agency acting on behalf of the funders of public education (taxpayers/chargepayers) — to ensure that public money is being used cost-effectively for the ends for which it was intended, and that education of appropriate quality and relevance is being provided;
- parents and students — both as customers and to provide them with information on which they can base their choices.

There is no intrinsic reason why the quality assurance function should be undertaken by a local authority, provided that stringent accreditation processes can ensure that all these clients' needs are met. However, while schools are (partly) locally funded, the local commissioning and funding body (the local education authority) should be able to monitor the educational and financial performance of individual institutions, to intervene to secure improvements where performance is unsatisfactory, and to require a full inspection. If funding passes to the centre, local education authorities could still undertake a quality assurance role as agents. If local education authorities do not themselves undertake the quality assurance function, while continuing as funders, they would need access to all the results of inspections undertaken by others in order to assess how far and how well needs were being met by a mix of providers. There would also be advantage in quality assurance processes which supplemented the formal four-yearly full inspection prescribed in the Education (Schools) Bill 1992, although the extent of this would depend on the requirements of the client groups listed above.

Funding and resource allocation

There are two aspects to resource allocation. The first concerns the primary decision about the level of resources to be devoted to schools, as opposed to those devoted to other education services. The second concerns the distribution of resources between schools, an area where there is some uncertainty under a grant maintained system. Currently local education authorities make both decisions, and grant maintained schools are then funded (by central government) according to the local education authority's own formula — plus extras. With a fully (or nearly fully) grant maintained system, a case could be made for a nationally driven formula, perhaps with local variations, with neither the level of funding, nor its distribution, being driven at local level.

The remaining local education authority functions would then be to determine the funding and allocation to non-schools areas and to contribute to any decisions on the local variations in a nationally driven formula. There may be a parallel with the system proposed in the Further and Higher Education Bill 1992, which envisages a regional dimension to the Further Education Funding Council to allow regional considerations to be injected. For schools, with their much greater numbers, such a local dimension would seem to be more necessary, and could be provided by a body such as a local education authority. As such, the authority would be acting purely as a local agent of central government. The need for a local education authority to account to the local electorate for spending in the area of schools provision would accordingly diminish. Such a body would be less likely to need any directly elected members, accountable to a local electorate.

Summary

If the education system were to move further along the spectrum from local management to a grant maintained system, the 'enabling' role of local education authorities would change. There would still be a need for local bodies to provide strategic policy and planning, information and advice on provision, and services to pupils and students. There is a good case for such local bodies to be elected.

The strategic policy and planning functions would be undertaken from a new pespective, with the need for such authorities to work in close partnership with a wide range of providers (both from the state and independent sectors) to ensure that local community needs were identified and met. The functions of information and advice to parents and of services to pupils and students would also be akin to a role regulating the market. Services to schools and colleges could increasingly come to be provided by a range of providers operating in a market framework. A local role would remain for quality assurance and funding and resource allocation (unless, in the latter case, education were to become wholly centrally funded).

Even at the extreme end of the grant maintained spectrum, there is still a need for local, intermediate bodies between central authorities and individual institutions. It follows that, under anything less, there is a still stronger local role. With this in mind, the present review of local government structure will need to consider the form local education authorities should take for the 1990s and beyond. The next section of this chapter develops a set of evaluation criteria to provide a framework for this.

Future local arrangements for the education service

A number of models have been mooted in current debate about the future organisation and management of the education service. These include scenarios based on:

- elected local education authorities with responsibilities much as at present;
- elected local education authorities which focus mainly on services to parents, pupils and students, and support to primary schools;
- single-purpose local bodies or agencies which are arms of central government, with members appointed by the Secretary of State (along the lines of the health service);
- no local bodies of any kind: under this scenario, schools would form themselves into consortia to provide, secure the provision of, or pur-

chase, those services and functions which need to be provided at a level above that of the individual school.

The last model is probably not realistic or practicable, at least until schools have more experience of running their own affairs either under grant maintained status or under maximum local management. Moreover, it would mean abandoning the concept of a single local education service, shaped in response to all the needs of local communities.

In practice, the choice for the future most relevant to the review is between an elected local body or an arm of central government. The key issues are therefore the nature of local arrangements required in the future, given the changing strategic and enabling role of local education authorities; and the extent to which these arrangements should incorporate local democratic structures. The starting point for addressing these questions is to develop criteria which the arrangements need to satisfy.

Developing evaluation criteria

There appears to be a broad consensus (crossing party political boundaries) that the education system delivers economic, cultural, educational and leisure benefits at a number of levels: national, local, and individual, implying a legitimate plurality of interest in the education system at national and local level. The national interest is reflected at present in those elements of the education framework which are set centrally, e.g. the National Curriculum; rules and procedures on funding under local management; and national attainment targets. The local interest is reflected in the discretion over levels of education funding, and in the discretion for local education authorities to tailor the national framework to meet local needs, e.g. the requirements for each local education authority to develop and publish a curriculum statement. There are also areas where local education authorities have substantial discretion, e.g. non-vocational adult education.

Thus, *plurality of interest* is reflected in the allocation of powers and responsibilities to different levels in the system, and forms the first criterion to be applied in determining the future shape of the management, organisational and administrative framework for the education service.

The resulting allocation of powers and responsibilities to different levels needs to be accompanied by clear lines of accountability between different levels in the system, and between those with responsibility for managing, administering and providing publicly-funded educational services, those who fund them, and those who consume them. Thus:

- headteachers are responsible to governing bodies for the day-to-day management of the school;
- governing bodies are responsible either to the local education authority (under local management) or to the Department of Education and Science (under grant maintained status) for the overall performance, efficiency and effectiveness of the school;
- the Secretary of State for Education and Science and the Secretary of State for Wales are accountable to Parliament — and through Parliament to the national electorate — for those aspects of the education service which are centrally prescribed and funded.

It follows that a form of local education authority is required which similarly can be held accountable to the local electorate for those aspects of the education service which are funded and delivered locally. Schools themselves — and particularly governing bodies and headteachers — are also directly accountable to the consumers of education — the parents and students connected with the school.

There is frequently confusion about the respective powers and duties of central government, local education authorities and individual schools. Where lines of accountability are blurred, it may seem that no-one is responsible. This leads to the second criterion: *clear accountability* for responsibilities operating at the different levels in the system. The system should be comprehensible, transparent and open to influence by electors, taxpayers, chargepayers, parents, pupils and students.

There is consensus that the principle of local management of institutions should be developed further. Local management involves the maximum delegation of management responsibilities. Responsibility for operational matters and service delivery is already located at the institutional level, while responsibility for setting the framework within which institutions operate is located at the level of the local education authority (in the case of local management) or at the national level, in the case of grant maintained schools and city technology colleges. Local management and maximum appropriate delegation is desirable because it gives managers maximum discretion in deciding how best to use available resources to meet agreed objectives (and matches best management practice in other sectors). *Maximum local management* is the third criterion for allocation of responsibilities between different levels in the system.

Allocation of responsibilities for the education system cannot take place in isolation from responsibilities for other locally administered public services. Dividing responsibilities for closely related functions could lead to diseconomies because of the need to duplicate administration. The grouping together of different functions can encourage creative interaction, beneficial to consumers and taxpayers and charge payers. Thus the fourth criterion is *appropriate grouping of functions*.

The education system in England and Wales is already a mixed economy, with a large number of players. If any future local body is to be able to function successfully and effectively, it needs to be credible to other players in the system, as well as to parents, pupils and students. This gives the fifth criterion: *credibility*.

Finally, there is consensus that each level in the education system should be able clearly to demonstrate that it adds value to the system as a whole and that it can secure effective and efficent use of resources. So the sixth criterion is: *added value and cost-effectiveness*.

Applying the criteria

In summary, the criteria to be applied in determining the allocation of responsibilities and accountabilities between different levels in the education system are:

- plurality of interest;
- clear accountability;
- maximum local management;
- appropriate grouping of functions;
- credibility;
- added value and cost-effectiveness.

Plurality of interest

By tradition, the education service in England and Wales is a national service, locally administered. While recent developments have seen a shift in responsibilities from the local to the national level, aspirations and needs for educational services still vary between different parts of the country. Thus, if local communities are to exert influence over the development of educational opportunities in their area, there remains a key role at the local level and a need for education authorities to be accountable at the local level to those communities. This is best done through elected bodies, particularly for the strategic policy and planning functions.

Clear accountability

Plurality implies that education authorities will continue to be accountable to the local electorate. However, local education authority responsibilities would change if there were a further substantial shift to a system where grant maintained schools predominated, and the nature of an authority's accountability to its electorate would also change. Its primary focus might be to promote local interests to providers not under its direct control, rather than itself to be the major service provider. Even at the extreme grant maintained end of the spectrum, there are still provider functions to be undertaken at the local level (e.g. adult education). Under local management, however, primary responsibility for the quality of service provided to individual customers would lie with the institution, whose governing body would be primarily accountable to parents and students.

Under a fully (or nearly fully) grant maintained system, central government would be accountable to the electorate for the level of funding and performance of the school system as a whole. Local education authorities could act as agents of central government under this scenario to discharge aspects of central government's responsibilities for the performance of grant maintained schools.

Maximum local management

The concept and principles of local management can be applied equally to the allocation of responsibilities between the Department of Education and Science and any local bodies. This would reinforce the case for local involvement.

Appropriate grouping of functions

Particularly given the Children Act, there is an increasing need for local authority education and social services to work closely together, and with other external authorities. Grouping functions together also allows for the achievement of economies in providing common support functions (e.g. finance, personnel and information technology). This criterion points away from setting up local education authorities of the future as freestanding single-purpose bodies and towards them remaining an integral part of local government.

Credibility

To carry out the 'enabling' role effectively, local authorities need to have credibility with other players in the system. They should be of a weight and scope comparable to other bodies concerned with the administration and funding of education provision at the local level — particularly Training and Enterprise Councils and the proposed Regional Further Education Funding Councils. Local education authorities also need to be credible in the 'enabling' role to local electors and consumers, able to exercise real influence in the interests of local communities.

Added value and cost-effectiveness

All things being equal, the maximum value added is obtained where the size of the authority is sufficient for it to be able to offer and manage effectively a range of functions running across many schools, or which must be exercised independently. The more significant the range and weight of responsibilities, the more scope there is for the authority to secure added value from the enabling role.

Local education authorities are more likely to be able to achieve improved resource management performance if they are of sufficient size to be able to secure cost-effective and efficient purchasing or provision of services and maintain managerial and other specialist resources of high quality to meet the needs of their consumers.

Conclusion

Even at the extreme of an entirely grant maintained education system, therefore, there would be a legitimate enabling role for local education authorities in the 1990s and beyond. It follows that, under anything less, there is a still more important local role.

In summary, the analysis leads to the following conclusions:

- There is a need for some form of local education authority for the 1990s and beyond, even under a fully grant maintained system (plurality of interest and maximum local management).
- Given the need for decisions on provision to reflect the wishes and priorities of the local community, there is a good case for education authorities to continue to be elected bodies, accountable to their electors/funders, at least for those parts of the education service which are funded locally (plurality of interest and clear accountability).
- Local education authorities would be more effective if they were part of local government, not freestanding single-purpose authorities (appropriate grouping of functions).
- Local education authorities should be of sufficient size, and have the necessary authority and scope, to achieve and maintain credibility with other players in the system and with local communities (credibility and appropriate grouping of functions).
- Large authorities are likely to be able to secure and deliver benefits

more easily and more efficiently than small authorities (added value and cost effectiveness).

Even under a fully grant maintained scenario, therefore, the most appropriate arrangement would be local education authorities which are elected, which are larger rather than smaller, and which are part of local government. Though the need for elected authorities may be a matter primarily of political choice, it is in accordance with principles of accountability and responsiveness reflected in the Government's Citizens' and Parents' Charters.

The arguments in favour of larger rather than smaller authorities are less subjective. Within limits, the aggregation of functions into larger units within local government brings benefits in terms of reduced unit costs (economies of scale). This is as true for education as for other major local authority services. The key question in this context is whether the savings from the aggregation of functions into larger units are outweighed by a diminution in local responsiveness. In the case of education, local management has resulted in a distinction between accountability for service provision (for which institutions are primarily responsible) and for establishing the framework within which educational opportunities are planned and developed (for which local education authorities and central government are responsible). Since local management already delivers effective local responsiveness, strategic functions can be carried out by larger rather than smaller authorities, allowing economies of scale to be secured. Any move away from existing arrangements would result in substantial transitional costs and disruption. More fundamentally, any alternative arrangements would still need to:

- provide an effective means of carrying out the enabling role locally, as set out earlier;
- meet the six criteria set out above.

The key point for the review of local government structure is therefore that there are no clear advantages or benefits to be gained from dismantling existing local education authorities, and considerable disadvantage in so doing. The above analysis points to a strong case for retaining existing local education authorities, either in a unitary or a two tier system.

Existing authorities face a significant challenge in adapting and responding to changes in the education system and the demands made of them. They can build on recognised strengths, including a record innovation and substantial customer satisfaction. They will, however, need to address a number of difficult issues:

- moving to a more consciously strategic planning role;
- changing processes and machinery for quality assurance;
- defining more explicitly the respective roles of members and officers;
- further improving their responsiveness to customer demand — both for pupils and parents as consumers of the service, and for schools and colleges as clients.

Perhaps the only certainty is that the future will see change. Nationally there is the possibility of integration of some Department of Education and Science and Department of Employment activities. Locally there is the present review of local government structure. At institutional level, there is the continuing process of achieving maximum delegation of management and budgets to schools and colleges and the implementation of schemes of local management, incorporation, and grant maintained status. Local education authorities must continue to anticipate and manage such changes innovatively and effectively.

This last point is paramount. Innovation in education development has historically taken place through individual education authorities taking local initiatives — sometimes against the policy direction of the government of the day. A system which removed the ability to innovate through local initiative would be seriously flawed. Any new structure should continue to allow local diversity, growth, development and experimentation to occur.

Bibliography

Association of District Councils *New Horizons for Education*.
Audit Commission (1989) *Losing an Empire, Finding A Role* HMSO.
Brooke, R. (1989) *Managing the Enabling Authority* Longman.
Bush, T., Kogan, M. and Lenney, T. (1989) *Directors of Education — Facing Reform* Jessica Kingsley Publishers.
CIPFA Education Statistics 1990/91.
Clarke, M. and Stewart, J. (1989) *The Enabling Council* LGTB.
Clarke, M. and Stewart, J. *Choices for Local Government for the 1990s and Beyond*.
Coopers & Lybrand (1988) *Local Management of Schools*.
Flynn, N. (1990) *Public Sector Management* Harvester/Wheatsheaf.
Hollis, G. et al. (1990) *Alternatives to the Community Charge* Joseph Rowntree Foundation.
Lister, E. (1991) *LEAs — Old and New: A View From Wandsworth* Centre for Policy Studies.

Maclure, S. (1988) *Education Reformed: A Guide to the Education Reform Act* Hodder and Stoughton.

Morris, E. R. (1990) *Central and Local Control of Education After the Education Reform Act 1988* Longman/BEMAS.

OECD (1990) *Public Management Developments: Survey — 1990* OECD.

Rao, N. (1990) *Educational Change and Local Government: The Impact of the Education Reform Act*, Joseph Rowntree Foundation.

Education Acts.

HMI Annual Reports.

Education; Times Educational Supplement; Times Higher Education Supplement.

5 Caring for the community: the role of local government

> To leave the world a bit better, whether by a healthy child, a garden patch, or a redeemed social condition; To know even one life has breathed easier because you have lived; This is to have succeeded
> (Ralph Waldo Emerson)

Introduction

This chapter considers the role of local authorities in the provision of personal social services for individuals, families and communities.

Since the reorganisation and unification of personal social services in England and Wales in 1971, local authorities have developed services and expertise in response to increasing and more complex needs, the wishes of more demanding and articulate users of services, and the requirements of legislative change. Personal social services are now a major local authority service, second only to education, accounting for expenditure of some £3,500m a year in England and Wales in 1989 and employing the equivalent of over 250,000 full-time staff.

Recent legislation is bringing about further profound changes. The National Health Service and Community Care Act 1990 makes changes in the way social care is provided to people who are affected by ageing, mental illness, mental handicap or physical/sensory disability. Its objectives are:

- to ensure the delivery of high quality services by means of a proper assessment of need and good care management;
- to promote the development of services that enable people needing care to live in their own homes wherever feasible and sensible;
- to ensure that service providers give a high priority to practical support for carers;
- to promote the development of an effective mixed economy of care;
- to clarify the responsibilities of agencies and hold them accountable for their performance;

● to secure better value for money by introducing a new funding structure for social care.

At the same time the Children Act 1989, the provisions of which are seen as consistent with and complementary to the community care legislation, establishes a new framework for the care and upbringing of children. It is based on the philosophy that children in need are best supported within their own families whenever this is feasible and sensible, and that this should be undertaken in partnership with parents or carers. The Act draws together local authorities' responsibilities in relation to:

● the identification and assessment of children in need;
● the safeguarding and promotion of children's welfare;
● the nature and range of servies that can be provided along a continuum from family support to the provision of substitute care for the child in need.

Both pieces of legislation have given local authorities new or enhanced responsibilities in the personal social services. Within the context of the many other trends and influences affecting these services, this chapter describes the nature and range of these reponsibilities under the two broad functional groupings defined by recent legislation and by other developments in local government: those associated with the enabling role, and those associated with the direct providing role. It then considers their implications for the structure of local government.

The enabling role

Whilst recognising that local authorities will continue to have an important part to play in direct service provision, the Government's community care legislation provides for an enhanced enabling role for them. This section considers the key activities associated with this role:

● anticipating and measuring service needs within their population;
● planning strategically how to meet these needs within service guidelines and resource constraints;
● securing provision in line with service plans;
● establishing arrangements for regulating and monitoring service quality.

Anticipating needs

Anticipating community needs requires the development of an appropriate categorisation of need and methods of measuring their prevalence in the population.

Needs are not immutable objective conditions but vary in response to social and demographic change, professional developments, user and carer expectations, legislative change and public opinion. Significant changes have taken place in family structure in the UK over recent decades which include, for example, increasing levels of divorce and subsequent remarriage. In addition, there has been a substantial growth in the number of single parent families. There have also been demographic changes such as the growth in the number of very old people, and the increase in the number of people with learning disabilities now surviving into later life. All these changes create new needs to which social services have to respond.

The influence of professionals has also been important, Investigations into child care strategies during the 1970s and 1980s, for example, have led to broader definitions of child abuse than the initial concept of the 'battered baby syndrome'. Recognition of users' and carers' needs has grown over recent years, mainly through the work of representative organisations and self help groups. Carers' needs are now defined separately from those of users.

Legislative change can also lead to developments in the categorisation of need. The Children Act recognises that young people leaving care have specific needs which require action. In the past, services to this group have been ad hoc and uncoordinated, in part because of this lack of legislative recognition. Public opinion, often influenced by the attention drawn to an issue by the media or campaigning pressure groups, can also change to recognise new or enlarged categories of need. For example, public perceptions of old age have changed. In the past, services for elderly people were provided solely on the basis of age. This is now considered an insufficient criterion in itself for provision of domiciliary services such as home care. The categorisation of need is also influenced by value judgements about the proper function of the family and the responsibilities of individuals. For example, changing attitudes to working mothers have led to greater recognition of the need for day care for young children.

Whilst need categories may have become more precise, methods of quantification of need remain relatively under-developed. There is little precise information about the prevalence of need, even when based on broadly defined categories such as frail elderly people, people with a learning disability, people with a physical disability, people with a mental health problem, or children and families. In most instances, demographic data is used as a proxy indicator, rather than an attempt being made at actual measurement. For example, the number of people in the population aged over eighty years of age may be used as an indicator of the extent of mental infirmity among the elderly.

Demographic data, however, is of limited use in measuring needs such as the number of people with a learning disability. In these instances, the level of need at the local level is often estimated from data from national studies. Local authorities have established registers of people with different forms of disability but it is often difficult in practice to keep these up to date. Different services and different agencies may also use different definitions of need, which may mean that response is triggered at different points along a continuum.

Notwithstanding these problems, both the National Health and Community Care Act and the Children Act require local authorities to assess the level of need in their populations. This will involve a range of activities to obtain relevant and reliable information including:

- undertaking small-scale market research surveys to obtain information about special needs in their area to supplement demographic data;
- collecting and collating information from individual assessments of need;
- developing effective consultation machinery with service users and carers;
- establishing registers of rare populations, perhaps jointly with health authorities;
- analysing data from these activities to produce an integrated picture of needs;
- developing information systems to assist with these activities.

Even assuming that levels of current need may be reliably established, they may not be good indicators of levels of future needs, for many different reasons. For example, future need may be related to carers' economic status or health rather than the social need itself. Admission to residential care is a good example. It is frequently a response to a breakdown in support mechanisms, rather than a change in the coping level of the person being admitted.

Secondly, new needs emerge that are difficult to predict. For example, people with AIDS were first defined as a new need group during the 1980s, and the social needs of people with AIDS, or who are HIV positive, will be identified in more detail in the 1990s. No one could have foreseen the increase in inter-country adoptions resulting from the changes in Eastern Europe. Emerging trends in other countries may also lead to the identification of needs in the UK. The recently recognised phenomenon of 'granny dumping' in the USA is likely to lead to its identification in this country, followed by proposals for addressing it. Needs may also not be identified until a crisis occurs. For example, the social and psychological needs of disaster victims and their families were identified during the 1980s, and specific skills have now developed in this area.

This level of unpredictability means that substantial resources are often required to deal with a need that had not previously been recognised and hence had not been planned for. The effectiveness of the social services response to these emerging needs depends largely on how far and how rapidly staffing and other resources can be switched from one area to another, without prejudice to those needs which had been anticipated.

Strategic planning

Under the 1990 Act, local authorities are responsible for producing a community care plan which sets out how they intend to meet identified needs within service guidelines and resource constraints. This will involve establishing the nature and mix of provision in terms of domiciliary, day care and residential services. It will include determining the specialist resources that are required within each of these service areas (for example, elderly people from ethnic minorities). Services will also need to be planned to meet the needs of very rare populations, such as adults with multiple and severe disabilities.

In developing these plans, the Act requires local authorities to collaborate with key statutory agencies, the independent sector and service users and carers. In essence, planning becomes a joint endeavour which emphasises the interdependence of local authorities, district and family health service authorities, and other agencies, in the provision of community care.

The relationship between local authorities and the health service is especially important. Whilst collaboration between these services has been encouraged in the past through administrative machinery (Joint Consultative Committees and Joint Planning Teams) and funding mechanisms (Joint Finance), the new legislation envisages a qualitative change in the nature of the planning relationship. The emphasis is on planning agreements which involve the development of shared objectives and policies, the establishment of the mutual responsibilities of each agency, and contract specifications and funding agreements for achieving effective inter-agency working between service providers. In some cases the two agencies have already developed one integrated community care plan.

In the future, the relationship will need to be even closer. New developments, involving joint management arrangements and the transfer of staff and functional responsibilities between health and social services, are likely to increase to facilitate the planning of 'seamless' packages of care for service users across agency boundaries. In addition, effective collaboration with FHSAs will help to ensure the involvement of general practitioners who have a key role in the provision of social care.

Inter-agency planning and collaboration between health and social services does not only apply to community care. The Government document *Working Together under the Children Act 1989* (DHSS 1991) provides clear guidelines for inter-agency cooperation in protecting children from abuse. This involves not only social services and health staff but also the police, education and key voluntary agencies. Similar relationships are developing with the criminal justice sector, comprising a range of agencies including the courts, the police, and the probation service, in measures to divert young offenders away from custody.

Planning for the implementation of community care also requires effective collaboration with the housing sector. The link between good quality, affordable housing and people's physical and mental well-being is increasingly recognised. Local housing authorities are, in most areas, the largest local landlord and therefore have a continuing role to play, notwithstanding the growing importance of housing associations in providing a significant level of new special needs housing.

The Government believes that 'housing is a vital component of community care and . . . often the key to independent living' (DHSS 1989). Local authorities have powers to help people to continue to live in their own homes and to provide specialised accommodation, where this is appropriate. They can:

- provide advice and help to elderly people on how to keep their homes in good repair, including the grant aiding of minor works;
- carry out structural adaptations to the homes of people with physical disabilities;
- provide ordinary housing and a range of specialised accommodation, together with warden and alarm services, to meet the needs of people with severe physical disabilities, people with learning disabilities and frail elderly people.

Many of these services are provided in partnership with other agencies. For example, consortia of social services, health and housing authorities have provided and supported group homes for people with learning disabilities. Social services and housing authorities have developed very sheltered accommodation as an alternative to residential care for frail people, and some social services have made grants to local housing authorities for this purpose. Local housing authorities have also provided adapted housing as their contribution to innovatory respite care schemes for children with disabilities.

Under the Children Act, social services have enhanced responsibilities for young people leaving care, and for young people over sixteen who are in need and whose welfare is otherwise likely to be seriously prejudiced. In meeting these responsibilities, they will have to collaborate with housing authorities to obtain suitable accommodation for these young people. The new Code of Guidance draws housing authorities' attention to the potential difficulties if there is a lack of coordination between tiers of local government in this area (see Chapter 3). Housing associations are now also contributing to schemes to meet the accommodation needs of young people leaving care.

The important issue for the future is effective planning with the housing sector as a whole, public, voluntary and private, in order to develop an appropriate and flexible range of housing meeting the needs of vulnerable groups and increasing choice for service users. In Chapter 3 it was argued that there was a need to ensure that housing, community care and planning perspectives were reconciled in order to assess housing demand fully and ensure all client group requirements are recognised. An important issue for the review is therefore to ensure that future structure enables an effective strategic response to housing need.

Securing provision

The 1990 Act gives social services authorities the main responsibility to secure the appropriate level and range of services from providers in line with service plans. It involves both the stimulation of provision by the independent sector, as well as commissioning activities. Existing agencies need to be encouraged to develop their services where appropriate, sometimes into new service areas, and new agencies need to be encouraged to enter the community care 'market' to extend user and carer choice and fill any gaps and shortfalls in provision. Market stimulation requires a strategic perspective to identify how the contribution of the independent sector should dovetail with statutory provision, and how to make the best use of the contribution of the independent sector to address service gaps and increase choice. Sound inter-agency relationships are required to facilitate negotiations with national and local voluntary and private agencies about their future role.

In future, this promotion role is also likely to become more significant, especially in the child care field, in the development of day care provision within the independent sector. Many local authorities already have experience of promoting the independent sector: at the local level, for example, by stimulating voluntary provision through local guilds of community service; and at the national level, by encouraging national child care charities to develop services in their areas.

Commissioning involves securing suitable provision of the appropriate volume and quality in the right place and at the right time. To achieve this, local authorities will need to specify clearly their service requirements and put in place arrangements for monitoring service delivery. These arrangements can take the form of a service agreement with in-house and external providers, or may involve competitive tendering and the letting of contracts. Commissioning requires skills in specifying the services to be delivered by providers in terms of quality, volume and price — as well as in 'contract' management, including quality monitoring. The overall aim is to create an appropriate 'market' for providing services to meet objectives in terms of effectiveness, efficiency and quality, as well as to provide scope for users and carers to exercise choice. Joint purchasing arrangements, especially with the health service, are likely to increase.

The responsibility for securing provision for individual users will lie with care managers. Within the strategic planning framework, managers will carry out individual assessments of needs, involving cooperation between appropriate professionals from relevant agencies. They will put in place packages of care to meet these needs, and monitor and track performance. They will provide advice, information and counselling. All these tasks must involve service users and carers and take their views into account. They must be needs, rather than service, led, taking individuals and their carers as the starting point.

This holistic approach to assessment must also be adopted in child care if local authorities' duty to give support for children and their families is to be carried out effectively. For example, in working with families from ethnic minorities assessments must take into account differences in the way family and social networks operate so that service provision builds on existing support mechanisms.

Giving care managers responsibility for putting packages of care into place facilitates the delivery of a responsive service by bringing operational decision-making as near to the user as possible. The devolution of budgets and the development of effective information systems will contribute to this. It requires skilled practitioners, operating within strategic policy and planning guidance, within a framework of effective inter-agency arrangements, and supported by effective training in key professional and management competencies.

Regulation

The final activity associated with the enabling role is regulation. This involves the registration of service providers and the monitoring and evaluation of the care they deliver. Under the Act, local authorities are required to establish inspection units, at arm's length from operational management, to monitor and evaluate provision across all sectors and to exercise a quality control function to ensure consistency in delivery. In addition, under the Children Act, authorities have increased responsibilities for ensuring the welfare of children who are looked after away from home, other than by the local authorities themselves.

This enhanced regulation role increases the scope of local authorities' intervention by placing on them a wider registration and/or inspection duty in respect of, for example, elderly persons' homes in all sectors, playgroups and childminders, and private boarding schools. This role is likely to develop to encompass a regulatory responsibility for domiciliary and day care provision in all sectors.

Alongside registration and inspection, local authorities have a duty to establish complaints procedures to enable service users and carers to have a say in the way services are provided to them. The objective is not only to address mistakes, but also to obtain feedback about service delivery from users and carers. This feedback contributes to quality control.

The direct provider role

Although local authorities are expected to develop a mixed economy of providers of community care, they will continue to provide services 'where this remains the best way of meeting care needs' (DHSS 1989). The Children Act also recognises the key role of local authorities in direct provision. This section considers local authorities' direct provider role in relation to changing patterns of service delivery, increasing staff specialisation, the development of a user and carer centred perspective, and its exercise within a mixed economy of care.

Changing patterns of service delivery

A review of the pattern of social care reveals a long-term trend away from institutional care — whether hospital or residential care based — for all user groups. For example, the provision of hospital-based care for elderly people with disabilities or mental health problems has diminished. More recently, this has been accompanied by a move away from residential care towards establishing and/or maintaining people in their own homes or a home-based environment. This change has been mirrored in child care, with fostering increasingly being viewed as the preferable way of providing subsitute care rather than residential care, and the increasing importance of preventative strategies aimed at maintaining children with their own families. These developments have been given fresh impetus by recent legislation.

In support of these changes, social services authorities have developed a range of domiciliary and day care services and facilities to enable people to continue to live in the community. Within their own homes people in need can receive assistance with personal care and domestic tasks, and be provided with disability aids and adaptations. Day care, leisure facilities and help with transport can also be provided.

The range and diversity of these services have greatly increased in recent times to meet more effectively the more complex needs and aspirations of service users and carers. For example, a number of local authorities have established 'tucking-in' and 'night sitting' services to provide personal care at times when other domiciliary services are not operating. Other local authorities have developed adult placement schemes where the host carers offer respite or long term care to people with a range of complex needs. In rural areas, some local authorities have developed mobile facilities to provide, for example, day care for elderly people.

Alongside these changes, local authorities are reviewing the contribution of residential care to meeting their responsibilities for people in need. They are seeking to focus the service more effectively on people who require more support than can be reasonably provided in their own homes, whilst, at the same time, deploying some beds for assessment, respite and episodic care. This integration of residential care with community care services has been further enhanced in some authorities by the integration of services for each client group — domiciliary, day, and residential — under a local manager.

Another development encouraged by the new legislation is the growth of inter-agency, multi-disciplinary approaches to service delivery. For example, a team providing services to a frail elderly person might comprise a social services occupational therapist and a member of the local authority housing department (providing aids and adaptations), a volunteer (providing meals on wheels), a local authority domiciliary care assistant (providing personal care and domestic help) and a health visitor or district nurse (addressing the person's health needs). Within this collaborative framework, information and expertise is shared with each staff member contributing to the total pattern of care. In some areas, for example, community mental health teams, inter-agency working has become more formalised with the establishment of multi-disciplinary teams working to a single manager.

Inter-agency approaches have also developed in the fields of child protection, juvenile justice and learning disabilities. Social services staff are sometimes out-posted to other agencies, for example placements in general practitioners' surgeries. These local authority operational staff in conjunction with their other agency colleagues form 'implementation structures' for the delivery of services in their specialist areas. The inter-professional relationships within these structures are becoming as important as the internal relationships within social services departments.

Increased specialisation

Alongside the developments in service delivery, services themselves have become more professionalised and specialised. There has been a move away from generalist approaches to client group specialisms and sub-specialisms, such as child protection, fostering and adoption. In response to problems with residential child care, the Government has given fresh impetus to the professionalisation of residential social work, together with an explicit recognition that residential social work with children is a specialism with specific skill requirements (SSI 1991).

There is a general recognition in respect of all client groups that service delivery is becoming more complex, and that much of the work is potentially of a 'high risk' nature. Specialist approaches to service delivery and staff supervision are viewed as the best way for developing sufficient skills and experience to inform good practice, and to command credibility with service users and carers, key agencies and the general public.

Government guidance accompanying the community care and child care legislation has emphasised that the delivery of personal social services is not a routine task that can be reduced solely to procedural guidelines. The point of worker/user contact calls for sensitive observation and judgement informed by an appropriate knowledge and skills base. Training, therefore, is an essential component in the development of a skilled specialist service, and its scope is increasingly embracing joint training across agency boundaries, as well as training within social services departments.

Developing a user and carer-centred perspective

The legislation also emphasises the importance of taking into account the needs and wishes of the consumers of social services — the user and carer — in planning, delivery and evaluation of services. The community care changes stress that service provision should support and complement the role of informal carers who provide most of the care in the community to children and adults in need.

Strategies for finding out the needs of users and carers were discussed in the previous section. But the establishment of an effective user and carer-centred perspective also demands that actual and potential users and carers are informed of what services are available. This requires the production of appropriate publicity material about available services and eligibility criteria, and effective communication channels for individuals and groups of users and carers. Increasingly, information provision is being recognised as an important service to users and carers who have to negotiate their way through a complex welfare system. Social services have taken on aspects of this role themselves, through the establishment of welfare rights posts. They are also beginning to develop formal consultation machinery with groups of users and carers. Other local authorities are encouraging voluntary organisations to take on the role of bringing users and carers together in networks and groups where their views can be expressed.

Different geographical areas or neighbourhoods within a local authority area can exhibit differences in social and economic characteristics. Authorities are therefore exploiting the benefits of decentralised management and budgetary arrangements to respond more effectively and flexibly to the specific needs of local communities, within the wider strategic policy and planning framework. Some have established area panels of local councillors in parallel with devolved management structures, to provide opportunities for two-way consultation and thereby inform wider policy-making fora with a user-centred perspective.

All these developments raise a number of important issues for the 'direct provider' role. In the first place, significant resources are being deployed, and more are likely to be required, to provide a service that is accessible and responsive to user and carer needs, whether to enhance access, or provide specialist skills ensuring an effective and responsive intervention. Secondly, redeployment of resources to develop more user-sensitive services may require long lead times, especially if it involves new buildings or the development of new skills. Thirdly, there is a continuing tension between the wishes of service recipients and professional judgement, especially in high risk situations such as child protection, and between the needs of users and of carers.

Direct provision within a mixed economy of care

In developing a mixed economy of care, a strategic view must be taken of the role of in-house provision in the profile of service delivery. Direct provision will continue to have a significant role in the future, but its emphasis is likely to change as it is increasingly seen as part of the wider pattern of care entailed by the 'enabling' approach. As such, it needs to be seen in the strategic context of planning to meet need in the most appropriate way and securing the most effective form of provision.

Against this background, direct provision could be targeted on high priority groups — those in greatest need within wider client groups, for example, such as elderly people who are very mentally infirm — or concentrated on meeting highly specialised needs not readily met elsewhere. For example, local authorities could leave much mainstream residential care for elderly people to the independent sector, and concentrate on developing in-house residential provision as resource centres, providing assessment facilities and episodic/short term care as part of a community care package for individual users and carers. A further in-house role might be the development of 'leading edge' responses to new needs, for example, those of victims of civil disasters and their families.

Apart from this change in focus, there is a continuing responsibility for ensuring that in-house services are delivered to the required standard of performance and quality. The relationship between in-house providers and commissioning staff is likely to become more formalised in the future through service agreements or other forms of contractual arrangements. Increasingly, in-house providers will have to justify service standards and costs. It will be important nonetheless for in-house providers to work in close collaboration at the operational level with external providers, so that professional contacts are maintained and developed, and skills transfer is effective across the full range of service provision.

Implications for local government structure

This section sets out the implications of the changing role of personal social services for the future structure of local government. The key issues are:

- the benefits of scale;
- the need for a responsive service;
- the requirements of a collaborative policy environment;
- the increasing complexity of the management task.

Benefits of scale

The new enabling role in personal social services involves a number of key strategic activities in relation to anticipating needs in the population, planning to meet those needs, and securing and regulating provision to put plans into action. There are benefits of scale in each of these areas.

Anticipating the needs of their population is a difficult task for local authorities. They will have to adopt a range of activities to assess need effectively, including new approaches to information collection and methods of integration and analysis. New skills will be required, for example in market research, and new technologies, such as improved information systems. A broader resource base will enable local authorities to invest in these activities.

Yet, however expert the planning and information-gathering process, new needs are bound to emerge unexpectedly. Social services departments must have sufficient resource flexibility to respond to changing needs, and to a high level of unpredictability, within an appropriate timescale. This requires responsive and flexible management processes, and the effective deployment of a range of scarce resources — physical, financial and staffing. Larger organisations are more likely to have a broad resource base to provide the necessary flexibility, at both the strategic and operational levels, to manage uncertainty effectively.

The issue of scale is also relevant to planning, commissioning and regulatory activities. If the full range of client needs is to be met by appropriate services, then local authorities require a population of substantial size to ensure that a range of specialised services is viable. Otherwise, choice will be limited, and client needs may not be met.

As local authorities embrace the enabling role, they will become more involved in promoting independent sector activity and securing services from agencies in this sector. Larger scale organisations have both greater commissioning power and the ability to vary contract sizes (and indeed to put together 'packages' of contracts). This gives maximum flexibility and value for money. Greater economic leverage makes for more effective commissioning, while the skills required — for example, drafting specifications and managing contracts — are specialised and relatively scarce. Other things being equal, it is more efficient to concentrate these skills in a relatively small number of bodies, where they can be drawn on as required by a large number of care managers.

At the operational level, the tasks of individual assessment, care management and supervisory management are becoming more skilled and more specialist. Staff who undertake these tasks require appropriate training and effective professional support from senior people with the relevant expertise and experience. These staff are in short supply, and the relevant skills and expertise could become unacceptably diluted if they had to be distributed across a large number of small authorities.

Finally, the regulatory functions of registration and inspection have to be at arm's length from service delivery. Staff working in this area need to take a broad view of services to compare them effectively. If they are working very locally it is difficult to ensure objectivity and to develop a strategic view about issues of service quality.

The benefits of scale are also significant from the direct provider perspective. First, the direct provider role means even more specialisation among staff at all levels, as the new legislation is implemented. Specialists may simply not be available to service a larger number of authorities than currently exist. Even if they were, maintaining full and productive use of their skills could prove difficult because of the potentially lower level of demand for such specialist help made on organisations serving smaller geographical areas. In general, there is a risk of losing economies of scale, reducing productivity and increasing unit costs.

More particularly, effective delivery of specialised services, especially to rare populations, may require a large catchment area to be viable, because of the limited number of people within the area who will need the service, and the specialist training which service providers require. Furthermore, services must be provided on a sufficiently large scale to ensure that support, back-up and 'front-line' monitoring is available both from colleagues and from specialist advisors.

It has been argued that benefits of scale could be adequately achieved by smaller local authorities cooperating with each other, either informally or through joint boards. Evidence of the extent and value of inter-authority cooperation, on anything like the scale likely to be needed for social services, is limited, however. Joint boards tend to lead to diffusion of democratic accountability and to a lack of clarity in management responsibility. It cannot be assumed that such arrangements could readily match the greater simplicity of a structure of larger scale authorities.

A responsive service

Local authorities must respond appropriately and sensitively to the needs and circumstances of users and carers. In much of the discussion of this issue, however, 'responsiveness' is often equated with service planning and provision at the level of 'local community'. But the concept of 'community' is highly problematic as a basis for policy development or as the framework for service planning and delivery. Too little is known about what determines the shape and style of informal networks, and there is no single way of knowing or serving communities (Nisbet 1973).

Because of this complexity, decision-making on behalf of the 'community' is not straightforward. It has to take account of both narrow and wider interests, and be sensitive to both individual and collective needs. Inevitably, conflicting needs will be identified, not all of which can be met. This conflict has to be managed. It requires decisions addressing the balance between the achievement of equity in provision and the targeting of scarce resources on those in greatest need (Davies *et al.* 1989), and is complex. It needs an organisational capacity for effective policy formulation and broad strategic planning, so that these issues are addressed as objectively as possible and key decisions are not influenced inappropriately by forms of 'local' special pleading.

Operationally, responsiveness clearly requires services to be delivered locally. The degree of 'localness' is, however, likely to vary with different forms of service. For example, the management and delivery of a range of domiciliary and day care services to people with social care needs could be based at a resource centre serving a relatively small community. Adoption, in contrast, could be more centrally based because of the benefit of scale. The deployment of scarce expertise more centrally is likely to help the adoption service user receive a skilled intervention and so a responsive service. It may not be feasible to provide effective services locally which are targeted at small numbers of people.

The development of responsive social services must avoid a simplistic 'central versus local' debate; nor must it be seen as a function of structure. It is fundamentally about competent management. It needs to consider in turn each type of service and the most appropriate way the enabling and providing tasks associated with it should be carried out within resource constraints. This process will establish the appropriate level of devolved management and service delivery, and identify those tasks that need to remain more centralised. 'Decentralisation ought to take place within an organisational structure which is big enough to allow for the formation of a strategic view, a degree of coordination of service delivery, monitoring and evaluation, and liaison with other agencies of key importance' (Laming 1945). Currently, social services departments have decentralised service delivery through the establishment of local and area offices. This is supplemented by a substantial presence at the local level, of, for example, day and residential facilities.

A collaborative policy environment

The planning and delivery of social care and children's services requires effective inter-agency linkages at the strategic and operational levels. Social welfare is inherently an inter-agency endeavour. The structure of local government must therefore promote, and preferably enhance, effective collaboration. The key issues influencing the success of inter-agency collaboration include:

● agreement on the clients served;

- the complementarity of services provided by the respective organisations and the manner in which the services are offered;
- the degree to which organisations have shared goals, similar values and status among senior members and officers, and complementary technologies and resource needs (Whetten 1977).

Progressively, social services departments have built up strategic relationships with health authorities and are developing links with the new family health service authorities. Effective inter-agency working at the planning and operational levels has been facilitated by, though it does not absolutely require, coterminosity of the respective agencies' boundaries. Indeed, the incidence of coterminosity is increasing with some district health authorities forming purchasing consortia based on county boundaries, as FHSAs already are. Where agencies are of comparable size or have coterminous boundaries, relationships at both member (whether elected or appointed) and officer level are reinforced by equivalence of status and influence.

Many voluntary bodies, with whom local authorities will increasingly need to work closely, are also organised on a county basis. In addition, collaboration with the criminal justice system in work with young offenders and in child protection has been assisted by the comparable size and influence of the participating agencies.

It has also been argued in this chapter that planning for the implementation of community care requires effective collaboration in particular with the housing sector — public, voluntary and private. Though housing is only one aspect of the multi-dimensional environment of community care, there is nonetheless considerable advantage from this perspective in moving to a unitary structure, since this would further facilitate common perceptions of housing need and the development of an appropriate response across the expanding range of housing providers.

Collaboration is needed not only between local agencies, but also between local authorities and central government, which exercises a developmental, advisory, monitoring and evaluation role in relation to local authority social services departments. This role is increasing as policy and procedural guidance from the centre becomes more prescriptive, and new powers are taken to ensure that community care plans are open to inspection and to call for reports from local authorities. A recent report examining the wide variations in levels of social services between different local authorities shows the very considerable task involved in ensuring consistency of service quality across the UK (Policy Forum 1992). This task is likely to be made easier by a local government structure that results in a smaller number of social services departments.

Management complexity

A key determinant of successful implementation of the new legislation will be the effectiveness of senior and middle management. The management task in social services is growing in complexity. New demands include:

- Need has to be balanced against scarce resources in the implementation of community care. Most evidence suggests that for a similar quality of service, community-based provision is more expensive than institutional forms of care which achieve some economies of scale.
- These changes do not necessarily lead to improvements in services to users, unless the targeting of an appropriate level of services to those in priority need is achieved through managers establishing effective assessment and care management procedures (Davies *et al.* 1989).
- To respond effectively to the changing environment, new skills and expertise must be developed in, for example, marketing, commissioning, business planning and project management.
- Operating increasingly in a more complex and developing multi-agency environment, and integrating different professional contributions within a holistic pattern of care.
- The need for appropriate human resource strategies for the recruitment, retention and development of the required level and mix of staff.
- The incorporation of self-determination and choice for users into service development, requiring an element of risk-acceptance for both users and staff.
- The development of management frameworks which give staff an appropriate level of discretion whilst ensuring accountability.
- Putting in place new department structures and new working practices in response to the new legislation, and making them work.

The cumulative impact of these tasks amounts to a qualitative and quantitative shift in the complexity of management. The development of the necessary skills and expertise to carry them out effectively will require significant human, financial and material resources. There must be a significant risk that dealing with major structural change will divert time and energy away from the successful implementation of significant policy initiatives of high priority to central and local government, and of considerable importance to users and carers. This implies at minimum a presumption in favour of continuity in the scale and nature of social services authorities.

Conclusion

This chapter has described the major and unprecedented policy changes currently facing local authorities in the social services field. At a time when social services are attempting to balance changing and increasing levels of need with scarce resources, they are being asked to take on new and enhanced responsibilities which involve, in many instances, a qualitative change in the way the service is delivered and managed.

Major structural change could therefore have significant implications for the personal social services. The key points for the review of local government will be to ensure that:

- the benefits of scale of the current structure are maintained or enhanced;
- the task of further developing a responsive service is addressed realistically, avoiding a simplistic 'local versus central' debate, and instead considering in turn each type of service and how best to carry out the associated enabling and providing tasks, within resource constraints;
- the collaborative environment of social and child care policy and provision is promoted and, preferably, enhanced, through the maintenance and development of existing links with external agencies, with central government, and, in the field of housing, through a move to a unitary structure;
- there is minimal risk of successful implementation of new legislation being compromised by structural change.

References

Davies, B. *et al.* (1989) *Resources, Needs and Outcomes in Community Services: an Overview* PSSRU.

DHSS (1989) *Caring for People (Community Care in the Next Decade and Beyond)* HMSO.

DHSS (1991) *Working Together under the Children Act 1989* HMSO.

Laming, H. (1985) *Lessons from America: The Balance of Services in Social Care* PSI Discussion Paper II.

Nisbet, R. A. (1973) *The Sociological Tradition* Heineman.

Policy Forum (1992) *Great Expectations . . . and spending on social services*.

SSI (1991) *Children in the Public Care* HMSO.

Whetten, D. A. (1977) 'Toward a contingency model for designing interorganisational service delivery systems' *Organisation and Administrative Sciences*, **8**.

General bibliography

(1989) *An Introduction to the Children Act 1989*, HMSO.
Rao, N. (1991) *From Providing to Enabling: local authorities and community care planning* Joseph Rowntree Foundation.
Smith, B. C. (1985) *Decentralisation* G. Allen & Unwin.

6 Partnerships in prosperity: local government's role in economic development

> Enterprise only pretends to itself to be mainly actuated by the statements in its own prospectus, however candid and sincere. Only a little more than an expedition to the South Pole, is it based on an exact calculation of benefits to come . . . if spontaneous optimism falters, enterprise will fail and die. This means . . . that economic prosperity is excessively dependent upon a political and social atmosphere which is congenial to the average businessman. In estimating the prospects of investment, we must have regard therefore, to the nerves and hysteria and even the digestions and reactions to the weather of those upon whose spontaneous activity it largely depends
>
> (J. M. Keynes)

Introduction

This chapter examines the role of local government in economic development of local areas. It describes how economic development has evolved as a local authority activity since the early 1970s and examines the roles of the different tiers of local government. Economic development involves many activities and partners and the chapter considers their relationships and the legislative framework for undertaking economic development. It concludes by assessing the local authorities' economic development role in relation to the local government review.

The importance of economic development as an activity of local government lies not only in the direct promotion of economic activity in a given area, but also in focusing on the economic dimension of other council services. The first aspect is about creating the right environment for both the continued well being of industry and commerce in the area and the attraction of new investment. The second recognises that whilst most local authority functions are not inherently concerned with promoting enterprise, they can nonetheless have a major impact on economic development through the provision of services (such as education) and regulatory activities (such as consumer protection).

While economic activity is largely the purview of the private sector, economic strategy is not. The operation of the market may require intervention, assistance and regulation, not least to compensate for a lack of private sector activity. Involvement can take many forms, adapted to local circumstances. It can range from tackling directly structural, economic or sectoral weaknesses, to ensuring that the economic needs of the area are taken into account across a wide range of policy areas to achieve a positive climate for economic activity.

The role of local authorities in economic development is likely to become more important and more complex. The reasons include a growing understanding of the relationship between the private and the public sectors, and a new willingness on both sides to enter into partnerships to achieve common objectives. The objectives include balancing wealth creation and environmental protection, promoting enterprise while conserving the local heritage and helping the local community to adapt effectively to new demands. The advent of the Single European Market is also a key factor here.

Local government will have to adapt as well. Liaison between communities and markets requires understanding of and response to changing expectations on all sides. Adaptation requires monitoring and maintaining a detailed awareness of trends in the local economy. It may also mean reshaping local authorities' own structures to ensure that the most effective arrangements are in place. The local government review must be based on a clear understanding of the economic role of local authorities in order to reach conclusions on future structures best suited to maintaining a positive economic environment into the next century.

The emergence of economic development initiatives

Local authorities have a long-standing involvement in promoting the economic well-being of their areas. During the 1950s and 1960s the most active authorities were generally in assisted regions. The majority of economic development activities were planning led, mainly concerned with industrial restructuring. The emergence of economic development as a discrete activity, with associated management structures and budgets, has been a significant feature of the last two decades.

For much of this period local government was virtually alone in dealing with economic development at local level. Central government's role was primarily concerned with regional development policy. The private sector was not seen as a partner, to be actively nurtured in developing local areas, although its absence in specific areas was a stimulus for local authority action.

From the 1960s economic decline in important areas of the country resulted in closer examination of the economic problems of smaller geographical areas. By the 1970s the decline of the inner areas of major cities added a new dimension. It became more widely accepted that tackling the problems of an area involved the local economy, as well as the land use and housing issues which had been the main focus of most local authorities up to that time.

The local economic development role of local authorities grew rapidly from the 1960s, but individual authorities have pursued such activities to varying degrees, depending on:

- the severity of economic problems including high unemployment;
- the absence or low level of private investment and development activity, demanding alternative economic stimulus;
- commitment to intervention in the market stemming from political perspectives;
- designation of selected areas, or parts of them, by central government, reflecting national views on priorities for investment;
- the availability of skills through which individual authorities could initiate and sustain economic strategies.

By the end of the 1970s, local authority economic development activities fell broadly under five headings:

- land use policies and development control, using planning powers to ensure the availability of an adequate amount of land for new or expanding industry;
- direct involvement in the development of infrastructure, primarily to provide roads and services, assemble and prepare sites, and build factories;
- business advice and promotional activities (including: the provision of information for existing companies, or companies considering relocating to an area, on premises availability, work force, employer forums etc.; general advice to small businesses; promotion of an area's image to a wider audience);
- employment-related activities such as careers advice and special training schemes;
- investing in and operating businesses by providing grants and loans or loan guarantees, and providing 'risk' capital or owning and managing (municipal) enterprises.

These economic development activities raised a number of policy and organisational issues. First, there was a need to integrate them into the overall policies of the authority. Second, an organisational framework was needed for this expanding function. Many authorities established economic development units in their planning department or chief executive's office. Others introduced new, separate departments. In parallel, specific committees were designated to consider economic development issues.

While much of the activity was characterised by fragmented initiatives, individual authorities began to design and implement coordinated economic development strategies, which they sought to integrate into their strategic and local plan framework. By the 1980s the production of coordinated local economic development strategies was widespread.

The legal framework for economic development

Reflecting the piecemeal emergence of economic development activity, legislative powers were adapted from other purposes rather than designed for the new purpose. Not until 1989, with the Local Government and Housing Act, were local authorities given specific permissive powers to promote the economic well-being of their areas.

Before then, the power most commonly used to promote direct local government economic development was s.137 of the 1972 Local Government Act. It provided authorities in England and Wales with the ability to spend up to the product of a 2p rate on activities which were:

> in the interests of their area or any part of it or all or some of its inhabitants. (Local Government Act 1972, Part VII, s.137(1))

The provisions of the Local Government and Housing Act, 1989, were introduced in response to the Widdicombe Committee Inquiry, which expressed dissatisfaction with the nature and use of economic development powers by local government. The Act was intended to clarify the situation.

It permits authorities to undertake activities appropriate to the promotion of the economic development of their area, including the participation in, encouragement of, and provision of financial and other assistance for 'the setting up or expansion of any commercial industrial or public undertaking situated in the authority's area or likely to increase the employment opportunities of persons living in that area, and the creation or protection of opportunities for employment' (s.33, Local Government and Housing Act, 1989). This is a permissive, not mandatory power, and some powers are geographically limited.

An authority is deemed to have offered financial assistance if it provides grants, loans, loan guarantees, liability indemnities, or property services, and if it invests in any undertakings. It must also produce a document before each financial year specifying the steps it proposes to take for the economic promotion of its area in that year, and identifying the associated capital and revenue expenditure together with anticipated financial and other benefits. Commercial and industrial interests in the area need to be prominent among those consulted on this document.

A key element of the 1989 Act (Part V) is the rules on local authority involvement in companies. This reflects government concern at the growth of such enterprises, many directly undertaking local government functions. A distinction has now been drawn between those companies which are truly independent and those which are local authority controlled or influenced, to which the normal local government expenditure rules apply, including government controls on spending.

The requirement to produce an annual economic development plan for each area where qualifying expenditure is contemplated, and to circulate that plan for consultation, is a positive step which encourages greater coordination of area-specific programmes. In many counties liaison already exists between the county council and district councils to form county-wide development strategies. There is also extensive liaison with other agencies such as Training and Enterprise Councils (TECs) the Rural Development Commission (RDC), and the Urban Development Corporations (UDCs), though this is not required by law.

Current economic development initiatives

During the 1980s new links developed between local and central government, the private sector and a range of other agencies, as a growing number of bodies involved themselves in economic development. Local authorities have continued to respond to the changing relationship in order to promote coordinated, focused initiatives. Many of the bodies involved, whether established by government or from the private sector, pursue complementary programmes to those of local government and seek to work closely with it.

Central and regional initiatives

In recent years central government has become more active within local economic development, mainly through its inner city programmes and the establishment of Urban Development Corporations. The most recent initiative, the competition for City Challenge funding by designated local authorities, is targeted on stress boroughs in the major urban areas. These however have had little impact in shire counties.

More widespread in impact was the government's launching of the Training and Enterprise Councils. The administrative boundaries of TECs are, in most cases, coterminous with those of counties. While primarily concerned with training issues, TECs operate in a wider sphere and are intended to contribute substantially to local economic development.

A consistent theme of government in the 1980s was a growing expectation that the private sector should play a more active part in the promotion of local economies. The TECs are an example of this approach, but a more general belief prevailed that sustained development could only occur where the private sector took the lead and developed an enterprise culture.

It remains however for local authorities to encourage private sector activity or, where this is absent, seek to provide alternatives. Much emphasis is laid on the partnership between individual authorities and their local, industrial and commercial interests. Bodies such as Business in the Community were formed by the private sector to facilitate this relationship.

Government also sought to support economic development through a number of Local Enterprise Agencies, companies limited by guarantee, managed by a board drawn from both the public and private sector. Their basic remit is to provide advice to new or existing businesses, but many go beyond this and offer training, trade directories, business clubs and even loan funds. Their functions may thus overlap with some of the small business advisory work undertaken by local authorities, but for the most part they are complementary, given different scales of operation and perspectives.

In addition, a number of government agencies have a role in economic development. The Rural Development Commission, English Estates and the Tourist Boards play significant, but very different, roles in promoting economic activity. These bodies, and the equivalent Welsh agencies, seek to liaise with and work alongside local authorities. In most cases relationships are well established and effective.

The Rural Development Commission (RDC) is an important stimulator of smaller enterprise in rural areas. Its key functions are:

- advising government on economic issues affecting rural areas;
- developing sites in conjunction with English Estates and providing work spaces for small enterprises;
- offering grant or loan assistance for the conversion of redundant agricultural or other rural buildings;
- supplying general business advice and lobbying or promoting rural industries in a wider market.

The RDC operates at sub-regional level through a network of offices. It works closely with private, voluntary and public sector bodies at county and district level. This liaison is carried out both on an informal basis and via Rural Development Programme Committees which meet quarterly to promote agreed economic strategies in their areas. County councils and district councils are represented on these committees, the former frequently undertaking coordinating, initiating, and secretarial functions.

English Estates, similarly, has a regional structure and liaises with all tiers of local government. Its primary function is the preparation of sites and the provision of industrial and commercial workspace where this is lacking in economically disadvantaged areas. English Estates takes a strategic view of market demand in specified areas, and works closely with county councils to determine future demand. Where effort is directed towards creating a ladder of accommodation for new and expanding enterprises to occupy, English Estates and individual local authorities work well together in devising suitable development programmes.

In an effort to coordinate its own mainstream activities, central government has itself formed a number of new bodies such as Task Forces and City Action Teams to focus the activities of different departments. These bodies aim at the more effective targeting of government's existing initiatives, rather than new intervention. County councils have in some cases played an important role in helping to establish and orientate these organisations.

EC initiatives

European Community policies to promote economic development, and the provision of Community funds to implement these policies, have become of increasing importance to local authorities in the UK over recent years. These funds, known as the Structural Funds, comprises the following:

The European Regional Development Fund (ERDF)

This aims to distribute EC resources to the poorer areas of the European Community so as to ensure a more balanced distribution of economic activity throughout the regions of Europe. The fund grant aids industrial infrastructure projects such as road schemes, industrial estates, factories and tourist facilities. The fund can also provide assistance to small and medium sized enterprises engaged in industry, craft industries and tourism.

The European Social Fund (ESF)

This grant aids vocational training, retraining and job creation schemes.

The European Agricultural Guidance and Guarantee Fund (EAGGF)

This assists in the reform and restructuring of agricultural regions.

Not all these funds are available throughout the whole of the United Kingdom. Some are linked to defined priority areas such as the undeveloped region of Northern Ireland, certain areas of industrial decline, and a small number of rural development areas.

In 1989 the Structural Funds were the subject of major reform designed to increase their effectiveness. These reforms were based on five main principles:

- the doubling of the funds by 1993;
- better coordination of the funds by using them in an integrated way through operational programmes in the context of Community Support Frameworks;
- concentrating the funds on the more needy regions of the Community;
- the setting up of partnerships, involving the EC, central government and local/regional authorities, to manage the operation of the funds;
- the simplification, greater flexibility and transparency of fund procedures.

County council roles

Central to the reforms is the concept of 'partnership' and the need for local/regional authorities to be actively involved in the effective operation of the funds. In non-metropolitan areas of England and Wales, county councils have largely fulfilled the role of the regional partner, for two main reasons:

Firstly, county councils are relatively large in terms of their population, the extent of the areas they administer, and the GDP produced by their areas. Not surprisingly the European Commission deals with county councils as the local/regional partners rather than a multiplicity of smaller councils.

Secondly, county councils provide a wide range of services, many of which relate to economic development (e.g. highways and education). Many of these services are also eligible for European funding.

Consequently, county councils have been actively involved in developing the operational programmes (such as the Integrated Development Operations Programmes and the RENAVAL and RECHAR programmes) which are now essential for accessing European Structural Fund grants. County councils are frequently among the leading members of the partnerships that manage and implement the programmes. County councils have also identified and been able to utilise other European Community initiatives for the purposes of economic development, such as the PETRA initiative on preparing young people for adult and working life and the FORCE programme for continued vocational training.

Through their active involvement in European matters, county councils have developed a level of European expertise which other local authorities lack. This expertise is not only of great advantage to county council services, but is also used to assist other organisations involved in economic development in the counties concerned.

Local authority involvement

Within this framework, the current core activities of local authorities are:

- *strategic planning, coordination and monitoring;*
- *land, premises and infrastructure provision;*
- *business development and financial assistance;*
- *marketing, promotion and tourism;*
- *research, advocacy and lobbying;*
- *training and education;*
- *attracting inward investment;*
- *liaison and linkage.*

Strategic planning is at the heart of local authority work in economic development. It requires an understanding of economic trends at a macro level, as well as their impact on the local economy. A successful strategy depends upon understanding industry by sector, and recognising the opportunities and needs for stimulating indigenous business or inward investment. It also has to be sensitive to the needs and preferences of local communities.

Regular analysis and monitoring is required to ensure that policies are still relevant and targets are being met. Effective strategic planning also demands coordination between the public and private sectors, and bringing together competing interests in a coherent framework. County councils are well placed to exercise this coordinating role over a wide range of services.

The effective deployment of industrial land and property is central to the well being of the local economy. Local authorities are better placed than any other body to marshall that resource. Their planning powers and investment programmes enable them to embark upon site assembly and development. The latter is increasingly carried out in partnership with commercial bodies, or with agencies such as English Estates. Experience of the rise and fall of the property market has led many local authorities to a better understanding of the need to work with specialists as well as to maintain genuine expertise in-house.

The land assembly and site development capability of local authorities is often used to stimulate rather than respond to demand. This again highlights the need to understand and retain a close contact with both the local market and the broader regional or national economy. The capacity both to plan strategically and carry out project development requires a scale of resources and breadth of technique which favours larger administrative units. Added to this is the need to promote and lobby for these resources at sub-regional, national and European levels.

Many local authorities provide advice and financial support to businesses. The size of authority determines the scale of this involvement and the depth of expertise deployed, but most authorities can offer some useful support to their business communities. Supplemented by, or in some cases in partnership with, some of the agencies referred to earlier, local authorities provide a key link between community and business. As an elected forum, local government is an important channel of communication for business opinion and information.

In addition to advice, direct financial assistance is made through grants and loans. For smaller authorities the limits on direct financial assistance to businesses are very tight indeed. Sums over £1,000 may be out of the question. Counties, in contrast, routinely consider assistance on a scale fifty times as great. Grants of this kind are generally related to premises or equipment. Currently, local authorities commit a substantial proportion of their economic development budgets to incentives of this kind. Advice is also given about other sources of funding, whether from within the UK or from the European Commission.

Most local authorities now engage in marketing their area. The extent of this activity varies very substantially from one authority to another. No set pattern is evident. Some authorities have jointly or individually established specialist agencies to market their regions and to lobby government both in the UK and at the European level. Some authorities pursue a general programme of marketing their area to promote a positive image to attract both investment and tourism. Other authorities, particularly those trying to overcome severe problems of under-investment, obsolete infrastructure and industrial closure, generate highly targeted programmes sometimes aimed at one particular company or industry. Some of the more notable successes in recent times have involved major Japanese industries seeking European locations.

The creation of specialist agencies to attract investment, such as the Northern Development Company in the north-east, the Yorkshire and

Humberside Development Agency and the West Midlands Development Agency, has introduced cross-boundary working at the county level. Establishing and participating in such a forum is both a demanding and efficient use of resources. Duplication is avoided and a strategic view can be taken of opportunities.

Increasing competition demands that marketing should be clearly focused internationally particularly because of the advent of the Single European Market. The scale and complexity of the task involved means that only larger administrative units are capable of sustaining an effective programme. Much of the work involved in this kind of strategy is long-term and requires consistent profile-raising.

Strategic considerations

Commercial investment hinges on both business and non-business issues, the latter including the quality of the environment, housing, social facilities, labour force, transport infrastructure and many other aspects of an area, which a local authority is well-placed either to marshall or to stimulate. The strategic and enabling role of major local authorities is not replicated by any other body and cannot be underestimated in its implications for economic development. Promotion and marketing in a narrow way is unlikely to be successful.

All economic development activity must be backed by genuine and authoritative knowledge and understanding.

An effective research and information capacity need not be maintained in-house, but where research is carried out externally it needs to be properly commissioned, which requires in-house expertise. Because of the increasing complexity and trans-national nature of economic activity, the scope of research is broadening. Targeting scarce resources, identifying all possible sources of investment and support, maintaining close liaison with key agencies, accessing Europe-wide data banks, and maintaining an awareness of competing players, all suggest that the broad research capability of local authorities is likely to have to grow markedly. Consequently relatively few smaller local authorities can or do undertake their own research programmes. There is increasing reliance upon county-level authorities to maintain research programmes to which others can subscribe.

A key task for local authorities in economic development is to help develop a skilled workforce. This means a close relationship between schools, colleges and further education establishments, and industry and commerce. The local authority also concerns itself with those in the community who do not have skills which are readily marketable. Training, retraining and education are thus central issues in the evolution of the economic development strategies of most local authorities.

With the advent of TECs, there needs to be a partnership with the local authority to ensure that the training requirements of the area are being met.

New investment is important to the well-being of all areas. Some local authorities have concentrated almost exclusively on inward investment. In practice relatively few industries are footloose, and relatively few major international companies are looking to develop large new plants in the UK. Competition for these is therefore fierce. Individual local authorities need to foster indigenous business investment as well as external investors. For this reason any local authority putting together a comprehensive economic development strategy must give substantial thought to all possible new investments, ranging from cooperatives to small-scale local businesses, and from medium-sized firms to multi-nationals. This broad-based approach to creating a more robust economy needs a wide variety of skills, policies and proposals.

Local authorities remain the one consistent dimension in the development of local economies. As circumstances change and new programmes emanate from government or elsewhere, it is local authorities who maintain a dialogue between central and local interests, and business and social agencies. Whether as service providers or as coordinators of the work of others, local authorities are pivotal in achieving economic well-being. Neither central government nor small local authorities could carry out this role. Central government would be too remote, and could not focus its attention locally on all areas through UDCs and Task Forces. Current experience suggests that small local authorities would not have the capacity to carry out all aspects of the economic development role effectively. It is difficult to conceive of any other agency replacing this role of liaising with, and linking between, the many interests involved, whether in the current environment, or in the future. In determining the preferred structure of local government, these are crucial considerations.

Shaping the future

The context within which local authorities operate their economic development function has changed considerably since the 1960s. They have benefited from a growing understanding of the issues to be tackled, and growing recognition of the different agencies which must contribute to the process. The location of any expertise or service delivery function should be less of a preoccupation than the need to accept that local authorities remain central to effective strategic planning and coordination.

Despite the growing emphasis on partnership local authorities have a lead role in promoting their local economies. Leadership and vision are essential in focusing resources and competing interests on shared objectives. Economic development is more than achieving industrial and commercial growth; it influences local authorities' thinking over a wide range of social and environmental issues.

Economic development will become even more important over the coming decade. The increasing mobility of the population, fundamental changes in the relationship between urban and rural areas, industrial restructuring and the advent of the Single European Market, all mean that local economies will face growing turbulence. Adjusting to new trends and unexpected pressures will lie at the heart of the local authority role.

Resources may be a limiting factor. It must be assumed that the UK will, with important exceptions, achieve relatively low priority against some of the poorer regions of the European Community. Public expenditure constraints cannot be expected to ease to a significant degree, nor will economic development rank highly against other social priorities such as health, education and housing. Marshalling scarce resources, achieving economies of scale and ensuring effective targeting will all be vital endeavours. The future structure of local authorities in the context of economic development must take account of this need. Achieving economies of scale and maintaining critical mass must be the driving force in determining the future organisation.

The future picture therefore looks like this:

- increasing importance for economic development in local and central government;
- a growing range of specialist agencies and bodies, both in the public and the private sectors, incorporating specialist capabilities;
- rising expectations in the community of high standards of service and high quality environments;
- increasing complexity brought about not simply by the number of participating bodies, but by a widening European framework within which development is promoted;
- wider understanding of the requirements for successful economic development, taking into account social and environmental factors;
- recognition of the inter-relationships between economic development and other dimensions of social change, particularly with the restructuring of agricultural and other industries, together with population shifts (urban/rural, inter-regional, international);
- intensifying competition between different parts of the country for footloose industries and inward investment.

The local authority which will best respond to the many demands implicit in the new economic development environment will have the following features:

- economic development viewed as a mainstream function, under-taken by experienced and specialist staff, but as part of an integrated policy planning process;
- the capacity to undertake a full range of direct service provision from policy development to operational activity, alone or in conjunction with other bodies;
- sufficient expertise and experience for the authority to function effectively in all EC matters;
- ability to liaise and maintain an equal dialogue with a large variety of agencies and enterprises, public and private, to achieve complementary programmes aimed at common objectives;
- of sufficient size to achieve critical mass in terms of research and analysis, including the ability to monitor and evaluate investment and to commission external assistance where necessary;
- internally structured to ensure that local communities are not forgotten in the promotion of wider economic development goals;
- orientated towards indigenous business development opportunities as well as to inward investment from UK or other origins.

Larger scale units of local government, with their substantial resources and expertise, will dominate the economic debates which lie ahead. Whatever organisation is put in place for local government in the UK, it must have the capacity to link the local and the trans-national so that neither is compromised or neglected.

The decision on local government structure is in many ways as important to the economic well-being of the community as external market circumstances. As the challenges of the 1990s unfold, it will be the efficient and effective authorities who secure benefits for their communities. They will do so because they can bring together many disparate interests into a coherent strategy and because they can deploy the resources needed to sustain that strategy. It is essential to national economic well-being that any new local government structure specifically addresses responsiveness to the full range of interests and tasks which will confront local authorities and their partners over the coming decades.

Bibliography

ADC (1987) Economic Development Initiatives and Innovations — Economic Development by District Councils: Best Practice Paper Six.

Audit Commission (1989) *Urban Regeneration and Economic Development* HMSO.

Bennington, J. (1985) 'Economic development: local government initiatives' *Local Government Studies* **12** (2) pp 3–8.

Bramley, G. *et al.* (1978) *Local Economic Initiatives* School for Advanced Urban Studies, University of Bristol.

Campbell, M., Hardy, M., Healy, N., Stead, R. and Sutherland, J. (1987) 'The economics of local jobs plans' *Local Economy*.

Carley, M. (1990) 'Business in urban regeneration partnerships. A case study of Birmingham' *Local Economy* pp 101–115.

CLES (1988), 'Economic development — sentence first: verdict afterwards' *Local Work* November 1988 (2).

CLES (1991) 'Local economic strategies' *Local Work* April 1991.

Cochrane, A. (1990), 'The future of local economic strategies' *Local Economy* pp 133–141.

Coulson, A. (1986) 'Getting started in economic development' *Local Government Policy Making* **12** (3) pp 31–37.

DOE (1980) *Review of Local Authority Assistance to Industry and Commerce* HMSO.

DOE (1988) *Action for Cities* HMSO.

DOE (1989) *DOE Inner City Programmes 1987–88. A report on achievements and developments* HMSO.

DOE (1991) *Local Government Review. The structure of local government in England* A consultation paper.

Emmerich, M. (1990) 'The 1989 Local Government and Housing Act and its implications for economic development' *Local Work* (16).

GLC (1985) *The London Industrial Strategy* GLC.

Gordon, P. (1987) 'Urban and economic development policy, effective management — The differing perspectives of the Audit Commission and the London Borough of Hackney' *Local Government Policy Making* **14**. No 1, 1987.

Griffin, D. (1990) 'Economic development' in *New Directions in Public Services — The County Council Experience* Published for the ACC by the Policy Studies Institute.

Hayton, K. (1984) 'Economic Initiatives: Strathclyde's Strategy' *Local Government Policy Making*, Vol 11, No 2, 1984.

Hayton, K. (1990) 'The future of local economic development' *Regional Studies* 23 pp 548–564.

Healey, P. (1990) 'The future of local economic strategies' *Local Economy* pp 133–141.

Heseltine, M. (1991) Speech delivered by Michael Heseltine at the Annual Dinner of the Tyne and Wear Development Corporation, 23 May 1991.

DOE (1977) White Paper, Policy for the Inner Cities, *Cmnd 6845*, June 1977.

INLOGOV (1986) 'Economic Development — The Future Role and

Organisation of Local Government' *Functional Study* No 6. March 1986.

Johnstone, D. (1986) 'Programme of research and actions on the development of the labour market: The Role of Local Authorities in promoting local employment initiatives' Office of official publications of the European Communities, 1986.

Keays, P. (1990) 'Encouraging the Partnership Approach' Paper presented at ADC Economic Development Conference, Hull, October 1990.

LEDIS (1987) Economic Development Companies, The Planning Exchange, July, 1987.

LEDIS (1989) 'New Economic Development Power for Local Authorities in England and Wales — a Consultation Paper', The Planning Exchange, October 1989.

LEDIS (1989) Local Government Training Board Economic Development Project, The Planning Exchange, May 1989.

Martinos, C. H. (1979) 'Tools for economic development policies', Proceedings of Seminar — Planning for Employment and Economic Development, 9–12 July. University of Warwick.

Martinos, C. H. (1988) 'Identifying local economic development research priorities', Paper presented to ESRC Conference. London 2 February 1988.

Newman, I (1990) 'Surviving in a cold climate' *Local Authority Economic Strategy Today* Local Economy.

Rural Development Commission, *Annual Report 1990–91*.

Shutt, J. (1991) 'Local Economic Strategies', *Local Work*, pp 1–7.

Turoki (1988) 'The Limits of Financial Assistance, An evaluation of local authority aid to industry', *Local Economy* 2 (4) pp 286–297.

7 The new Europe: implications for UK local government

No man is an island, entire of itself; every man is a piece of the continent, a part of the main

(John Donne)

Introduction

The 1990s will see the growing influence of the European Community (EC) on the political and economic life of the United Kingdom. This will continue the trend begun in 1973 when the UK joined the EC and will have important implications for local government and its structure.

During the 1980s local and regional government developed closer links with the EC as sub-national tiers of government assumed various responsibilities for implementing EC primary and secondary legislation, for example in trading standards and environmental protection. The EC also became increasingly important as a source of funding, particularly through the structural funds. In addition, there was growing pressure for increased recognition of the views of local and regional government in EC policy-making.

Yet the relationship between the EC and local and regional government has received little attention. Discussion has focused on the respective responsibilities of national governments in member states and of the EC institutions. This is not altogether surprising since the Treaty of Rome makes no mention of the role of either local or regional government. This attitude has been particularly true of the UK as a unitary state whose government's primary concern has been to protect the UK's sovereignty rather than to establish a closer relationship between the EC and local government.

The 1990s are likely to see increasing pressure for closer links between the EC and local and regional government. A 'Europe of the Regions' is in gestation. The agreement at Maastricht confirms this trend. It extends EC competence into important new areas and gives formal recognition to the role of local and regional government in EC policy development by creating a 'Committee of the Regions'. When elaborating new policy proposals, the EC's institutions will be able to consult with local and regional government through this committee.

The implication is clear. The structure of local government in the UK must enable it to establish an effective and valuable relationship with the EC's institutions. The purposes of this chapter are to analyse likely developments in the relationship between the EC and sub-national tiers of government and to consider their implications for the structure of local government in the UK.

In doing this, the chapter is concerned with all sub-national tiers of government. In the UK, however, the absence of a 'regional' tier of government means that the link between local government (and counties in particular) and the EC's institutions is especially important because it is effectively the regional link as well. Therefore, the way in which regional government in other member states relates to the EC is also important so far as local government in the UK is concerned.

The paper starts by comparing local and regional government in EC member states in terms of powers, structure, functions and finance. There follows an analysis of the current relationship between the EC and local and regional government and an assessment of how this is likely to develop in the foreseeable future. The final section considers the implications for local government structure in the UK if it is effectively to contribute to, respond to and implement EC policies.

Local and regional government in the member states of the European Community

Powers

The powers of local and regional government in the EC derive from three main principles: the right to local self-government, the power of general competence and subsidiarity.

As a general rule, local government in the EC is safeguarded within each country's (written) constitution. Most national constitutions embody the right to local self-government, a principle given official recognition in the European Charter of Local Self-Government (1985). Local self-government is defined in the Charter as the right to '... regulate and manage a substantial share of public affairs under their (local authorities') own responsibility in the interests of the local population'. The Charter sets out the basic tenets which any system of local government should embody and provides that the principle of local self-government should be enshrined in the constitution. All EC member states have signed and ratified the Charter except Belgium, France and the Netherlands who have as yet only signed, and the Republic of Ireland and UK who have done neither.

The power of general competence is also the norm in most parts of the EC. It empowers local government by enabling it to take any action in the interests of the local community unless specifically prohibited by statute from doing so. In the United Kingdom, the opposite is true. Local authorities are only empowered to carry out activities specifically assigned to them by Parliament. Other activities are 'ultra vires'.

The principle of subsidiarity provides the basis for identifying 'where the demarcation of responsibility should occur between a higher and a lower authority' (Foreign Affairs Committee Report on the Operation of the Single Market). It implies that responsibility for activities should wherever possible belong to the lowest level of government. Subsidiarity has become increasingly influential in determining the allocation of responsibilities between the national and supranational tiers of government (individual member states and the EC as a whole), and national and sub-national (regional and local) tiers of government.

The principle of subsidiarity is not contentious, but its interpretation is. The factors that make a tier of government competent to fulfil a particular role are debatable. On occasions subsidiarity has been used by national governments in member states to protect their national sovereignty against undesired incursion of EC powers. It has also been used to justify the transfer of power from local and regional tiers of government to higher levels to maximise efficiency. This ambivalence explains the enthusiasm for the principle: it can be used to support different motives. The UK Government's support derives from its interpretation of subsidiarity to offer some protection against EC competence impinging on UK sovereignty. However, the UK Government is less enthusiastic about the application of the principle to establish the respective responsibilities of central and local government.

The application of the principles of local self-government, general competence and subsidiarity in the EC is reflected in the increasing devolution of responsibilities to sub-national (local and regional) tiers of government. Countries which were once highly centralised, such as Italy and Portugal, have adopted programmes of decentralisation to move away from the authoritarian regimes of their modern histories. Most countries, particularly in Northern Europe, but with the exceptions of the UK and the Republic of Ireland, are devolving central powers to local authorities in the spirit of local self-government.

Structure

The structure of local government in all member states of the EC shows little homogeneity (see Table 7.1). In all countries, however, except Luxembourg and Greece, and parts of Portugal and the Republic of Ireland, there are at least two tiers of local government. Moreover, Greece is considering the creation of a further tier of government. The creation of unitary local government in the UK would mean that the UK would move away from the general pattern.

There has been a strong trend towards regionalism made more significant by the EC's increasing desire to establish contact and policy dialogue directly with sub-national units of government. All EC member states of a comparable size to the UK are either federal states (Germany) or have a constitutionally designated regional tier of government (Italy, France and Spain). For example, Italy embodied the

	Population (millions)	Tiers of government	Number of lowest tier authorities
Belgium	9.9	N + 3	589
Denmark	5.1	N + 2	275
FR Germany	61.9	F, S + 2	8,506
France	54.3	N + 3	36,393
Greece	9.9	N + 1	6,036
Italy	56.7	N + 3	8,088
Luxembourg	8.4	N + 1	118
Netherlands	14.3	N + 2	702
Portugal	10.1	N + 3	305
Republic of Ireland	3.5	N + 1 or 2	77
Spain	38.4	N + 3	7,270
United Kingdom	56.4	N + 1 or 3	11,072*

Key: N = National
      F = Federal
      S = State, Province or Territory (in a federal system)
      * = Parishes and community councils in England and Wales; districts in Scotland and N Ireland
Note: 'Special districts' or equivalent units created for the provision of a limited number of services are not included

Source: Coopers & Lybrand Deloitte 1990

Table 7.1: Local government structure in the EC

concept of regionalism in its constitution drawn up after the war, although most regions were not created until the 1970s. France created planning regions in the 1970s and members of regional councils were first elected following the reforms of the early 1980s. Spain established a regional tier of government after the death of Franco in response to the popular call for autonomous governments, based on historical kingdoms.

What constitutes a region in EC terms is still a matter of debate. The Council of Europe has defined a region as '. . . a territorial authority situated immediately below the national level and administered by an elected council'. The Commission of the European Communities defines three levels of regions in member states for economic and social comparison and policy development. Both the Council of Europe and the European Parliament treat the English counties as equivalent to regions, and the Commission in effect acts as if they are.

The degree of correspondence between the Commission's three levels of regions — known as NUTS — and the boundaries of local and regional government varies between member states (see Table 7.2). In some cases, for example in Germany, there is a close correspondence between the boundaries of the different tiers of sub-national government and those of the Commission's regions. But in other member states the boundaries are not coterminous. In the UK, for example, the definitions of regions are artificial because they are based on central government's standard (planning) regions — which are not uniquely defined and have boundaries which bear no resemblance to those of elected councils — and combinations of counties.

The physical definitions used by both the Council and Commission do not always correspond with member states' own regional boundaries (where these exist). Nor are the competencies of the designated regions similar. Their powers and authority also vary widely. Some, such as the German Länder, have legislative powers, whereas French regional authorities have not and are equivalent to upper level local authorities.

Despite these ambiguities, the EC's relationship with regions is growing in importance. The slogan 'Europe of the Regions' is indicative of the EC's commitment to greater integration, which can be achieved only if the EC strengthens the capacity of the weaker regions to reap its benefits. This requires their closer involvement in the development and implementation of EC policies.

Functions

Table 7.3 shows the distribution of functions between tiers of government in nine of the EC's member states. Two features are evident.

Member state	NUTS 1		NUTS 2		NUTS 3	
Belgium	Régions	3	Provinces	9	Arrondis-sements	43
Denmark[1]	–	1	–	1	Amter	15
Germany[2]	Länder	11	Regierungs bezirke[3]	31	Kreise	328
Greece	Groups of development regions	4	Development regions	13	Nomoi	51
Spain	Agrupacion de comunidades autonomas	7	Comunidades autonomas + Melilla and Ceuta	18	Provincias	52
France	Zeat +DOM	8 / 1	Régions	22 / 4	Départements	96 / 4
Republic of Ireland	–	1	–	1	Planning regions	9
Italy	Gruppi di regioni[4]	11	Regioni	20	Provincie	95
Luxembourg	–	1	–	1	–	1
Netherlands	Lansdelen	4	Provincie	12	COROP – Regios	40
Portugal	Continente + Regiões autonomas	3	Comissaoes de coordencao regional[2] + Regiões autonomas	7	Grupos de concelhos	30
United Kingdom	Standard regions	11	Groups of counties[4]	35	Counties	65
European Community		66		174		829

1 A breakdown of Denmark into three regions is given in most of the tables and maps
2 Regions of the former GDR are not included (5 Länder, 15 Bezirke, 218 Kreise)
3 26 Regierungsbezirke + 5 Länder not subdivided into Regierungsbezirke
4 Grouping for Community purposes.

Source: Commission of the European Communities

Table 7.2: Correspondence between community regions (NUTS levels) and national administrative divisions in the Community

First, there is no clear pattern in service provision responsibilities. Subsidiarity is either not used to allocate responsibilities between tiers of government; or, where it is used, its application varies from one

Service	Belgium	Denmark	FR Germany	France	Italy	Netherlands	Republic of Ireland	Spain	UK
Primary, Secondary Education	PC	CM	sm	NHD	pm	M	N	PM	CB
Housing	R	V	VC	M	pM	pM	CB	M	MB
Health
— Hospitals	M	C	NS	R	R	pm	–	PM	N
— Others	P	C	CM	D	R	M	–	PM	N
Welfare	MP	M	sm	D	pm	M	–	NP	N
Refuse Disposal	m	m	m	m	m	m	CB	M	C
Water Supply	R	M	m	m	R	P	CB	M	–
Roads	P	CM	CM	MD	R	pm	CBM	PM	CB
Transport	–	m	CM	MDR	M	m	–	M	–
Leisure (e.g. Parks, Sports)	rm	m	sm	m	pm	PM	M	M	BM
Culture (e.g. Theatres, Museums)	PC	cm	CM	MDR	RM	PM	M	M	PM
Police	m	–	S	MD	RM	M	–	M	C
Fire	m	m	M	MD	–	m	CB	MP	C
Electricity	R	–	CM	–	M	P	–	(M)	–
Ports	R	–	sm	–	R	m	–	M	–
Airports	N	–	s	–	m	m	–	N	–

Abbreviations: Nn = National
Mm = Municipality/Commune/UDC/Shire District
Pp = Province
Ss = State
V = Voluntary Sector
Cc = County (Community in Belgium)
Rr = Region
Dd = Department (France)
Bb = Borough
(M) indicates that although the function is a municipal responsibility it is significantly constrained by central government.
– denotes service performed by organisation other than those listed.

Other Notes: Upper Case = Source = Coopers & Lybrand Deloitte Survey 1990
Lower Case = Source = Paying for Local Government (Cmnd 9714, HMSO, London 1986 p 131)

Table 7.3: The pattern of service provision

country to another, depending on their views as to the competence of different tiers to undertake particular service functions. Second, more services tend to be the responsibility of national government, state agencies or the private sector in the UK than elsewhere. This confirms the centralised nature of government in the UK.

Finance

There are significant differences between EC member states in the scale of local and regional (state) government's revenue relative to GDP — and by implication its spending — and the sources of its funding. Tables 7.4 and 7.5 summarise the position. The key features are:

● sub-national government's revenue as a proportion of GDP tends to be highest in the federal countries — the UK lies in the middle of the range;

	Total government revenue (per cent GDP)				Local government revenue (£ per head)			
	Central	State	Local	Total	Taxes	Grants	Other	Total
Belgium	44.4		2.8	47.1	175	276	39	490
Denmark	42.2		19.1	61.3	1,298	1,105	283	2686
FR Germany	27.1	9.7	6.5	43.3	278	204	275	757
France	43.4		5.8	49.2	324	251	156	731
Greece	34.1		0.4	34.5	15	0	0	15
Italy	37.4		2.0	39.4	51	838	103	992
Luxembourg	46.8		6.3	53.1	524	366	78	968
Netherlands	51.5		3.3	54.8	81	1,115	175	1,371
Portugal	36.6		1.9	38.5	77	0	0	77
Republic of Ireland (1987)	43.6		4.2	47.8	42	484	152	678
Spain (1987)	31.0	0.0	4.3	35.3	181	85	49	315
UK	36.3		6.8	43.1	327	425	229	981

Source: OECD Revenue Statistics (1965–1990)

Table 7.4: Government revenue sources (1988)

- the heavy dependence of local government on grants from central government in the Netherlands and Italy and, now, in the UK;
- the widespread use of more than one local tax in other parts of the EC (in particular, the extensive reliance on local taxes on income and profits) whereas the UK has only one local tax;
- the sharing of tax proceeds between tiers of government.

Local government in the UK is strongly constrained by central government. It is highly dependent on funding from central government, and its effective discretion over local taxes is limited. This clearly reduces the degree of local autonomy. Moreover, EC moves towards fiscal harmonisation threaten to constrain further local government's ability to achieve greater financial freedom. Already, member states have agreed not to extend sales taxes.

The relationship between the EC and local regional government

The differences between local government in the UK and in other EC states provide important background to an analysis of the relationship with the EC. Also relevant is the EC's desire to foster closer links with local and regional government.

Current position

There are two main aspects to the current relationship between the EC

		Income %	Social Security %	Payroll %	Property %	Goods %	Other %	Total %
Belgium	Local	76.8	7.2	0.0	0.0	16.0	0.0	100.0
Denmark	Local	92.1	0.0	0.0	7.8	0.1	0.0	100.0
FR Germany	Local	81.9	0.0	0.0	17.1	0.7	0.3	100.0
	State	61.8	0.0	0.0	6.5	31.7	0.0	100.0
France	Local	14.6	0.0	4.2	33.9	13.2	34.0	100.0
Greece	Local	0.0	0.0	52.1	0.0	47.9	0.0	100.0
Italy	Local	41.7	0.0	0.0	0.0	58.3	0.0	100.0
Luxembourg	Local	84.3	0.0	0.0	3.9	11.8	0.0	100.0
Netherlands	Local	0.0	0.0	0.0	73.0	27.0	0.0	100.0
Portugal	Local	42.9	0.0	0.0	23.3	33.3	0.4	100.0
Republic of Ireland	Local	0.0	0.0	0.0	100.0	0.0	0.0	100.0
Spain	Local	31.7	0.0	0.0	27.1	39.3	1.9	100.0
UK	Local	0.0	0.0	0.0	100.0	0.0	0.0	100.0

Source: OECD Revenue Statistics (1965–1990)

Table 7.5: Government tax revenue sources (1988)

and local (and regional) government. The first relates to local government's ability to influence the EC's policy-making process. The second is the impact of EC policy on local government finances and responsibilities. Each aspect is considered separately.

Policy development

Local government's involvement in the EC's policy-making process has developed in a pragmatic and uncoordinated way because local government has no formal position from which to input to the process. In contrast, the German Länder and the Belgian regions, as federal states, have observer status at meetings of the Council of Ministers. Although this does not give them a formal input into EC decision making, it is a powerful means of ensuring that their national government take their interests into account.

Given the current division of responsibilities between EC institutions (summarised in Table 7.6), local government's collective input can only be advisory. Latterly, the focus has been the Consultative Council of Regional and Local Authorities. This was set up in 1988 as the official forum in which the Commission may seek the views of representatives of European local and regional government. As such, the Consultative Council has had an important influence on the development of EC policy, not least in the lead-up to the decision to set up the

Level	Body	Responsibility
Legislative	Council of Ministers	Decides on policy issues and EC legislation
Executive	European Commission	Policy initiation and implementation
Advisory	European Parliament	Mainly advisory role — power of codecision on budget and some legislation
	Economic and Social Committee	Advisory capacity
	Consultative Council of Regional and Local Authorities	Advisory capacity

Table 7.6: Community policy-making responsibilities

Committee of the Regions at the Maastricht summit meeting in 1991 (see below).

The Consultative Council brings together the different interests and perspectives of all categories of local and regional government. The members of the Consultative Council are jointly nominated through two separate international associations — the Council of European Municipalities and Regions (CEMR) and the Assembly of European Regions (AER). These represent the overlapping interests of local and regional government in the EC, albeit from different perspectives. The Consultative Council was established to give the Commission a coordinated input from the sub-national tiers of government. It has achieved a significant degree of unity. Nevertheless, some underlying tensions between the two groups remain.

The English counties are in a special position. Both the EC and the Council of Europe recognise them as both 'regions' and part of 'local' government. Increasingly, the Commission has grown to respect and recognise the counties as key points of contact with sub-national government in the UK. This has enhanced their formal influence in the EC.

Local and regional government seek to influence EC policy by lobbying the EC institutions and national government individually and collectively. Sometimes individual authorities seek to ensure their own particular interests and the needs of their areas are taken into account. Local and regional government also expresses its views collectively through national and Community-wide associations. The effectiveness of the lobbying depends on several key factors.

One is the clarity, authority and force with which sub-national government communicates its message to the EC's institutions. The Consultative Council is primarily charged with ensuring that this is done effectively. In the UK, local government views are developed by the individual local authority associations, and coordinated through the Local Government International Bureau (LGIB), which presents UK views to the Consultative Council. The AER also plays a part, though as an informal grouping, representing the larger, strategic, democratically elected units of sub-national government in Europe (including some from outside the EC), it lacks a constitutional position. At present, individual county councils and, in some cases, groups of counties and metropolitan authorities are eligible for membership of the AER because they are regarded as effectively the 'regional' tier of government in the UK. Nearly half the County Councils in England and Wales are members and the number is growing. The CEMR, of which all UK local authorities are indirect members through the LGIB, also has an important representative role. It was the prime mover in getting the Consultative Council established, and makes a significant input to its work. In addition, it orchestrates other input to the Commission and the European Parliament.

Within a particular member state, local and regional government's ability to provide a coordinated and concerted input also affects its influence over the EC policy-making process. Thus, where authorities are able to provide an agreed response to, or input into, the policy development process, they are more likely to be an effective influence.

The attitude of national governments is a second important factor in local and regional government's ability to shape EC policy. Some member states give sub-national tiers of government freedom to deal directly with the EC, even to the extent of representing member states in EC decision making. Local government in the UK is more restricted in its EC links and influence. Any such influence is largely despite, rather than because of, the UK Government.

Local government also seeks to shape EC policy indirectly by influencing the position of its national government. The Audit Commission has pointed out that time devoted to lobbying UK Government is valuable because of the UK Government's ability to influence the EC policy-making process.

However, there are some policy issues on which individual units of sub-national government lobby the EC's institutions and national government in support of their own particular interests. This situation arises particularly where EC policy is expected to have a differential impact between areas, for example economic development. Individual units of sub-national government have no rationale nor incentive for cooperation and coordination of effort in these circumstances. In effect, they are competing with each other. To be influential, individual local

authorities need to ensure that their views are effectively and persua-
sively communicated.

Looking at the situation the other way round, the influence of EC
policy on local and regional government is more significant in two
respects:

- financial
- regulatory.

Financial relationship

The current financial relationship between the EC and local and
regional government in the member states is based on an economic
partnership between the EC, the member state and the local authority.
The main basis of the relationship is structural funding — the Regional
Development Fund and the Social Fund — but there are other funding
sources.

EC structural funds have become an increasingly important part of
local and regional government's funding, particularly in certain disadvantaged areas. The recent doubling of the structural funds, and the
likelihood of further increases, mean that this relationship will continue
to be significant even if there is further enlargement of the Community,
Table 7.7 shows the allocation of structural funds to the UK for the
period 1989–1993.

The 1987 reform of the structural funds gave the regions a more formal and enhanced role in their operation. In the UK, local authority
representatives now sit on the Community Support Framework (CSF)
committees. These committees oversee and advise on the disbursement
of EC monies in accordance with member states' regional development
plans, and assist with the implementation, monitoring and assessment
of the programmes.

The EC and local and regional government also have an important
relationship in other EC funding initiatives, most notably:

- support for businesses, in particular small and medium-sized companies;

    — research and development;
    — training and education.

In the UK, the availability of funding depends critically on local
government's ability to bring forward projects which meet EC objectives and can absorb the funds earmarked for the UK. This depends on
local government:

- *understanding the EC's policy objectives;*
- *identifying suitable projects and programmes;*
- *having the power and influence to secure the support and cooperation of other organisations in the private and public sectors;*
- *advocating projects effectively to national government and the Commission.*

The recent Audit Commission survey in the UK suggests that local government may be missing opportunities to secure EC funding, notably from non-structural sources. This is because local government has not fully recognised the potential significance of the opportunities and organised itself accordingly. Although there are around 400 non-structural fund programmes, only 22 per cent of councils were found to be involved in a scheme, the greatest participation being in education and training programmes such as COMETT and LINGUA. Counties however were considerably more likely to have received EC funding than districts, particularly shire districts. This is partly because of their close involvement in education provision.

A key issue in the UK is the treatment of EC funding within the local government finance system. At present, local government receives EC funds to support specific projects and programmes designed to meet EC policy objectives. These grants are generally transferred to the national exchequer first. This allows the UK Government some control over these funds, leading to recent controversy over the UK Government's contravention of EC rules on addi-

	Less developed regions	Industrial conversion areas	Objective Combat long term unemployment/ integrate young people into job market	Promote development of rural areas
ERDF	348	1,935	–	277
ESF	315	610	1,820	48
EAGGF				
(Guidance)	130	–	–	26
Total	793	2,545	1,820*	350

*The 1993 figure is estimated

Source: Department of Trade and Industry

Table 7.7: UK structural funds allocation 1989–1993 (million ECU)

tionality by using EC money to replace funds that the UK Government would otherwise have provided to local government, rather than adding to the overall level of local government expenditure in a particular area. The effect is to weaken the significance of the financial link between local government and the EC.

Regulatory relationship

The second way in which EC policy affects local and regional government is through the regulatory relationship, especially following the Single European Act 1986. This opened the way to the completion of the Single European Market (SEM). Due to come into force in January 1993, it aims to promote socio-economic growth and to develop cohesion within the EC by removing physical, social and legal barriers.

The SEM programme recognises that greater cohesion will be achieved by strengthening the role of the regions, by encouraging greater partnership between the EC and local and regional government, and by devolving responsibility for implementation of some SEM legislation. Specific aims include:

- *ensuring the additionality of EC funds;*
- *encouraging greater regional (and local) involvement in EC funding decisions;*
- *ensuring local inputs into EC needs assessments;*
- *ensuring the implementation of EC actions through the application of the 'subsidiarity' principle.*

Legislation arising from the SEM has grown considerably in importance. It affects local and regional government in two ways. First, it impacts directly on its operations, for example by requiring open competitive tender for many more projects. In addition, in the area of social affairs, despite the UK's national stance, the Community's Social Charter may affect local and regional government's employment practices. Second, local and regional government is increasingly required to monitor, implement and enforce EC legislation, for instance on:

- trading standards, where UK local government is responsible for enforcing EC Directives and Regulations;
- environmental health, where the demand for higher standards has heightened the responsibilities and obligations of local government.

A further 30 out of the 282 measures in the EC's White Paper affecting local authorities have still to be implemented, according to the Audit Commission.

The indirect effects of the SEM are also important. Completion of the SEM is expected to have a positive overall effect on the EC's economy, but not all local economies will benefit equally. Local and regional government needs to appraise the likely impact on the local pattern of economic development, and to consider what to do to ensure that as many benefits of the SEM as possible are realised, and adverse effects are moderated. The evidence from the Audit Commission survey indicates that counties have been more active in assessing the way in which the EC will affect them: only 19 per cent of shire districts have carried out a review compared with 63 per cent of counties.

Likely future developments

Relationships between the EC and sub-national government will grow stronger as the SEM becomes reality and as European Political and Monetary Union comes closer. Significant other developments are likely to take place on both political and economic fronts.

Political developments

The build-up to the Inter-Governmental Conference at Maastricht stimulated debate about the role of local and regional government, with proposals from several sources to change the political relationship between the EC and local and regional government. The Consultative Council made proposals to give local and regional government greater constitutional recognition in the Treaty of Rome, and hence in EC decision making. Both the European Parliament and Commission made similar proposals to enhance the role of local and regional government, although they differed in detail.

The Maastricht Conference agreed to establish a Committee of the Regions comprising 189 representatives of regional and local authorities. The Committee will have an advisory role. Representatives will be appointed by their national governments for fixed terms and UK representation will be 24 compared with the six current members of the Consultative Council. However, two issues are still the subject of debate.

The first is the matters on which the Committee will be consulted. The present Consultative Council believes that the Committee should have a wider role and be consulted as of right on all matters affecting local and regional government responsibilities, rather than where the Treaty so provides and where the Council and/or Commission consider it appropriate.

The second outstanding issue is the actual representation on the Committee. There is concern that the agreement could be taken to allow national governments to nominate their own representatives, rather than elected members from local and regional government.

Another aspect is the balance of representation between local and regional government. Previous tensions about the respective roles of local and regional government have been heightened by the enhanced recognition given to sub-national interests following Maastricht. Unless sub-national government is able to cooperate effectively it may lose the opportunity to be influential.

The significance of these points is made all the greater by the extension of EC competence into various policy areas, such as environmental protection and economic development. Local and regional government potentially therefore has a greater opportunity to influence EC policy development. Equally, there are more policy areas in which EC policy will influence it.

Looking further ahead, the prospect that the EC will be enlarged, to include additional countries from Scandinavia and Central and Eastern Europe, may have implications for its political structure.

Economic developments

Political developments in the EC are likely to impact on economic developments. For example, as the EC assumes greater responsibility for aspects of industrial policy, this will have important implications for the prospects of local economies. Growing EC competence in environmental policy will not only strengthen the link between sub-national government and the EC but will also highlight the economic impact of environmental policy.

One uncertainty affecting future economic development is the degree of success of the SEM. Whether the SEM meets its aims depends, in part, on:

- how the issues of subsidiarity, sovereignty and devolution of central functions are resolved;
- the ability of local and regional authorities to respond to their proposed and emerging roles.

A key factor influencing the pattern of economic development in the EC is the desire for a 'Europe of the Regions'. Not all regional or local areas will be affected by the SEM in the same way. Some will benefit, others will lose. Some areas are better placed than others to deal effectively with EC institutions. Nevertheless, an effective and coordinated grouping of sub-national government could derive considerable benefit from EC policy, and exert a powerful influence over its development.

The issue of additionality of EC (structural) funds will determine just how significant an economic impact these funds have in the UK. The UK Government does not favour direct fiscal transfers between

EC institutions and local government as happens, for example, between the Federal Government and the Länder in Germany. Unless this changes, the impact of EC structural funding will be reduced.

In the longer term, if the EC is enlarged, this could change its economic character significantly. For example, if the countries of Central and Eastern Europe gain membership, the EC's economic centre may shift eastwards and so too may the support provided to the EC's disadvantaged regions. Whether or not this happens will depend on how, if at all, the structural funds are affected. This will have important implications for the financial relationship between the EC and units of subnational government, and for the pattern of economic development. Local government will need to be alert to these possible changes if it is to ensure its views are taken into account in policy development.

Implications for UK local government structure

The implications of EC relationships for the structure of UK local government depend, to some extent, upon the constitutional role envisaged for local government within the UK. Although the present Government asserts the superiority of national government, defenders of local government argue for a move towards practice elsewhere in the EC which, as has been shown, gives greater recognition to the right to local self-government. If UK local government is to fulfil an active role, its future structure must ensure that it can provide an essential source of pluralism in an increasingly complex and diverse EC policy environment, and promote active local participation in government. It must also provide a focus for community identity and a mechanism for resolving local conflicts of interest, as well as preventing too great a concentration of power at any one level of government.

Both the EC's institutions and local government wish local government to have the scope to play an active role. The Commission envisages the establishment of a partnership involving it, national government and local and regional government to develop and implement EC policy. Local government believes that it can and should be allowed to make such a contribution.

It may do this at two different levels. First, it may act collectively to provide a unified local government contribution to policy making. Second, individual authorities may seek to ensure that their own particular interests and perspectives are considered. Which of the two levels is most appropriate depends upon whether or not authorities face incentives to cooperate and coordinate effort to achieve mutual benefit. In some cases, authorities will be concerned that their own particular interests differ from those of other authorities, and will wish to ensure that they are fully taken into account in decision making.

The constitutional issue is crucial but whatever its outcome local government in the UK must establish a relationship with the EC which enables it to:

- *influence EC policy development effectively;*
- *ensure the best use of EC funding for projects and programmes;*
- *deal effectively with the responsibilities arising from EC legislation.*

Influence

To be influential in the EC, local government needs to develop and sustain effective relationships with EC institutions and to be perceived by them as a valuable partner. Local government will be more influential if it:

- *has the skills and resources needed to identify and analyse EC policy issues;*
- *is recognised as a competent and credible source of views on these issues;*
- *represents a wider, strategic viewpoint rather than a limited, local interest;*
- *is able to coordinate its views and advocate them effectively.*

A smaller number of larger authorities covering broader areas is likely to be more influential with the EC. Such authorities are likely to be better resourced to analyse major policy issues and develop a strategic overview in a cost-effective way. A large number of smaller units of government, often with conflicting local interests, would need to make special collaborative arrangements to lobby the EC. This is unlikely to be effective. The Audit Commission has noted that influencing the EC requires specialist inputs and knowledge which can be provided at significantly lower unit cost in larger areas better able to reap economies of scale. The EC institutions will also benefit from receiving a smaller number of more authoritative views rather than wholesale localised special pleadings. It is hard to envisage the Commission welcoming the need to deal with a large number of smaller authorities. For this reason alone, large authorities are likely to be more influential.

Funding

Local government's ability to make the best use of the available EC funding depends on it developing an understanding of the EC's policy objectives, having the ability to put together projects and programmes that meet them, and being able to lobby in support of them. There is an important distinction between the structural funds and the many other available sources (non-structural funds).

For local government to be effective in securing structural fund support, it must be capable of identifying and developing schemes which meet the EC's and national government's regional policy objectives. This requires it to be responsible for local economic development policy at a strategic level, rather than focusing (only) on localised problems. It must also have effective liaison with UK Government.

Local government's ability to secure non-structural funding requires it to be aware of the funding opportunities available and to be able to bring forward eligible projects. These objectives are more likely to be achieved by larger rather than smaller authorities which can monitor EC policy developments more cost-effectively and can then identify potential projects eligible for the available funding.

Implementation responsibilities

Local government's main responsibilities under EC legislation involve implementing and enforcing EC policies. Larger units of local government are likely to be more able to carry out these responsibilities efficiently and effectively because they can:

- develop a partnership with national government and the EC which is essential to the successful and sensitive implementation of EC measures;
- implement more effective regional economic development strategies so essential to the successful integration of the EC;
- maintain the specialist skills and resources needed to fulfil their regulatory responsibilities in a cost-effective way;
- coordinate their activities with those of other units of local government;
- achieve and maintain international identity and visibility.

If local government in the UK were to comprise many smaller authorities in a unitary system, it is hard to envisage how the EC could develop the effective partnership required to implement EC policies successfully. The administrative effort alone would be burdensome and a deterrent. The requirements of efficient and effective implementation and enforcement of regulations mean that a smaller number of larger authorities is likely to be more successful at a coordinated approach, to achieve greater economies of scale and to liaise effectively with those responsible for setting the regulatory framework.

Conclusions

There can be little doubt that as its competence extends in the 1990s and beyond, the EC's influence over local (and regional) government will become ever greater. Regardless of the constitutional position in the UK, it will be essential for local government to establish an effective and valuable relationship with the EC's institutions. In the UK, the larger county authorities are more active in their assessment of the likely impact of developments within the EC and also more successful in developing actual partnerships and relationships with the EC's institutions. This confirms the analysis that a smaller number of larger authorities is likely to be better placed to influence EC policy development, to make the best use of available EC funding for projects, and to respond to and implement responsibilities arising from EC legislation and initiatives.

The implication is clear. If UK local government is to provide an effective link with, and counterbalance to, the EC's institutions, its structure must contain larger authorities able to operate effectively across the whole range of interdependent financial, economic and political interests.

8 Making the most of parish and town councils

One sees great things from the valley; only small things from the peak

(G K Chesterton)

Introduction

The Government has expressed interest in enhancing the role of parish councils as part of the proposed change in local government structure. The current local government review presents an opportunity to take a fresh look at the smallest and most local level of local government and consider role, functions and relationships with other components of the local government structure, whether these are the current two tier authorities, or, as the Government would prefer, unitary authorities. But an essential pre-requisite for so doing is an understanding of the contribution that can be made at this level to local government's democratic purpose.

Chapters 1 and 2 of this book considered the historic development of local government's role as part of the British constitution, and explored local government's changing style. It was argued that the starting point for the review must be the requirement for future structure to support a continuing and active constitutional role for local government:

- *as a source of pluralism in a complex and diverse environment;*
- *as the means whereby individuals and communities could participate in the day-to-day business of government;*
- *as the focus for community identity and as the means of resolving conflicts within communities;*
- *in preventing too great a concentration of power at any one level of government.*

It is in terms of these fundamental 'design criteria' that any enhanced role for parish and town councils must be defined and developed, as an integral part of the system of local government as a whole.

By way of background, this chapter first examines the historical development of parish and town councils, and considers the range of current activities compared to the European experience. It then examines ways of enhancing the contribution made by authorities at the most local level to effective service delivery and active local democracy. It draws attention to the need for a flexible approach, reflecting the diversity of communities and of their aspirations for self-government. It identifies a range of ways in which parishes and towns can work together with principal authorities as an operational and a democratic partnership in order to ensure that, at the most local level of local government, the criteria set out above can be successfully met.

The background

It is generally accepted that the structure of local government should ensure an effective contribution to democratic processes at a very local level, and that some kind of independent and very local forum is necessary to ensure that service delivery is sensitive to local needs, and that local communities' voice is heard. In the present structure, this is the role of parish, town and community councils.

Though it is not at present the Government's intention to initiate changes to the structure at this level, or to change the legislative framework which provides for parish status and powers, there is considerable scope within existing legislation to develop an enhanced role for parish and town councils, and thereby to encourage communities at the most local level to play an increasingly active part in the wider system of local government. Appropriate legislative change would clearly create even more scope for this enhancement. The review's main task, in this area, will be to determine the role of such authorities, and their relationships with authorities in the wider structure (termed here 'principal authorities'). Such authorities may be unitary, or may be two-tier. The issues and approach set out in this paper will be relevant to both.

The emergence of the parish

It is sometimes forgotten in the long-running debate about local government structure that the parish council level provides a substantial historical tradition of participation in self-government, and a solid foundation of experience, on which any wider structure may build. There is a well-established frame of reference within which to consider the development of local government at this level, in ways appropriate to future needs.

Parishes are extremely old administrative entities. They evolved out of the need for communities to look after themselves as best as they were able, within the demands of a wider social, legal, administrative and eventually democratic system. The needs and communities varied, as they do now, and the pattern which has emerged over the centuries remains very diverse, even today.

From the various forms of medieval village government developed the 'parish vestry', a group of villagers, usually the larger ratepayers, who met about monthly in the church vestry or elsewhere, usually with the vicar presiding. They were not established by any Act of Parliament and there were no rules governing their operation. Their prime functions were to set the parish rate, to disburse it to relieve poverty, to help the sick, old and homeless, and to oversee all aspects of village life. To carry out their functions they appointed unpaid officials including church wardens, highway surveyors and constables. Not until the 1819 Poor Relief Act were they empowered to have paid officials and then only the 'assistant overseer' whose job was to assess and collect the poor rate.

The period which led up to the 1819 Act marked the beginning of the end of this traditional approach. The social and economic changes of the Industrial Revolution were leading to increased unemployment and putting greater pressure on the poor rate. Ratepayers resented large increases in their rates to pay for local poor relief. The Royal Commission on the Poor Law reported in 1834, leading to the Poor Law Act of 1834, and the creation of the Poor Law Guardians. During the middle years of the nineteenth century further ad hoc 'local authorities' were established, including library commissioners, burial boards, highway boards, school boards and local boards of health. All these removed functions from parish vestries.

The anti-centralisation backlash, stressing the ancient concept of parish self government, helped form the thinking behind the Local Government (England and Wales) Bill which was published in 1893 and which had a long, stormy and highly controversial passage through Parliament. When it was finally passed in 1894, the Act called into existence 'parish councils' for all parishes (defined in terms of their ability to set a poor rate) in rural districts where the population of the parish was 300 or more in 1891. Smaller parishes were to have parish meetings which could ask (if their population was less than 100) or require (if their population was 100–300) the county council to establish a parish council for their parish.

This served to emphasise the democratic functions of parish authorities, as well as their more traditional role in the administration of local services. The first parish council elections were controversial, with a high turn-out of both candidates and electors. Parish councils had significant powers and, in the early days at least, many used them to make wide-ranging improvements to village life. In later years, enthusiasm waned, turnout at elections fell and the activity of many parish councils settled into a routine often involving lobbying other bodies or individuals to take action, as well as directly performing their own functions.

Between 1894 and 1972, powers of parishes changed considerably. They gained the power to subsidise post office facilities, to appoint managers of voluntary schools, and powers relating to commons, open spaces, fishing harbours, war memorials, clocks, bus shelters, roadside seats and litter bins. However, they lost their role as rating authority, they lost the power to provide libraries, to appoint constables, and to run the fire service. They gained a discretionary spending power but, at 1/5 d, it was smaller than that of other authorities.

During the period from 1945 to 1971 structural reform of local government was seldom off the political agenda, with parishes being put forward in a number of roles. For example, the Redcliffe–Maud Commission considered in 1969 that, within the context of their proposals for a predominantly unitary structure (other than in metropolitan areas), parishes' role as the expression of the voice and views of local communities would require greater emphasis:

> Our conclusion that local councils must be part of the new system is unanimous. We do not see them as having statutory responsibility for any local government service; but we do see them as contributing a vital element to democratic local government. Their key function should be to focus opinion about anything that affects the well-being of each community, and to bring it to bear on the responsible authorities, but in addition they should have a number of powers to be exercised at discretion . . .
>
> (Royal Commission on Local Government in England 1966–69,
> Cmd 4040)

The Government, however, did not adopt Redcliffe–Maud's wider recommendations. The 1972 Local Government Act established the present two-tier structure, with little change for parish councils (to be called community councils in Wales). Existing rural parishes were retained, and some towns which were previously borough or urban district authorities also became elected councils at parish level. Oversight for boundary issues transferred from counties to districts, reporting to the Local Government Boundary Commission for England.

Current situation

Thus throughout their long history, parishes have generally been regarded as an important dimension of local government, but their actual development has been very patchy. To an extent variety is a

Measure	Smallest	Largest
Population	Stone (PM)0	Bracknell 48,681
Penny Rate Product (1988)	Stone (PM)£1	Bracknell £93,315
Area (acres)	Guys Cliffe (PM)12	Whittlesey 22,265
Wales		
Population	(not available)	Llanelli (not available)
Penny Rate Product (1988)	Llandyfeisant £30	Barry £40,111
Area (acres)	Narbeth 121	Llanddewi Brefi 28,115

Source: Municipal Year Book 1991

Table 8.1

healthy reflection of the differences between local communities, but there may also be differences in the levels of support and encouragement being given to parishes in different areas. Some evidence of this is provided by the extent of the country which remains un-parished and the slow progress of parish reviews in some areas. The Local Boundary Commission for Wales was charged with a Special Community Review, which was completed in September 1983. In England the process is still underway with roughly a third of districts yet to undertake a review of parishes in their area as required by the 1972 Act and detailed in circular 121/77 issued in December 1977.

There are currently some 10,200 parishes in England, the substantial majority of which have a parish or town council. They vary considerably in size, as shown in Table 8.1.

In Wales there are some 800 community councils and town councils. As in England there is a considerable range of size, as illustrated in Table 8.1.

Parish councils and community councils are still predominantly rural in character, covering some 30 per cent of the population. The Local Government Act 1972 included enabling legislation for additional parishes to be created in previously unparished areas outside London and circular 121/77 specifically referred to the requirement for metropolitan districts to carry out reviews of parishes in their area. However, progress on such reviews has been slow and few parishes have been created in large urban areas. Nearly half have populations of less than 500, though there are equally a few with populations over 20,000.

Parish and town councils have no specific duties, but a wide range of powers to provide local services. These are generally concurrent powers with district councils and the extent to which they have been taken up varies significantly. The most active, however, may engage in a wide range of consultative and representational activity, in addition to direct service delivery. Activities include:

- articulating local concerns and lobbying of principal authorities on issues affecting their area;
- liaison with other statutory or voluntary agencies or private individuals;
- statutory consultation, especially in the planning area, and consideration of unauthorised development and associated enforcement issues.

The most common areas of service provision are in the area of local amenities, such as seats, shelters, open spaces, village halls, community centres, outdoor recreation facilities, and the maintenance of churchyards. There is also increasing interest at the parish level in wider issues, including social matters, information services and environmental concerns, as part of an increasing role in stimulating community development in the widest sense. Parish and town councils also nominate representatives to local organisations, such as school governing bodies.

Parish and town councils are thus able to work within the local government system both by persuasion and by exercising permissive/concurrent powers. Indeed, large, active parish or town councils feel they have the competence and mandate to do more, and this is sometimes a cause of conflict with district councils. It is important to recognise, however, that equally many councils at the other end of the spectrum of activity tend to be reactive rather than proactive, and have limited administrative and management resources. Few employ full-time staff. This section draws upon, inter alia, *Parish and Town Councils in England*: A survey, undertaken for the Department of the Environment by the Public Sector Management Research Centre, Aston Business School, and published on 13 February 1992 by HMSO for the Department of the Environment.

European comparisons

A further insight into what is possible at very local level is provided by experience in other European countries. Local government in the rest of Europe is multi-tier almost everywhere, exceptions being parts of Ireland, Luxembourg, Portugal and Greece. The number of tiers and their sizes vary widely. A group of countries follow the 'country, county and commune' model; others have a generally uniform four tier structure. A large number of communes/municipalities have populations of less than 500 although there are commonly very large ones as well, for example Madrid, with a population of over 3 million. An average size of about 10,000 is not uncommon.

From the perspective of UK experience, it is perhaps surprising that, despite the very small size of a large number of communes, there are examples of all major functions of local government in the UK, as well as hospitals, other health services, electricity and ports, being a commune/municipal responsibility. In some cases a municipality's freedom is rather constrained by a central government framework, in others the only constraint is its ability to raise finance. Finance can also constrain the general power of competence which is commonly given to the lowest tier authorities.

A general sharing of functions between different tiers of local government is not common, exceptions being Germany and Italy. However, in some cases functions are split with different aspects being the responsibility of different tiers. For example, the communes in France are responsible for primary schools except the staff, who are civil servants and thus the responsibility of the State. There are also examples of (generally small) local authorities of the same type working together to provide services more effectively (e.g. Belgium, France and Finland). In some cases (e.g. Belgium) the formation of such groups is provided for in the country's constitution and (as in Finland) they may have a separate legal status.

There is therefore sufficient evidence from Europe to demonstrate that, given the will to make them work, a wide range of sizes, relationships and competencies for the lowest tier local authority can operate successfully, though this has to be seen in the context of structures developing over time in response to the varying culture, history and geography of each area. This underlines the importance in the present review of taking an evolutionary approach to further development of the parish council role, building empirically upon past and present experience and the current strengths of local communities.

Key issues for the review

The review will need to consider the extent to which existing structures and relationships (and indeed any proposals for change) in any individual area provide adequately for an effective contribution at the most local level. In some areas, parish and town councils are content to work within the existing framework of roles and relationships. Others believe that they could, and should, do more to influence local services and provide a distinctive voice for their local community. Some do not do enough. Furthermore, not all areas are parished. The review will therefore need to consider:

- how best to build on historical strengths and learn from those parishes and towns which operate effectively;

- how to address shortcomings in present arrangements leading either to frustration or to inaction;
- the most appropriate way to expand coverage.

Much has been said in the past about the potential for authorities at the most local level to contribute more to local government. There is now the opportunity, in a comprehensive way, to consider their role and functions, and their relationships with principal authorities, in the context of wider structural change.

The next sections of this chapter set out how parish and town councils might realistically develop their role, and thereby enhance their contribution. Three main areas are considered, building upon present activity:

- the consultative role
- service delivery opportunities
- increasing numbers and coverage.

It does not seek to present a universal model for all parish and town councils. To do so would be inappropriate to the diversity of local communities and to the need for flexibility in encouraging their wider participation in local government. Nor does it attempt to define in detail a comprehensive list of possible additional functions, whether within the current legislative framework or under any extended powers. Its purpose is to provide for the review a basis upon which those considering future structure can develop proposals for an area, consistent with local communities' tradition, capacity and aspirations.

Enhancing the consultative role

In general terms, the role of parish and town councils as a 'local voice' embraces the right to be consulted about issues which affect their area, acting as an advocate for the community, and influencing decisions about the nature and extent of services provided within the area. Issues about which parishes already have a right, or may expect, to be consulted include local planning applications, school closure proposals, bus routes, the frequency of refuse collection and road repairs. Some authorities are already going beyond this to develop other kinds of communication channels, both formal and informal. Examples, established and experimental, include the following.

Locally based information points, both freestanding or within services already community-based, which also provide direct access to other statutory authorities. These serve as 'one stop shops' which help all levels of local government to be more responsive to local concerns as well as providing a point of contact between the various authorities concerned. They provide a means of communicating information to the public, both regularly and on specific issues, and also enable members of the public to put forward their views.

'Pairing' between representatives of principal authorities and parish councillors. This gives individual members a role in liaison and two way communication with parish councils. It may be formally structured, with invited attendances at meetings, or operate less formally on a 'surgery' basis.

Area committees: larger authorities particularly may wish to establish locality-based committees either as well as, or instead of, service or issue-based committees, to strengthen democratic links with local communities. Such a structure could provide the opportunity for parish representation of some sort; a variety of constitutional options is possible, depending upon the role and powers of such committees within the authority's decision-making structures.

County-wide or other area 'senates': principal authorities could bring together parish council representatives in a wider forum to discuss local issues and provide the opportunity for presentation by the principal authority of key policies and wider initiatives relevant to local communities' interests.

Individually, parish and town councils could agree rights of consultation on specific issues, over and above those covered by statute. For example, communities particularly concerned about local environmental issues could agree with principal authorities a framework of consultation on key planning and transport decisions relevant to their area (in addition to the statutory consultation process).

Parishes and towns could also be encouraged to develop active involvement with principal authorities' service delivery points in their area. This could range from being active supporters of a 'friends' organisation for a local home for elderly people or people with learning difficulties, or exercising their right to appoint a school governor, through to taking over some aspects of running the service under delegation or agency agreements (addressed further in the next sub-section). Such arrangements could:

- by harnessing the goodwill of the community, help to improve the quality of service for those benefiting from it;
- open up possibilities for more flexible use of property, which may in turn relieve pressure on the principal authority's own resources;
- increase local understanding of the roles, priorities and pressures of the principal authority;
- enable the parish to influence the nature and extent of the service delivered, since their position as 'stakeholder' in its future is more clearly identified.

Active parish involvement in local services also enhances the feeling and reality of partnership between the parish council and the principal authority(ies) and provides additional channels for communication on general as well as specific issues.

A more radical approach might be to encourage parish and town councils to initiate proposals for service improvements in their areas, even where functions remained the responsibility of the principal authority, to be funded through an element of the budget specifically set aside for parish-initiated ideas. For example, mainstream services could be complemented in a particular town or parish area by additional facilities or services appropriate to the needs of those communities. Additional satellite information points could be created; the principal authority's facilities could be used out of hours for childcare or other community activity. Parish and town councils could be invited to put forward competitive proposals for ways of using the fund, so as to encourage communities to think about innovative and beneficial ways of improving services in their area, and to participate in wider policy and service issues. A scheme of this kind could provide for some response to local diversity without calling into question standards of service delivery throughout the principal authority. It would also smooth the financial impact.

Service delivery opportunities

All the foregoing enhancements to the consultative role of parish and town councils would also increase their influence on the levels and quality of services provided by other authorities within the area. There are however further specific developments possible. These involve using the present range of concurrent powers between parishes and principal authorities in a different way, as outlined below. One result of the approach suggested below would be different patterns of service delivery in different areas. This sort of local diversity has considerable value, in that it enables different areas to adopt the approach which most suits them. However, it should be sufficiently structured so that public confusion and blurred accountability are avoided.

The present (or indeed an extended) range of concurrent powers could be used to encourage variety, without blurring accountability, if they formed the basis of specific agreements between the principal authority(ies) and parishes in their area. These agreements would clarify in advance how concurrent powers were to be exercised in each parish area, and they could also cover:

- An agreement on 'top-up' improvements to baseline services, appropriate to community needs or reflecting community preferences, to be funded by the parish itself. For example, a parish or town council could fund the extra necessary for backdoor refuse collection in their area over and above the standard kerbside collection, or fund extra opening hours of library or other leisure facilities.

• An agreement on the services to be provided by the parish or town council itself, on behalf of the principal authority, under delegation or agency arrangements. The principal authority would need to formulate a policy determining those areas of activity in which they would encourage parish and town councils to take on additional responsibility for service delivery, to create a 'menu' of options from which parish and town councils could select those of most interest or concern.

Agreement would also be required on funding arrangements, appropriate to the nature of the various service agreements between the parish or town council and the principal authority, to avoid 'double rating'. For example, in exchange for taking over delivery of a local service, a parish might seek a reduction in the principal authority's community charge/council tax in its area, discuss the amount involved and then decide on its course of action in the light of the decision reached.

In developing an approach on these lines, principal authorities would need to be prepared to sustain a high level of variety in the way in which services were delivered, from one area to another, and in the mechanisms by which this variety was achieved. Parish and town councils wishing to take on full delegated or agency responsibilities, or provide 'top-up' services, would need to demonstrate their capacity to handle this reliably on a permanent basis. Relationships between principal authorities and individual parish and town councils would need to be actively managed by both parties. In practice, to avoid the process becoming too bureaucratic and thus impeding development rather than encouraging it, agreements would need to be as simple as possible, based upon a common structure. For example, a principal authority could have an agreement drawn up to accommodate the most active town or parish, from which others could then select the particular provisions they wished to activate.

Such agreements could be suported by a range of different working mechanisms. For example, the parish and town council could itself employ staff to take on functions, or fund the staff of the principal authority to do so on its behalf. Beyond direct services, as the concept and practices of the enabling style of authority gain ground, there is scope for a wide range of delivery options. Contractors could contract directly with parish and town councils for delegated functions, with no further involvement from the principal authority; alternatively, those on contract to the principal authority for services in the parish or town council area could additionally take on related services under contract to the parish, or the principal authority could conclude and manage a series of contracts on behalf of all parish and town councils.

In this way a framework would be established within which each town and parish could choose the extent to which it played an enhanced role locally. Because the arrangements were agreed in advance, both authorities and the general public would be clear about local accountability for services. Parishes would be able to see, and indeed influence, the financial consequences of exercising their options before committing themselves. Large town councils could substantially increase their decision-making and service delivery role, whilst smaller, less well-resourced parishes could negotiate valuable enhancements to principal authority services to meet particular local needs.

The maximum limit of additional roles and functions would depend only upon legal constraints, and the degree of innovation and flexibility displayed by principal authorities. As communities developed their interests and abilities, agreements could be renegotiated to provide for additional responsibilities. Imaginative delegation arrangements are already being developed in some areas and these illustrate the potential which exists within the present structure. The minimum of the range of possibilities, on the other hand, would amount to current parish and town council duties.

Increasing numbers and coverage

It has already been noted that significant areas of the country are unparished, and this applies particularly to urban areas. All other things being equal, new parish and town councils should relate to the lowest level of 'community' to which people feel they belong, though this does not rule out two or more small communities joining together in order to provide a basis for effective self-government. Imposed unions, however, are likely to prove counter-productive. Particular difficulties arise in defining new councils at this level in urban areas, where sense of community may be weak, or where there may be difficulty in determining the most appropriate boundary for a new authority. There may be a high rate of population turnover, and quite small spatial areas may include highly diverse populations. Notwithstanding these difficulties, however, it is important to ensure that wherever possible 'real' communities are used as the basis for new authorities at this level, rather than those created artificially or for administrative convenience.

The extension of coverage therefore needs to be a managed process. As one community defines itself, this should not prejudice a sensible approach to the whole area. Principal authorities will need to take a view on the potential divisions of unparished areas into new parish and town councils, on the basis of 100 per cent coverage, even though it may be some time before local people achieve such a goal. In some areas, it may be appropriate for the principal authority to take a more active role, by defining a number of potential parish and town council boundaries, and encouraging the community within each to develop an active council, within the framework of an appropriate agreement about consultation and services. This will require sensitivity and flexibility. Communities must feel free to make the choice to exercise powers of self-government. Much will depend in practice upon principal authorities' ability to put together suggestions for roles and responsibilities which local communities find attractive.

Conclusion

An elective, and flexible, approach of the kind set out in this section is essential if the parish and town council contribution is to be enhanced in a way which is compatible with local diversity and with the inevitable variations in size, resources, and interest among authorities at this level. The keynote of the approach is the development of an effective and accountable partnership between principal authorities, and authorities at the most local level, based on the twin presumptions of maximising local participation in decision-making, and seeking every opportunity for devolution of responsibility, wherever local communities were willing and able to take on these roles.

The task of managing potentially a large number of varying relationships with parish and town councils will have important implications for principal authorities themselves. The final section of the chapter considers this further, and assesses the implications for future structure.

Implications for principal authorities

The facilitation role

It will be apparent from the foregoing that principal authorities have an important role to play in supporting and facilitating the development of parish and town councils, and enabling them to take on an enhanced role. This requires not only enthusiasm and commitment to the ideals of participation and devolution, but also practical assistance. Parish and town councils will need information about the options for the future and the implications of alternative courses of action. They will need help in reaching a view on the right combination of roles to meet local needs and preferences.

This is likely to involve a considerable investment from both members and officers, as the scope of individual agreements is discussed and confirmed. Consultation with local people will also be required. Parish and town council attitudes to the development of an enhanced role are also likely to vary; though some will be very keen indeed to take on many new functions, others will prefer a more gradual approach. Principal authorities will need to form clear policies determining the range of options on offer, the scope for individual variation, and the approach to be taken to extending parish and town council coverage.

As new roles are taken on, parish and town councils are likely increasingly to need access to the professional and technical skills and experience of staff employed by a principal authority. Where this is significant it should be provided in a business-like way, charged for and subject to an agreement. Parishes may wish to use other sources of such skills or employ their own staff and, in the interests of preserving the partnership, this should be supported. However, provided the relationship between the authorities is good, it is likely that the specialist knowledge and economies of scale offered by staff from a principal authority will encourage parishes to use them.

Structural issues

Enhancing the role of authorities at the most local level does not of itself require structural change. It is a valid objective in its own right and is not contingent upon the adoption of a particular structural approach. The advantages to be gained by enhancing the role of parishes suggest that, even where the structure of the principal authorities remains (largely) unaltered, there is a case for adopting the approach set out in the previous section.

Not surprisingly, however, it has been seen in the present debate (and indeed before now, as the reference to Redcliffe–Maud indicates) as the natural corollary of any move to a unitary structure. It has been argued in Chapter 2 that it is essential within a unitary structure to ensure that adequate provision is made to understand local diversity and to secure effective local input to decision-making. Indeed, especially within a unitary structure, local government at the lowest level has an enhanced constitutional significance, in that it maximises participation and directly encourages a pluralistic approach.

In this context, the starting point must be a commitment to create and maintain a healthy structure of authorities at the most local level, to act as the foundation of the wider unitary system. The increased scope of a unitary authority, covering all local government functions and responsibilities, would enable a comprehensive approach to be taken to defining an enhanced role for parish and town councils across potentially the full range of local government activity. But, in a unitary scenario, it would also be important to ensure that there was adequate separation of roles and distinction of scale, between the two levels of authority.

If unitary authorities were relatively small, there would be a risk that the aspirations of more ambitious parish and town councils could lead to conflict, and frustrate the achievement of a more substantial role at the most local level, particularly while concurrent powers remain. Larger authorities, on the other hand, would have a direct interest in relying upon authorities at the parish and town council level to provide for representation of local communities and for local diversity. Any proposals to move structures towards a unitary model must therefore include careful consideration of the role of parish and town councils, and of the relationship with the unitary authority.

In either a two-tier or a unitary context, but especially in the latter, some formal processes are likely to be required to ensure that there is an effective democratic contribution from authorities at the most local level (the parish or town) to decisions taken at the strategic level (the county or unitary authority), as well as an effective operational relationship within the framework of current powers, as discussed in the previous sections. Processes will need to create and sustain close links between elected representatives at each level. They will need to operate in a number of ways since:

- the level of parish activity will vary;
- it will be necessary to accommodate different political attitudes;
- unitary authorities' internal management structures may vary — not all may choose to adopt an area committee approach;
- in some areas districts may remain within the current structure.

The following illustrates the potential for creating new links between parish and town councils, and the wider system of local government. Already, individuals can and do represent more than one authority. In a unitary scenario, it would be possible to develop this further, to integrate membership of both levels of authority, so that unitary councils would consist of representatives from parish and town councils. Two issues, however, are likely to limit this in practice. The first is the different attitude to party politics. Less than 5 per cent of local councils are political, whereas the majority of district councils and county councils have a political basis to their decision-making processes. Second, there will often be many more parishes in the area of a principal authority than seats on its council. It is therefore likely that the achievement of effective liaison will almost certainly require some other form of 'articulation mechanism' to bring together elected representatives of the two levels, in a realistic and manageable way, avoiding common membership as such. Furthermore, in the unitary scenario there is a good case in principle for keeping the membership of both levels of authority constitutionally separate, so that each is an independent authority.

The alternative approach would centre upon developing and enhancing consultative and service links between the principal authority and its parish and town councils. Smaller parishes and towns could link together into larger groupings, each having local ties. Such a grouping could have a number of specific roles, as well as providing the basis for general democratic linkage between levels of local government. For example, it could develop an area view on a development plan, or on education or social services policy or delivery. It could facilitate joint service delivery contracts between parishes or between parishes and principal authorities. It could also have a role in the allocation of the 'parish initiatives fund' referred to earlier. Such a forum would need a specific remit: consultative roles and responsibilities would need to be clearly defined and any decision-making powers determined.

In democratic terms there are a number of ways in which such groupings could be constituted, depending upon the circumstances in each area and upon the role of the grouping. They could comprise local members of the principal authority for the area concerned, representatives of the parishes and/or towns involved, or, probably most effectively, they could be some combination of the two. They could be formally constituted as 'area sub-committees' of the principal authority, with each parish and town in the area represented as of right, although probably without any voting rights because the decisions would formally be those of the principal authority. If the meetings of these 'area committees', or a less formal equivalent, were open to the public, this would allow local communities both to be reassured that their views were being represented and to understand the reasons behind decisions affecting their locality. Less formally, members of the principal authority could be given a general liaison role with parish and town groupings, meeting their representatives on a regular basis to discuss issues of common concern.

However, such groupings should be seen as clearly subordinate to both the principal authorities and the parishes, and not in any sense as another tier of local government. Their role would be essentially consultative and communicative. Nor could, or should, they supersede legitimate and necessary relationships between individual parish and town councils and their principal authority arising on a statutory basis on specific issues, such as planning applications, or on any delegated functions. It will therefore be important for principal authorities to develop relationships on a bilateral basis, especially with larger parish and town councils taking on a significantly enhanced role, as well as building wider links among parish and town councils generally.

Membership

If the role of parishes is enhanced as suggested, parish and town councillors will play a much greater role in the whole local government system. There is the prospect of a significantly increased contribution to wider decision-making, and a more extensive role in providing for the needs of the local communities they represent. For those people with the time to devote to it there is the possibility of a more varied, influential and demanding role than in the past. Increasing the variety and influence associated with being a parish and town councillor should help to retain good calibre members and to encourage other people with a wider interest to supplement the experience already present on most councils. This would in itself further encourage and support the development of the parish and town council contribution to local government as a whole.

Conclusions

An appropriate independent and very local forum is essential to effective local democracy. Parish and town councils provide a substantial historical tradition of participation in self-government upon which to build. There is now the opportunity to consider the role and functions of parish authorities and their relationship with principal authorities, in the context of wider structural change.

Parish and town councils have considerable potential to support an enhanced role, provided that a sufficiently flexible approach can be developed to accommodate the inevitable variations in size, capacity and interests of local communities. Further developments are possible in both representative and service-related roles. Within existing powers, parishes and town councils can agree with principal authorities a range of additional roles and responsibilities appropriate to local circumstances and aspirations. Agreements would:

- set out consultation rights on issues over and above those covered by statute;
- clarify how concurrent powers were to be exercised;
- cover any parish-funded 'top-up' to principal authority service levels or quality in its area;
- define the options taken up by the parish or town of delegation or agency arrangements for services on behalf of the principal authority;

- set out funding arrangements appropriate to the degree of additional responsibility assumed by the parish, avoiding 'double-rating'.

Principal authorities would have an important role in supporting and developing parish councils in taking on an enhanced role within this flexible approach, and also in ensuring that parish council coverage is extended as far as possible. Principal authorities will need to form clear policies determining what options are on offer for an enhanced role, the scope for individual variation, and the approach to be taken to the extension of coverage.

Such changes do not of themselves require a change in structure, though they would be an essential dimension of any move to a unitary model in any area. In the unitary context, it is essential to create and maintain a healthy structure of authorities at the most local level, as the foundation of the wider unitary system. It is important to ensure adequate separation of roles, and distinction of scale, between town and parish councils, and the unitary authority, to avoid the risk of conflict and of frustrating the achievement of an enhanced role at the most local level.

In either a two-tier or a unitary context, but especially in the unitary case, principal authorities will need to develop new 'articulation' processes to ensure that effective operational relationships are paralleled by an effective democratic contribution to strategic decisions. Close links will be required between elected representatives through a range of mechanisms appropriate to local circumstances, whilst maintaining the independence of authorities at the different levels. In this way authorities at the most local level will be enabled to make an increasingly significant contribution to local government's constitutional and democratic purpose.

9 Information technology: issues in the review of local government

Introduction

This chapter examines one of the means by which services are provided — information technology. The purpose of this paper is to: examine the information technology issues involved in local government restructuring; and identify how benefits obtained from use of this technology can be optimised.

Although the precise form which local government reorganisation will take is not yet established, the role of information technology (IT) should be to facilitate the introduction and operation of any new structure rather than constrain the options. However, the present and future use of IT within authorities is likely to complicate reorganisation. For this reason the impact of IT has been examined early in the review process.

This chapter examines the current position and future requirements for information technology and refers to published research material where available (SOCITM 1990). (The term IT is used to encompass not only traditional data processing and text processing facilities but related technologies such as voice, image, cable TV and radio.) Technological developments will have a significant impact on the opportunities offered to local government. Significant trends, and the views of major suppliers, are also covered.

Existing position of IT in local government

IT investment

Local government increasingly uses IT to support service provision to the public. Investment in IT on 31 March 1990 had grown seven fold in the previous decade. It had more than doubled since 1986, when it stood at £640m. It is projected to increase by 19 per cent in the current year, to £760m. (See Table 9.1.)

	No	Total spend 1990 (£m)	%	Average spend (£m)
Shire Districts	333	225	35	0.7
County Councils	47	158	25	3.4
Met Councils	36	145	23	4.0
London Boroughs	33	112	17	3.4
Total	449	640	100	1.4

Table 9.1

Published material indicates that of this spending, 85 per cent is on central IT and 15 per cent on departmental IT. This is probably an understatement: the level of investment in departmental computing is more likely to be between 30–40 per cent of the total rather than 15 per cent, which is often funded from office equipment budgets. Assuming 30 per cent spent on departmental computing, the total spending in 1990 would rise to £750m, with a predicted increase in the current year to £890m.

Standards and methods

Over 30 per cent of this investment is on computer hardware and software, and a significant proportion is on mainframe computing. Whilst mainframe expenditure as a proportion of the total is declining, total spending is still significant. The three main suppliers — ICL, IBM and Bull — operate in different proprietary environments, which reduces application portability and can lead to authorities getting locked into one supplier.

In contrast, at the departmental and personal levels, standard environments predominate. Almost all local authorities adopt MSDOS for personal computing, and 60 per cent have a UNIX policy for departmental computing.

This has encouraged software houses to develop application packages for the UNIX environment. Together with the increasing power available on mini and microcomputers, this is a driver of the migration away from mainframes, except where high volumes demand mainframe processing power.

Control and accountability

Whilst most authorities have a member sub-committee dealing with IT, most elected members feel they are dealing with a technical subject which they find difficult to relate to service delivery issues. The result is that control often operates at officer level, with reference to members only when substantial investment is required.

Most authorities still hold large central budgets for IT which are transferred to departments outside of the cash limited budgets. Accountability for IT costs and related benefits is still unclear. Though the preparation of investment appraisals prior to making investment decisions is the norm, most authorities do not have adequate mechanisms for ensuring that benefits are realised.

Organisation and service delivery

The changes in the role of local government brought about by legislation, and in particular compulsory competitive tendering, are recognised by IT managers. However, only 7 per cent have changed the organisation of central IT to reflect the new requirements and less than 40 per cent of authorities are considering doing so. Small councils have found it difficult to release management time to tackle the issue.

Some authorities are moving towards commercial operation to address the accountability issues or to achieve greater cost effectiveness. There has been a growth in contracting out all or part of information technology service provision to commercial organisations (facilities management) in order to:

- *make cost reductions;*
- *achieve service improvements;*
- *release senior management time to focus on core activities;*
- *alleviate IT staffing problems;*
- *ease migration to a new technical environment;*
- *escape the limitations of capital controls.*

However, successful use of FM arrangements requires an organisation which:

- separates client and contractor functions;
- ensures strong client side IT management is in place;
- clearly defines service requirements;
- explicitly specifies performance criteria.

Most authorities moving to FM have had to put these systems in place quickly to set up the contract. Protection of the authority's interests has sometimes been sacrificed to speed.

Central vs departmental computing

The role of central IT functions is changing, not always in a planned way, as a result of the growth in departmental and personal computing. This has been seen by some service departments as a way of breaking away from central control. The consequent tensions have created a danger that the value of investments may not be optimised, especially where there is no effective strategy in place.

Corporate systems, which are often mainframe based, tend to progress slowly because benefits are more difficult to identify and achieve, whilst initial costs tend to be high. In addition they need a wide body of support and involvement in their development, which runs counter to the trend of devolution of services. It is usually easier to relate costs to benefits on departmental computing, so the decision process is simpler.

Major changes have arisen in departmental system requirements as a result of devolution of management responsibility. Cost centre managers, such as headteachers or managers of direct labour organisations (DLOs), with a responsibility to manage their resources of finance, people and property and reduce central overheads, are challenging the assumption that central management information systems need to be highly functional. This test of cost effectiveness of corporate systems will become increasingly important and may reverse the trend for increased complexity and functionality evident over the past decade.

The importance of data and network management is illustrated in schools and education departments which are now beginning to use local systems for finance, property and people. These systems should complement the central systems and vice-versa. Without this, there is a danger of overlapping but uncoordinated databases which will:

- *bring into question the quality of management information;*
- *substantially increase data capture costs locally and centrally;*
- *reduce the value of information as a key resource of a local authority.*

The need to share data with external bodies is increasingly recognised, but only those authorities with technology and network strategies are likely to be able to achieve this. The costs of not being able to share data will increase.

Strategy vs tactics

The Audit Commission review of IT strategies concluded that performance was unsatisfactory. Although over 75 per cent of authorities had IT strategies in place or in preparation in 1990, concerns exist regarding the method of preparation of these strategies. Managers of service departments were not consulted in 25 per cent of cases, and elected members not consulted in over 75 per cent of cases.

The legislative demands made on IT recently with Community

Charge, Housing Benefits, Education Reform and CCT have caused authorities to focus on tactical rather than strategic issues.

Local government has dealt with the challenges of the past few years by focusing sharply on short-term needs at the expense of longer term planning. The intended replacement of the Community Charge by the Council Tax creates a serious danger that the short-term approach will continue, leaving little IT management time to handle the wider implications of local government restructuring.

Applications

Most authorities now have a wide range of applications covering virtually all services. The way in which application systems have been developed has changed significantly over recent years, as Table 9.2 illustrates.

Many of the current bespoke systems are likely to have been developed before 1984, indicating that the proportion of new developments for which packages are used is now very high. Whilst experiences of package use have been mixed, there is increasing evidence that authorities are becoming better at selection and implementation and that suppliers are producing better packages.

At district council level, the introduction of Community Charge systems has changed the scale of district council computing. There has been an increase in machine power and cost, a large growth of network users, and greater experience with implementation of packages.

At county council level, the introduction of decentralised systems and equipment to support the local management of schools has been the forerunner to a major change in emphasis from centralised to decentralised processing for many services.

Although office automation has been around for many years, almost half of local authorities do not use it. Of those who do, less than 40 per cent use such facilities as electronic filing, document transfer, diary management and electronic data interchange. Most authorities regard office automation as a useful way of providing added value once a significant network of IT users has been established. There does not appear to be any evidence of office automation, other than at the simplest level, being cost justified in its own right.

Method	1984 (%)	1990 (%)
In-house bespoke	60	41
External bespoke	7	9
Package	33	50

Table 9.2

Technology trends

Technologies will continue to develop through further miniaturisation, improved price performance, introduction of new technologies and improvement of existing ones.

A number of these technologies offer facilities which are not currently available or economic to use:

- expert systems provide knowledge of procedures or technical subjects which are likely to play a role in bringing services closer to the public, e.g. facilitating single points of contact;
- portable computers, combined with improved communications and networks, will provide access to data and processing power at any location or even while travelling;
- smart cards can provide a cheap and portable means of holding data facilitating access to computer records.

Other technologies offer improved facilities and are of strategic importance:

- open systems — providing protection of software investment and greater market choice;
- office automation — providing a wide range of integrated functions to a large population of users;
- geographic information systems — becoming increasingly valuable and cost effective as they are shared between departments internally and with outside bodies such as utilities;
- document image processing — allowing integration of image with other forms of data. However, the absence of an agreed international standard diminishes its strategic potential.

All of these technologies demand improved performance from and greater use of telecommunications networks. To keep costs down existing networks such as cable TV and radio will have to be used.

The effect of improving technologies over the past decade has been to increase investment in IT through increased price/performance, as it becomes economic to solve more and different problems. The drive for more cost effective services will accentuate this trend.

By providing more choice, technology trends have emphasised the need for high quality management capable of taking a strategic view of IT to:

- support business objectives;
- invest wisely by understanding both technology and business directions;
- procure cost effective solutions.

Local authority major IT suppliers — view of market

Suppliers' views are valuable because their business depends on their understanding of the IT market and their ability to apply developing technologies to meet local authorities' needs. A number of trends are evident:

- a move away from hardware towards software and services as the main revenue sources;
- continuing decline in mainframe and increase in mini and micro sales;
- growth in office systems products and image processing in particular;
- forecast that over half of PC sales will be in small portable systems, e.g. laptops and notebooks;
- increased demand for network products;
- consolidation of the facilities management market with fewer suppliers.

Technology has already reached the stage where price/performance of hardware is not an issue. Hardware is being chosen after the selection of applications software. Suppliers are therefore concerned that there is a wide portfolio of software available to run on their hardware.

Suppliers recognise that greater standardisation in the mini and micro market is leading to more package developments. The environment itself is simpler and machines will continue to increase in power and capacity. They are, therefore, fuelling the move to this distributed approach.

Although office systems have not yet taken off to the extent predicted, the market will grow because:

- needs are growing through decentralisation and management devolution;
- the products are improving steadily;
- hardware economics will continue to improve cost effectiveness;
- the growth in networks will allow office systems to be offered as 'added value' products.

Miniaturisation continues, allowing suppliers to provide significant power and capacity in genuinely portable machines. With improved network facilities, lap-tops can be used to collect, control and transmit data, as well as providing local processing facilities away from the office. PCs will increasingly become multi-media: voice, data, text and image. Networks will grow, both within local authorities and for communications, by bridging to supplier networks which offer value added services.

Most suppliers take the view that there are too many facilities management companies operating in local government, and that consolidation is likely. They also expect growth in the market, however, and recognise a need to offer FM as part of their comprehensive range of services.

In general, suppliers expect local government to continue to be an important market where the trend of increasing investment will continue. They are planning changes in their portfolio of products and services to reflect the changing technology and the opportunities it provides.

In summary:

- changes in local government role and culture are driving a need for more accountability, more data transfer, improved networks, simpler systems and greater cost effectiveness;
- in response to this, there is an emphasis on departmental and personal computing by local authorities and suppliers;
- despite financial constraints, IT costs are rising without an associated improvement in benefits realisation procedures;
- despite these difficulties, IT has played, and will continue to play, a vital role in the implementation of new legislation, often against tight deadlines and last minute changes in requirements;
- pressures to meet short-term legislative needs have reduced the capacity of many authorities to undertake longer term planning and to implement essential organisational change, at a time when these are needed more than ever.

The focus of change

The nature of local government IT in future will be influenced by:

- changes in the structure of local government;
- the changes in the role of local authorities and the way in which services are procured and provided;
- the opportunities offered by technology;
- the impact of financial constraints and the development of the internal market.

These changes will impact on several aspects of the use of IT.

Investment

The investment growth rate has been particularly high over the past three years, due to the introduction of Community Charge and associated systems. In the commercial market, investment in IT has shown signs of decline. It is possible the rate of increase in IT spend in local government will slow down because:

- the internal market will result in less complex central systems and lower net costs for computing;
- processing power will become cheaper to purchase, implement and use, particularly at personal computer level;
- the proposed Council Tax is intended to be simpler than the Community Charge and is likely to require fewer network users.

Despite this, levels of investment will still increase, rather than decline overall, because of:

- the IT support costs of continued decentralisation and devolution;
- likelihood of new legislation;
- opportunities offered by advances in technology to improve service delivery;
- the skill of technology suppliers in persuading authorities to invest.

The growth of local computing, often with a single application operating on a mini computer, offers the opportunity to simplify the investment decision process. IT investment will move away from mainframe processing capacity towards distributed computing facilities and data networking.

Control and accountability

The introduction of the internal market in local authorities will bring together responsibility and accountability for investment proposals and realisation of benefits. These will, in future, become the responsibility of a single unit, cost centre or DSO, charged with responsibility for effective service delivery.

Where budget holders are responsible for, and have control over, all IT costs, there will be an increased emphasis on costing proposals, identifying benefits, and ensuring that all benefits are achieved. Management will need constantly to ask the questions:

- *can we afford it?*
- *will the benefits outweigh the costs?*
- *when will the costs arise and the benefits be obtained?*

Compromises will be needed in selection of information systems. The adage that 80 per cent of the benefits can be achieved for 20 per cent of the cost still often applies.

Organisation and service delivery

The proposed application of compulsory competitive tendering to computing, and/or the effect of the internal market, will bring about changes to the organisation and management of IT. It will increasingly operate in a commercial market, and services are likely to be provided on a trading account basis, with business and investment plans based on sound business criteria, including:

- *understanding of the potential market;*
- *status of the order book;*
- *level of satisfaction of current customers;*
- *competition;*
- *cost effectiveness of proposals.*

A reduction in investment on corporate systems and mainframe computing is likely, together with an increased emphasis on decentralised processing, networking and package acquisition to support independent service units. As a result of this, IT units need to reassess the client and contractor roles and the appropriateness of current skills and services in the changing marketplace.

Client support services will be required across a number of areas:

- *development, agreement and maintenance of strategy;*
- *recognition of opportunities offered by technology;*
- *preparation of specifications;*
- *procurement of solutions;*
- *project management of the implementation process;*
- *management of the contract with the IT supplier.*

The extent of this support will vary according to the competence of the client department and the size and complexity of systems. However, a move towards support rather than production services may be required, with a resulting change in emphasis from technical to interpersonal skills.

The in-house IT contractor services will need to operate as a DSO and compete with external suppliers. This means:

- tendering for work against specifications;
- providing services in accordance with service level specifications;
- levying charges to achieve an agreed return and to win business rather than reallocating costs;
- deciding on services to be provided to maintain profitability;
- managing resources of people and equipment to match business demands.

The survival of in-house IT contractors will depend on their success in competing with external suppliers. They will need to provide a service which:

- *is comprehensive;*
- *meets service targets;*

- *is cost effective;*
- *is customer orientated.*

They will also need to be allowed to compete on a level playing field, and have the ability to:

- *hire and fire staff to meet the workload;*
- *pay competitive rates;*
- *purchase and dispose of equipment to meet customer needs;*
- *fix prices on commercial grounds;*
- *refuse non-profitable work;*
- *carry out research and development, e.g. pilot studies.*

The formalisation of business arrangements between each authority and its IT unit through the introduction of service level agreements will assist any newly created authorities to make informed decisions regarding the future source of IT services. Urgent action is required in most authorities, to ensure that the transfer to a more commercial form of IT operation can be completed in time to support the demands of user departments in such new authorities.

Strategy

IS/IT strategies will have an important role to play in ensuring that:

- *data sharing needs are identified and the value of data optimised;*
- *incompatible technologies do not limit the ability to share data;*
- *the authority can take advantage of emerging technologies;*
- *information systems are selected on a sound basis;*
- *the corporate core can obtain the information that it needs;*
- *there is appropriate and cost-effective information sharing with outside agencies.*

Improvements required to ensure that investment is optimised include:

- rigid and disciplined investment appraisal where benefits are quantified and their delivery date projected and planned;
- user department accountability for both the containment of costs and the achievement of benefits, where appropriate by reduction of the budget;
- development of IT strategies and determination of priorities for investment, based on meeting corporate and service objectives.

Technologies

One view of the relevance of each of the newer and developing technologies is set out in the previous section. To exploit new technologies, local government will need to:

- develop and maintain flexible strategies which enable technology to be used efficiently and effectively to achieve maximum business benefits;
- keep abreast of developments;
- define requirements carefully and procure cost effective solutions;
- recognise the need to communicate between departments and with the outside world;
- carefully define costs and benefits and take a pragmatic approach;
- carry out carefully controlled pilot studies where appropriate;
- ensure that net benefits are obtained;
- provide appropriate training and support to users;
- manage the IT providers to achieve agreed service levels within contracted costs;
- take a prudent view on write-off periods and leasing terms for investments.

Developing technologies will facilitate the processing and storage of additional forms of information, such as image and voice. This will make possible the better use of information and the improvement of services. Value-added network facilities to external users will be enhanced by additional information and improved network performance. Subject to legal requirements, it may be possible to sell information to third parties.

Network facilities and open systems interconnection will be the key to unlocking the potential of IT. This could transform business processes and facilitate the sharing of information with outside bodies — government departments, service providers, the NHS, and suppliers to local government. This is likely to be one of the most important roles for future technology, and is also one of the most challenging to local government management responsible for IT development.

The consequence of these factors is that local authorities need to be large enough to:

- support the organisational structure demanded cost effectively;
- recruit and retain high calibre management and technical staff.

Implications for local government restructuring

Based on the foregoing, the strengths and weaknesses of two major organisational options are analysed below.

Unitary authorities based on existing counties would:

- build on existing infrastructure and economies of scale enjoyed by counties;
- give rise to low transition costs;
- exploit existing scarce management and technical skills;
- reduce the number of authorities and makes standardisation and data sharing more practical.

However, they would also:

- cause significant redundancies of duplicated IT management and staff;
- cause short-term disruption in standardising district systems.

Unitary authorities made up of one or more district authorities within an existing county would:

- reduce the number of authorities, eventually leading to easier standardisation;
- avoid complex organisation structures.

But they would also:

- cause high transitional and on-going costs through the break-up of county services and networks;
- result in wasteful duplication, with around three times the number of IT strategies and systems implementations required by Option A;
- reduce compatibility between authorities;
- require more strategists and IT contractor managers than are likely to be available.

The short-term and long-term implications are explored in more detail below.

Short-term

The present position of IT in local government may complicate restructuring because of incompatibility of systems used by merging authorities. There is a well documented case in the private sector where two building societies had to abandon merger plans simply because they each utilised incompatible systems which could not be merged at an acceptable price. The problems which need to be addressed are:

- different proprietary operating system and network environments;
- wide variety of application systems used for major applications such as financial management, payroll and personnel and property;
- specialised skills restricted to proprietary environments;
- restrictive IT investment plans which limit opportunity for change.

Because local authorities now depend on information systems and networks to provide services, local government restructuring will create a need to ensure that existing systems can be merged with minimal effort and disruption. The existing position cannot be changed significantly in the short-term, but new major developments (such as the proposed Council Tax) should be introduced with the new structure in mind.

Steps could be taken to minimise disruption and avoid any unnecessary waste in expenditure on hardware and software. It would be advisable to:

• know the likely form of local government structure before decisions are made on new Council Tax systems;
• impose a set of standards covering interfaces, languages, database methods and operating systems;
• form consortia of existing authorities to implement and operate the Council Tax.

Longer term

Although the structure of local government will not be determined primarily by information technology issues, the effective exploitation of IT is essential to the efficient delivery of services. Local government must be able to successfully exploit IT investment for service gain. The critical success factors are:

• *ability to recruit and retain the calibre of management and staff required;*
• *effective networks for data and voice communications;*
• *successful transition from the present arrangements;*
• *a stable and effective local government environment;*
• *an acceptable level of compatibility between authorities today.*

A decade ago, IT staffing issues concerned the development and delivery of information systems. Changes in the economic climate, and in the way in which systems are developed and maintained, have helped local authorities to overcome this problem. The infrastructure required to support today's IT environment is more complex:

• *more sharing of data between systems;*
• *more technologies to interface;*
• *wider choice of technology;*
• *greater user awareness;*
• *faster pace of technology development.*

This places emphasis on the employment of smaller numbers of higher calibre staff, capable of developing and maintaining sound strategic directions, whilst enabling IT service delivery to meet current requirements. Small authorities unable to offer career development opportunities have experienced great difficulty in recruiting personnel with these skills. This problem will worsen rather than improve.

The present structure of IT in local government is piecemeal because:

- over 400 authorities are each determining their own strategic direction;
- there is a current need for many authorities to focus on short-term legislative demands;
- the growth of departmental computing is taking place in many authorities in an unstructured way.

The result of this is that even between authorities within existing counties there is a lack of compatibility in information systems. Although data can be shared, the lack of technical skills has prevented this in practice.

To exploit IT in the future, a balance needs to be struck between using available technology to meet business needs, and ensuring that individual solutions can contribute to achievement of longer-term strategic benefits. The agenda for the past decade has been centred on the efficient delivery of IT services. For the future, the challenge is to realise the opportunities of IT and ensure that investment is targeted at the achievement of maximum service benefits.

References

Audit Commission (1990) *Preparing an Information Technology Strategy — Making it Happen* HMSO, February.

Foundation for Information Technology in Local Government (1990) *Delivering services to the Customer — using IT for Strategic Advantage* FITLOG, November.

Society of Information Technology Managers (1990) *IT trends in Local Government* SOCITM, December.

10 Local government's role in leisure and recreation

All intellectual improvement arises from leisure

(Samuel Johnson)

Introduction

Local government is a major contributor to the provision of leisure and recreation outside the home in the UK. But, despite revenue expenditure in excess of £2bn in 1991/92, and the contribution this provision makes to health, well-being, and cultural enlightenment, local government's activities in this area are often given less importance than they deserve from a policy perspective.

There is little legislation that requires local government to be involved in leisure and recreation. Its involvement is largely discretionary and motivated by social and political objectives. As a consequence, the type and coverage of provision varies extensively between local authorities. Furthermore, expenditure on leisure often has a low priority in budgets and may not even feature as a separate category.

Local authorities have long promoted the policy of 'leisure for all' during a period of growth in leisure provision, starting after the Second World War. Four decades of great social change have led to considerable depth and variety of public sector involvement. The most pressing issue now for local authorities, and hence a key concern for the review of local government structure, is whether, and how, to continue to provide highly varied services in conditions of constant change, increasingly sophisticated consumer expectations, greater private sector involvement in some aspects of the market, and increasingly severe constraints on public funds.

This chapter reviews this central issue by:

- *describing current patterns of leisure demand and provision, with particular reference to the role of local authorities;*
- *specifying the changes which will present a challenge to local government provision in the future;*

- *setting out the different ways in which local government is meeting the challenge of leisure provision;*
- *drawing out the implications for future local government structure.*

Leisure today

Defining leisure

Leisure is the use of time and opportunity for relaxation and recreation. This broad description includes home-based activities which are beyond the scope of this chapter. Here, leisure is defined as the use of facilities and services provided in connection with the following:

— libraries and archives;
— museums and galleries;
— sports;
— arts;
— outdoor open space;
— tourism;
— play.

Facilities include premises and equipment, such as sports halls, books and play equipment. They are complemented by services such as sports coaching, information research and theatre booking agencies. Many of the categories listed above are themselves combinations of widely differing activities, some with broad appeal, others more specialised in terms of the facilities offered, and specialist in their appeal. Examples of the activities within categories are:

- *arts: dance, jazz, fine art, sculpture, theatres, orchestral and chamber music, pop concerts, bandstands;*
- *outdoor open space: playing fields, town parks, country parks, footpaths, bridleways, coast, common land, national parks.*
- *sports: swimming pools, all-purpose halls, climbing walls, ice rinks, saunas, marinas, golf courses.*

The pattern of provision in each leisure sector, together with an indication of current issues, concerns and trends, is summarised in Table 10.1. This chapter does not seek to examine each service area in depth. Some of the services covered here meet other needs as well as those of leisure and recreation: for example, library services provide for important educational and economic needs through the provision of information to pupils, teachers and businesses, as well as having a cultural dimension. Its purpose is rather to examine the general characteristics of the leisure sector as a whole and to consider the implications of changes in this sector for the review of local government structure.

Local authority provision

All levels of local government may provide for, and are responsible for, important aspects of leisure and recreation: county councils, district councils, metropolitan districts and London borough councils. Most authorities provide a much wider service than they are obliged to by law. The nature and scale of provision depends on the characteristics of the leisure market in the local area, on an individual authority's level in the local government hierarchy and on its political stance and policies.

One consequence of this variety of providers, each responding to local need and demand, is that the objectives of provision and the resulting facilities and services are highly diverse. Local authority expenditure on leisure activities is not purely an end in itself. It is frequently justified by reference to a mix of different social, economic and political objectives such as:

— improvement in the quality of life;
— alleviation of social deprivation;
— support to education;
— attraction of tourists;
— attraction of new investment;
— development of civic pride;
— promotion of health;
— reduction of crime;
— conservation of the heritage.

One consequence of these different justifications for leisure expenditure is that responsibility for leisure provision by local authorities is typically interspersed through the departmental structure. In addition to conventional departments, departments of planning, education, social services and public health may also be responsible for facilities and services used by the public in their leisure time. This makes it difficult to identify readily or accurately from collective published sources the total expenditure by local authorities on leisure facilties and services.

However, CIPFA's leisure and recreation estimates for 1991/92 provide a rough guide to the relative size and area of application of public funds in this field. They show that the three largest sectors of local government expenditure on leisure and recreation are sports, outdoor open space and libraries, with over £500m per annum spent on each. Annual arts expenditure follows with approximately £300m, whilst museums and tourism receive less than £100m each.

Leisure sectors	Key local government players	Other key players	Direct legislation	Indirect legislation	Main facilities, services and role provided by local government	Main issues, concerns and trends
Sports	County councils District councils Parish councils	Regional Park Authorities Sports Council Voluntary sector Private sector	National Curriculum Community use of schools	None	Direct provision of sports facilities: • pools • playing fields and outdoor facilities • dry facilities Enabling Lobbying/influencing	Increased trend for sporting activities Healthy lifestyle Diversification of sports type and choice Higher quality standards Decline in team sports Increase in dry facilities Concern over selling of playing fields Financial constraints/funding Fulfilment of social objectives Joint provision and integrated service with other providers CCT
Arts	County councils District councils	Arts Council Regional Arts Boards Central government Private sector sponsorship	None	National Curriculum Local Management of Schools	Funding of Regional Arts Boards Direct provision of: • theatres • concert halls • art centres	Increase audiences • theatres • classical music Financial pressures/funding Wilding Report 1989 Small scale operations cannot support large scale project or experimental work
Outdoors	district councils County councils	Forestry Commission National Parks National Trust	None	None	Functional • making safe trees, etc. Creative/Aesthetic • floral displays and parks Sporting	CCT • for ground maintenance • for management of outdoor facilities • conservation

Table 10.1: Pattern of provision in leisure sectors

Leisure sectors	Key local government players	Other key players	Direct legislation	Indirect legislation	Main facilities, services and role provided by local government	Main issues, concerns and trends
					• play areas • playing pitches Countryside • footpaths • country parks	
Tourism	District councils County councils	English Tourist Board Regional Tourist Boards Private sector	None	None	Funding of Regional Tourist Boards	Changing trends in demand • decline of two week holiday • introduction of short educational break • Channel Tunnel • recession
Archives	County Councils	National archives National libraries	Local government (Records) Act 1962		Direct provision of archives for the written word: • acquisition of material • secure storage • cataloguing and indexing • conservation Records management Education and outreach services	Increasing volume of data • expenditure to deal with it Increased interest from the general public in using archives Resource needs do not relate to standard indications for local government funding
Museums and galleries	County councils District councils	Independent providers Charitable trusts	Public Libraries and Museums Act, 1964 • discretionary only	Local Management of Schools National Curriculum	Direct provision of museums: • acquisition and care of collections • display and interpretation of collections • guardianship of the nation's heritage Education	Museum and Galleries Commission registration, April 1992 • expenditure required to meet criteria Local support of National/International collections Charging policies Financial pressure CCT

Table 10.1: continued

Leisure sectors	Key local government players	Other key players	Direct legislation	Indirect legislation	Main facilities, services and role provided by local government	Main issues, concerns and trends
Play	District councils County councils	Voluntary sector Private sector National Children's Play and Recreation Unit (NCPRU)	None	Children's Act, 1989 Education Reform Act, 1988 Local Government Finance Act, 1988 National Health Service and Community Care Bill	Direct provision of: • play grounds • playing fields • play schemes	Uneven distribution Enormous growth in last 20–30 years • social expectations and interest Changes in type, layout and presentation Increased demand • parents return to work • larger young children population Local school management • decline in after-school provision Children's Act • focus not on quality of play Financial pressure Lack of coordinated approach to play provision
Libraries	County councils Metropolitan district councils London boroughs City of London	Local education authorities Department of Social Services Regional health authorities (by cooperation and synergy with other areas of local government)	Public Libraries and Museums Act, 1964 'to provide a comprehensive and efficient library service for all persons who live, work or study in the authority's area' Library Charges Act	Education Reform Act, 1988	Direct provision of libraries: • lending books • reference and information services • 'outreach' library service • lending/provision of other media (magazines, newspapers, pamphlets, records, CDs, computer software, video tapes)	Demand for different media Demand from different groups • ethnic • disabled Increased demand for 'outreach' Charging levels and pricing strategies Rationalisation and economies of scale by cooperation, sharing of facilities Rationalisation of procedures and provision standards since 1974 CCT

Table 10.1: continued

Some expenditure is not recorded in these estimates: for example, music in schools is an important part of providing for the arts, but is funded from the education budget.

County Council expenditure dominates the libraries sector. Library services are one of the few leisure areas where legislation puts a statutory duty upon local government to provide 'a comprehensive and efficient service . . . for all persons who live, work or study in (an) authority's area'. Library services typically cover the provision of information services and of other media as well as traditional book-lending, and are widely used by agencies beyond local government, for example, in prisons and hospitals.

District councils have extensive involvement in providing and operating facilities for sports and outdoor open spaces (two of the largest expenditure items) and consequently bear the major part of expenditure on leisure as a whole. Shire districts in total spend more than metropolitan districts; together they spend about five times the amount recorded as spent by county councils.

Quoted expenditure on outdoor leisure is distributed between shire, London and metropolitan districts with county councils spending a very small proportion of the £546m (though expenditure in this area is also included in education, youth and community services, and planning budgets).

Arts expenditure is distributed relatively evenly between counties, shire districts, London boroughs (and the City) and metropolitan districts. Expenditure on museums is also distributed between all types of authority (except the City).

Tourism expenditure is almost all borne by shire and some metropolitan districts. However, in counties, expenditure on tourism is often subsumed within budgets for economic development.

In summary, diversity is the keynote of local authority leisure provision. The level and nature of provision is mostly discretionary (with the exception of libraries) but expectations now define a level of customary, universal provision. For residents of most parts of England and Wales this basic level of provision comprises access to a library service, a swimming pool and an all-purpose hall, and open space. Beyond this there is a wide range of facilities, reflecting the responsiveness of local authorities to their communities and the differences in user requirements within them.

Provision by the private sector

The private sector provides for and is involved in leisure and recreational facilities and services directly, indirectly, and through the planning system. Direct providers build, maintain and operate leisure and recreational facilities and services as profit-making concerns. The main areas of interest to them are entertaiment, pubs, catering outlets and, of increasing interest recently, sports. Examples in the field of sports include private health clubs, golf clubs and squash clubs. Access to these facilities is often restricted to members only, normally on payment of membership fees. In the field of arts, for example, the private sector owns and manages theatres and cinemas, and operates museums and galleries.

Leisure and recreational services are often used indirectly by the private sector to attract customers to other goods, services or facilities supplied by the provider. Examples include recreational facilities within new-build housing estates and office complexes to attract purchasers/tenants, play facilities in shopping centres and fitness/health centres in hotels.

Section 106 of the Town and Country Planning Act, 1990 enables local authorities to require developers to provide additional features to new developments before planning consent is given. The requirements can be extensive and may include leisure and recreational facilities, such as parks and play areas, sports centres, and community halls. Once developed, Section 106 facilities may be handed over for the local authority to operate.

Private sector involvement in leisure is overwhelmingly undertaken for commercial reasons, even if the commercial results are seen in parts of the business other than the leisure element. The private sector is selective in what it undertakes, and focuses on niche markets and largely on entertainment orientated sub-sectors with associated catering and retail opportunities. Its interface with the public sector is complex. Local government's more universal approach has, in contrast, provided 'for all' in often less fashionable and less commercial leisure areas, leaving the private sector to operate in the more obviously profitable markets. However, local government subsidy means that some leisure sectors are not subject to market forces; prices may be kept artificially low and the private sector effectively 'crowded out'. The market, in effect, is not tested.

Provision by the voluntary sector and clubs

If the boundary between the private and public sectors in leisure is defined by commercial potential, that between the public and voluntary sectors is largely defined by the breadth of social policy and the degree to which it influences provision. This is particularly so for the provision of leisure to disadvantaged groups such as the young, the elderly, handicapped people and racial minorities. At the local level, clubs provide and operate facilities and services for their own leisure time pursuits. In many cases they manage facilities which other providers have developed, notably local authorities.

Public sector other than local authorities

Several government departments have an interest in the provision of leisure facilities and services. In practice, national policy is achieved primarily at 'arm's length' from the political arena through a wide range of agencies and quangos, including the Sports and Arts Councils, the Tourist Boards, English Heritage and the Forestry Commission. Table 10.2 shows the network of interests in leisure throughout the hierarchy of government and the variety of relationships between local authorities and other interested parties. In general, these agencies and quangos establish a national framework and then work closely with local authorities: advising them, disbursing grants, and lobbying on their behalf.

Users of leisure facilities and services

Participation in leisure pursuits outside the home is, for adults, dependent on the availability of discretionary time and money. Table 10.3 gives available leisure tiime for a number of employment groups. The reasons people participate in leisure activities are generally personal, rather than community orientated; each activity has to be personally attractive and suit the individual as well as the fashion of the time. Motives for participation range from interest in health and fitness, culture and education, to relaxation, social gathering and entertainment. There is a correlation between available leisure time and the pursuit of out-of-home leisure. Local authorities have made particular efforts in the 1980s to cater for sectors not attractive to the private sector, notably increasing leisure opportunities among the unemployed and the retired.

Participation in each sub-sector of the leisure market is influenced by such factors as the age, sex, socio-economic standing, and family status of the participant regularly. Generally, people in higher socio-economic groups are more likely to participate regularly in leisure activities. The specific activities chosen reflect the supply of facilities locally as well as personal preferences. Tables 10.4 and 10.5 give participation rates for a variety of different leisure and recreation activities.

No out-of-home leisure pursuit, except walking, regularly involves a majority of the population. Most individual out-of-home leisure pursuits are minority interests, pursued by different sectors of society at different stages of the life cycle.

A consequence of this is that catering for out-of-home leisure pur-

Principal government department	Employment department group	Department of Transport	Department of Environment		Department of Education and Science	Office of Arts and Libraries	Ministry of Agriculture Fisheries and Food	Home Office	Department of Health
Central government body/ nationalised industry/ other public body	British Tourist Authority English Tourist Board	British Rail Transport and Road Research Laboratory	English Heritage British Waterways Board National Rivers Authority	Countryside Commission English Nature Rural Development Commission Inland Waterways Advisory Council	Sports Council	Arts Council Museums and Galleries Commission Crafts Council British Library	Forestry Commission Agricultural Development and Advisory Service		
Examples of national non-government organisations	British Hoteliers and Restaurateurs Association Tourism Society	AA RAC	National Trust Royal Yachting Association Council for Preservation of Rural England	National Angling Council Civic Trust Caravan Club RSPB	British Equestrian Society Cyclists Touring Club AAA	RSA ICA	NFU Country Landowners Association		
Regional body	Regional Tourist Board	Transport Region	DOE Regions		Regional Sports Councils	Regional arts associations	Regional offices		Regional health authorities
Local body	Local travel associations		National parks Local amenity/heritage societies		Local sports Clubs	Local arts societies/groups		Licensing Justices	District health authorities
Leisure interest	Tourism	Recreational traffic	Heritage	Local government Open space	Sports, play	Arts libraries museums	Countryside	Entertainment	Health/recreation

Table 10.2: Structure of leisure interests

	Male (hours)		Female (hours)
Employed full time	44		33
Employed part time (combined)		40	
Unemployed	88		72
Retired	93		82
Home makers (combined)		55	

Source: Social trends 21, 1991

Table 10.3: Leisure time in a typical week (1989)

suits requires a range and hierarchy of different facilities. Few cities have an opera house, not all towns have theatres but most towns have flexible spaces in which touring opera and theatre performances can be held if required. The public expects major cities to have collections of specialised reference books; at the other end of the hierarchy of provision users do not expect travelling library vans to stock such works.

Summary

Provision for leisure is guided, made, operated and promoted by a wide variety of organisations in the public and private sectors. With the exception of libraries, leisure is provided for at the discretion of local authorities, who are responding to the needs of their communities rather than to directing legislation.

The interaction of supply and demand factors means that leisure provision by local government is characterised by a wide variety of facilities and services over and above a base-load of provision probably comprising a library service, swimming pool and/or an all-purpose hall, and open space. Subsidies for leisure operations have generally been applied to facilities and services, rather than extended directly to users. Only selected, identified, individual groups such as the unemployed, the retired and the young have received targeted subsidies.

The private, voluntary and club sectors have clear objectives for their provision, and relatively focused target market sectors. Local authority provision in contrast, within the framework of broader national emphasis on 'sport for all' and wide access to arts events, has encouraged leisure for all. This is a highly challenging task when most leisure activities individually involve a minority of the population and when participation is closely linked to population profile, fashion and life-cycle stage. The next section of the chapter considers the current pressures upon local authorities in maintaining this stance.

Activities %	
Home-based leisure	
Watching television	99
Visiting/entertaining friends	95
Listening to radio	88
Listening to music	73
Reading books	60
Gardening	46
DIY	43
Dressmaking/knitting/needlework	27
Library visits	
All aged 16–69	26
Arts and entertainment	
Films	11
Plays/pantomimes/musicals	7
Ballet or dance	1
Opera/operetta	1
Classical music	2
Jazz/blues/soul/reggae	2
Other music shows	7
Galleries, museum and historic buildings	
Arts/galleries/museums	8
Historic buildings	8

Note: percentage participating in the 4 week period before survey

Source: Social trends 21 1991

Table 10.4: Leisure participation rates 1987

The current challenge

The pressures on local government in maintaining their stance to leisure provision are becoming acute. The reasons are both external and internal to the processes of government, and raise issues relating to strategic priorities and cost-effective provision. What needs to be provided? Who should be responsible for provision? How can provision be achieved effectively?

The key points shaping local authorities' strategic response are outlined in this section. The next section will examine the ways in which local authorities are developing a flexible and effective role in the delivery of leisure provision which suits the needs of their particular communities.

	Male %	Female %
Racquet sports		
Tennis	2	1
Badminton	4	3
Squash	4	1
Table tennis	4	1
Water sports		
Swimming/diving	13	13
Fishing	4	—
Yachting/dinghy sailing	1	—
Other	2	1
Team sports		
Soccer	10	—
Rugby union/league	1	—
Cricket	2	—
Netball	—	1
Basketball	1	—
Winter sports		
Skiing	1	—
Ice skating	1	1
Other sports		
Cycling	10	7
Athletics	1	—
Running	8	3
Golf	7	1
Horse riding	—	1
Cue sports	27	5
Darts	14	4
Tenpin bowling/skittles	2	1
Lawn or carpet bowls	2	1
Self defence	1	—
Weight training/lifting	7	2
Keep fit, yoga, aerobics, etc.	5	12
Motor sports	1	—

Note: percentage participating in the 4 week period before survey

Source: Social trends 21 1991

Table 10.5: Sport and physical exercise participation rates 1987

Demographic issues

Population profile is a key determinant of the scale and nature of
leisure facilities required in an area. Many leisure activities are highly
focused upon a narrowly defined group of participants, and so are

some leisure facilities, in both the public and private sectors. Changes in the population profile impact upon participation in activities and manifest themselves as changes in the use of, and demand for, facilities and services.

Three major demographic changes are currently prompting a response from the leisure industry. The increase in primary school and decrease in secondary school populations is leading to reductions in the latter's relatively high discretionary spending power in the leisure sector. Leisure facility operators are responding by targeting the family group as a whole, by offering family concessionary tickets.

Increasing numbers of retired people who are comparatively fit and mobile have a high proportion of their income available for discretionary spending. The recent shift in emphasis from sports to arts may, in part, reflect this demographic change. Increasing life expectancy is also having an impact upon numbers of library visits and creating pressure for additional services to institutions of different kinds.

Increasing numbers of working women have greater spending power than non-working women but less time to enjoy leisure pursuits. The leisure industry is responding by providing leisure opportunities after work hours, targeting family activities and recognising increased opportunities for home-based leisure through TV and magazine publishing.

A key issue for local authorities is the identification and management of current changes in demand and responding, as all leisure providers must, by being flexible in their approach.

Social issues

There is increasing recognition of the social and political value of local government's efforts in leisure provision. This active stance is more market led than previously, and seeks to suit the service to the potential user group rather than leaving potential users to conform to the provision made. Women, disabled people, minority racial groups, older people and people of different sexual orientations have all been targeted, to varying degrees, with the intention of increasing their access to leisure opportunities. As a consequence the variety of facilities and services provided or funded by local government is likely to increase. The key issue for local authorities is whether to provide universally a baseload of leisure services and/or to target provision, and if so, how to allocate priorities for such targeting.

User expectations

The 1990s are likely to be characterised by growth in home-based leisure activities. Those that have increased in popularity in recent years are:

- video usage, resulting from increases in home facilities and hire outlets;
- satellite and cable television;
- magazine reading, resulting from wider variety;
- Teletext and Oracle information services;
- DIY.

Spending on many of these activities operates in direct competition with other out-of-home leisure services. These activities are in large part supplied by the private sector where competition is likely to bring about innovations in products and services and downward pressure on real prices.

Outside the home, the user increasingly expects the following when purchasing a leisure service or opportunity:

- high quality;
- variety;
- good service;
- attention to fashion;
- value for money;
- services to complement facilities, for example sports tutoring, theatre workshops, information research in libraries, up-to-date booking systems.

These demands require constant investment in the upgrading of facilities and the development of staff. They are difficult to meet when user expectations change rapidly. A key issue for local authorities is how and to what extent they should make the investment required to meet the highest expectations of user groups.

Legislative issues

Specific legislation for recreation and leisure is minimal. Statutory obligations include the provision of libraries. Statutory frameworks, such as Section 106 of the Town and Country Planning Act 1990, exist at the interface with other services, in this case planning. Other legislation may have an indirect influence on leisure provision. For example, there has been recent legislation about play, including the Children Act, 1989, Education Reform Act, 1988, and Local Government Finance Act, 1988. All have implications for the provision of play facilities by local authorities.

Legislation having an impact on leisure provision may be sponsored by a variety of government departments and there is always the risk of a fragmented approach to policy and to provision. In the play area, for example, the National Children's Play and Recreation Unit (NCPRU) is advocating the coordination of all parties to ensure that provision is satisfactory. Though there may be little obligation to provide leisure facilities, once provision is made, a variety of regulatory legislation may have a bearing on its provision and its performance. Where there is no statutory obligation, the key issue is the level at which to provide for leisure needs, and more generally, how to integrate a coherent response to specific legislation as it impacts upon leisure provision.

Efficiency and management

Financial pressures on local government are increasing. Historically, the leisure industry has been one of the first to be affected during periods of financial stringency. Pressures to show economy, efficiency and effective delivery of services are likely to continue. Two key issues face local authorities as a result: using assets to the maximum; and managing facilities and services well.

Using assets

Ageing stock is becoming an increasingly important issue. The last three decades saw considerable expansion of leisure facilities in the community. For example, the Audit Commission's report 'Sport for Whom?' demonstrated that 70 per cent of swimming pools were built before 1981 and 50 per cent before 1972. Many buildings and a lot of equipment is at the end of its useful life, unsuitable for current activities or viewed as outdated. This decreases the appeal of the facilities to the general public, and both use and revenues therefore become more difficult to sustain. Considerable capital investment is required to refurbish the stock. Local authorities must consider increasing investment to maintain and expand the existing stock to meet more sophisticated and varied demands from users. The issue for local authorities is how to allocate scarce resources among increasingly costly leisure facilities and services.

Much leisure stock or potential stock is not owned and operated by leisure and recreation departments. It can be owned privately, by community trusts, by other departments in local authorities such as education, by other tiers of government, by quangos, by privatised companies and by regulatory authorities. Sharing facilities between schools and the public is now accepted good practice. Negotiating for use of facilities in the ownership of others is a more complex task facing local authorities than the direct provision of facilities.

Improving management

Government is keen to improve value for money in public services. The process of compulsory competitive tendering is designed to increase efficiency in the management of facilities and services, by focusing attention on achieving objectives.

Part of the process has been to invite private sector management to compete for tenders. However, the leisure and recreation industry in the private sector is generally young, entry thresholds are low, training has been poor and uncoordinated, and standards of management are only now beginning to be monitored. Against this background, the key issue for local authorities is how best to improve the management of their facilities.

Summary

In summary, the policy issues for local government in its provision of leisure facilities and services are:

- how to respond to the increasing variety of user requirements in a cost-effective and flexible way;
- whether it should be providing universally a base-load of leisure services for all, or targeting specific users not otherwise catered for, or some mixture of both, and if so, how to allocate priorities;
- whether and how to meet the highest and increasing expectations of users and to respond to private sector competition indirectly (in home-based entertainment and leisure activities) and directly (in out-of-home services);
- where there is no statutory obligation, at what level to provide for future needs, and more generally, how to integrate a coherent response to specific legislation as it impacts upon leisure provision;
- how to develop good management practice in the face of increasingly expensive and demanding investment decisions, increasing separation of ownership and control of leisure facilities, and in the absence of widespread good practice in the private sector.

Each authority will be developing its own response, according to the needs of local communities and social and political priorities. Taken together, however, these represent a set of fundamental political and strategic issues with regard to local government's leisure provision, to which the local government review will itself need to pay regard when considering options for local government structure. The next section considers the ways in which local authorities are responding to these issues through different approaches to provision.

Meeting the challenge

The trends outlined in the previous section suggest that local authorities are likely to face an increasing mis-match between their resources and user expectations. Policies will need to evaluate what should be provided, how and where. The debate is likely to focus on the scale and nature of provision and on appropriate target sectors of the community. It will emphasise the increasing importance of partnerships and the likely change in the relationship between facilities and services.

The ways in which leisure services are provided differs throughout the country and across the leisure sub-sectors. It does not follow party political patterns. There is a spectrum of involvement which may be categorised as follows:

— direct provision;
— enabling;
— influencing;
— passive.

Each category of involvement is discussed below in terms of its relevance against future requirements.

Direct provision

Local authorities commonly own, develop and operate leisure facilities such as swimming pools, sports halls, pitches, parks, play spaces and museums. The advantages of doing so are that: development can be relatively rapid because negotiations with others are kept to a minimum; service and quality are directly controlled by the authority and can reflect its social and political objectives; and innovative and experimental work can be promoted which would not, or would rarely, be funded by the private sector.

On the other hand, the disadvantages of direct provision are that it can be an expensive means of delivery for the local authority, and subsidised provision depresses market prices and deters additional provision by the private sector. Direct provision of major new facilities has been popular with local authorities in the past, but is becoming less common as financial pressures become more acute.

Enabling

Local government can enable others to provide for leisure. It does so by:

- *granting planning permission;*
- *distributing grants;*
- *providing information on sites and markets;*
- *providing advice and expertise in engineering, architecture, business development and marketing opportunities.*

Current examples include much of local government's patronage of the arts, assistance to sports clubs, grants to voluntary societies and grants of planning permission with section 106 agreements.

An enabling role suits particular circumstances. It works well where there is a dynamic population, thriving public, voluntary and club sectors, and in times and places of economic growth. Its advantages are that:

- schemes are likely to be developed in direct response to a perceived need;
- the risk of development and operation is shared;
- it is less expensive for the local authority both in capital and development costs;
- there is less likelihood of 'crowding out' of the private sector than with direct provision.

Conversely, the risks are that:

- no provision may result;
- provision may not result quickly, or in synchronisation with local authority budgets;
- provision may be adequate in some areas and not in others, perhaps over-riding perceived social needs;
- obtaining the desired level of control over quality, objectives and operating policy of the facility may not be possible or may require complex negotiation — currently, such skills are in short supply;
- accountability for operational performance through grant aid can be difficult to achieve.

On occasions, for example in connection with educational services for children, local authorities enable specific groups to use facilities provided by others, by subsidising the entry price. The advantage is that subsidies are targeted and may be more efficient in achieving the authority's objectives. Finely tuned targeting has been unpopular because it has been viewed as conspicuous means testing.

Local government has a considerable tradition of enabling others to provide services where they can do so effectively, efficiently and with a high degree of public involvement. It is likely that this form of provision will grow as greater emphasis is put on services which complement facilities.

Influencing

A local authority may also choose to influence others to provide leisure facilities and services, in particular central government, local industries, and the local population itself, as a substitute for itself providing or enabling provision.

Influencing central government takes three main forms. Firstly, local government can collectively lobby central government for changes in legislation. Secondly, individual local authorities can lobby central government to locate national facilities within their boundaries. Thirdly, local authorities can lobby to have their areas designated as areas of special need. Designated areas promote growth of leisure and recreational facilities by offering tax exemptions, wayleaves and special grants. This type of area designation is now relatively commonplace, as a means of promoting growth in deprived areas such as docklands and inner cities.

Authorities may also encourage local industry to provide leisure and recreational facilities. In the past, this type of patronage was widespread and often undertaken for both commercial and altruistic purposes. Bells in Perth and Boots and Players in Nottingham are examples of major local industries providing not only for their own workforce, but also for the whole local population. Today this approach can work best in a few, highly circumscribed situations, including:

- towns and cities where a few major industries dominate and draw heavily on the local workforce;
- where there is high level involvement in the local community of the chairmen or influential board members of an industry;
- periods of economic growth.

Greater attention to the lifestyle enjoyed by workers in industry might suggest that companies will invest in facilities for their own workforces during the next decades. On the other hand, changing patterns of work (including home working) with greater pressure on profit margins might suggest that they will not. It is highly questionable whether 'core' leisure provision will be forthcoming from industry of its own volition. Lobbying others to provide could, however, result in a few additional, specialist, high profile facilities for use by the wider community within the total framework of leisure provision.

Influencing the general population is perhaps the most exacting task for a local authority to undertake. Because local authorities have provided leisure facilities for many years, people expect the local authority to provide them; changing that perception is difficult. Nevertheless, in both leisure and other spheres some local authorities have been successful in influencing people to be active in providing and operating leisure services themselves. They have done so by:

- *appealing to a sense of duty: 'this is your facility/neighbourhood, why don't you . . .';*
- *raising awareness of what is required within the community;*

- *promoting voluntary action;*
- *marketing opportunities for involvement.*

Influencing others is the least costly approach available to local government in promoting leisure and recreation within its area. However, it is likely to be the least effective in the short term in terms of securing guaranteed provision. On a national or regional scale, it requires support from central government. On a local level, it requires members of the local community to champion schemes, and this may not often happen. Relying on this approach as a means of provision necessarily implies minimal control of leisure and recreation provision in terms of type, coverage and quality.

Passive provision

The remaining approach is a 'hands-off' option, in which the local authority chooses to exercise no control over non-obligatory leisure and recreation provision. This situation is similar to that in the United States where a large proportion of leisure and recreation is provided by the private sector. It assumes that users will be inclined and able to provide and support their own facilities. A company may provide facilities for its workforce; or tenants may pay ground-rent for the maintenance of facilities exclusive to their residential or commercial development.

Summary

Local government has played a major role since the war in increasing the access of many people to leisure facilities. To do so, it has often had to adopt an approach of direct provision and operation. It has also pursued alternative means of delivery as appropriate and expedient, including enabling others to provide for leisure, or accepting that in some areas of provision it will adopt no stance at all.

The position has now been reached where in many, perhaps most, local authorities sufficient facilities are available in most sub-sectors of leisure to enable access by larger user groups to the most popular educational, cultural, arts and sports activities. A key issue for the future, and hence for the review of local government structure, will be the position that local authorities choose to adopt along the spectrum of delivery. It is to be expected that different positions will be appropriate for different types of facilities and for different communities. Nevertheless, it is likely that to achieve objectives with constrained resources yet increasing expectations, local authorities will seek partners in direct provision and themselves adopt a more strategic and enabling role.

Implications for future structure

Leisure is one area of local government services where local authorities can readily respond to the needs of their communities and reflect their differences. The means of achieving their objectives have varied, both with the type of facility provided, and over time. They have provided for leisure in diverse ways.

During the 1990s, however, three main trends will force local authorities to review their role in the provision of leisure services. First, the constraint on resources will remain, perhaps increase. Second, the expectations of users and potential users will continue to grow, fuelled by experiences on holiday, private sector leisure provision and the experience of increased consumer choice. Third, local authorities have 'pump-primed' a major move into leisure for a wide cross section of the population; but their next role is unclear in any generalisable sense.

As leisure demands have increased, so the private sector has become more involved. The role of local authorities is not, and has not been, to duplicate private sector involvement, or to maintain exactly what has been developed in the past, but to find new ways of enhancing the quality of life and fulfilling diverse social and political objectives. Without local government involvement in most of its current leisure activities, the variety of choice offered to most people would diminish, certainly in sports, the arts, open air enjoyment and cultural activities in general. Access to these activities is expected in our society, albeit that individual activities taken up at any one point in time can be highly varied. A high value is placed on the existence and availability of these activities, even though individuals may not fully exercise the opportunities available to them.

Part of local government's role in the future will be to ensure that the expectations and requirements of different communities are met as far as resources allow in whatever way is appropriate to the area. The policy environment will be increasingly complex because there will be less emphasis on direct provision, and more on the roles of partnership, enabling, influencing and negotiating.

Increasing complexity argues for a structure of sufficient size and weight:

- to employ staff with specialist skills, for example, in funding, joint ventures, operating the variety of facilities and services required, organising and promoting a wide range of activities;
- to be credible in negotiations, particularly for funds, with central government, quangos, industry, domestic and European grant aiding bodies, and world leisure organisations (such as the Olympic Committee and Commonwealth Games);

- to balance the wider public interest with more parochial interests in considering policies covering the scale and spread of provision and in targeting resources on specific user groups.

The pressure to achieve more, and meet higher expectations, with fewer resources suggests that attention must be given to:

- allocating resources in the most appropriate way possible to achieve diverse social and political objectives, this may entail targeting resources on selected user groups;
- making greater use of assets and resources, including assets in the ownership of others, and aiding others to provide and manage as well as, or instead of, local authorities.

Addressing these issues argues for the organisational delivery of leisure services to be structured at a scale sufficient to give 'critical mass' in the optimisation of partnership and joint venture opportunities. The concept of critical mass is relevant from both the demand and supply perspectives. From a demand viewpoint, it is necessary to be able to draw upon and plan for a catchment population capable of supporting more than the lowest tier in the hierarchy of provision (if a full service is to be provided). From the supply viewpoint, it is necessary to be able to provide or procure the specialist skills and facilities required to lead in the field and constantly raise quality.

Achieving critical mass within the local authority unit enables strategic planning for the whole hierarchy of provision, so that:

- competition at the lower levels of the hierarchy are avoided, and competition, if it exists will be top level and between one type of leisure provision and another;
- specialist facilities can be supported;
- leisure delivery can be planned at the same level as other services which have facilities which can be used for public leisure activities; these may include education, social services, environmental health, and planning.

This has to be combined with flexibility and sophistication in operating in a complex local environment to respond to the needs of individual communities. Private sector companies provide a useful role model in suggesting how a strategic perspective and broad planning role can be married with effective local delivery. National and international strategy is combined with high quality local delivery through a variety of means from delegation to management agreement to franchise. Local requirements are met within a national or regional framework. In the local government environment, in addition to the localised service delivery by the principal authority, it would for example be possible to extend the role of parish and town councils in determining local community needs and priorities, in partnership with one another or with other interested parties locally, whilst developing a strategic approach over a wider area.

In the highly diverse field of leisure and recreation, it is difficult to define any single structural model appropriate to all sectors in all local circumstances. But the considerations above suggest that there are strong arguments for a future local government structure geared more readily to the achievement of scale and 'critical mass', able to satisfy demands at all levels in the hierarchy of leisure provision, and thus able to exploit economies of scale wherever appropriate to local needs. Future structure must:

- facilitate awareness of changing local needs across a highly diverse range of provision;
- develop and promote extended supply possibilities, seeking to optimise the use of available assets and improve the management of facilities to meet increasingly sophisticated expectations;
- ensure that a strategic approach is developed across the full hierarchy of provision.

11 Protecting the community: local government and public security

Nam tua res agitur, paries cum proximus ardet.
For it is your business, when the wall next door catches fire

(Horace)

Introduction

Maintaining the security of persons and property and controlling public nuisance have been functions of local government for many centuries. Today local government acts in a wide variety of ways to ensure that local citizens are protected from danger, fraud and abuse.

This is not purely a matter or law and order, or of response to emergencies. Decisions about environmental health services determine the approach to prevention and detection of human health and safety hazards; regulation of livestock movement and other preventative measures protect against animal disease. Highway design and maintenance contributes to accident prevention; schools teach road safety. Streetlight provision and sensitive design of buildings and open space deter crime; social services guard against child and elder abuse; recreation opportunities channel youthful energy constructively to individual and community benefit, rather than destructively. Consumer protection services ensure fair trading practice and protect against fraud; licensing and other regulation ensures proper standards are maintained across many trades to protect individuals from harm, abuse or offence.

Such functions are at base about striking the appropriate balance between the individual's interests (whether person or corporation) and the wider interests of the community at large, and are fundamental to communities' ability to provide for more sophisticated political, economic, personal, and social needs. In this sense protecting the community is the first and most critical of the functions of the state, and hence a key role for local government.

Communities, however, are diverse and multi-layered and people belong to more than one community simultaneously. Local government, as the agent of the state, must respond equitably to universal needs. As the agent and voice of local communities, it must equally respond sensitively to special needs and local circumstances. Individuals and communities of all kinds require and expect a common standard of public security as an integral part of living in a developed society. But vulnerable groups, such as the ill, the young, or the elderly, may require enhanced protection to safeguard their quality of life. Ethnic groups may require special measures to accommodate cultural and behavioural differences. Local communities may be in conflict and demand protection from each other.

Public expectations in this area are increasing and people demand a high quality of service. Effective public security is increasingly seen in terms of the need to ensure that protection is founded upon the consent and participation of those whose behaviour is regulated. This in turn requires those who exercise powers of public protection and regulation to be held effectively to account. At issue in the review of local government structure is how local government should be organised in order to secure the most effective relationships at the strategic and operational level with key protective agencies, taking into account the interests of central government and of local communities.

This chapter deals with relationships with the Police, Fire and Rescue Service, the Magistrates' Courts Service and the Probation Service. It identifies the principal issues impacting upon the way in which local links with these services may develop in the future, and the implications for local government structure. Chapter 12 considers local government's role in regulating business activity and in securing the economic well-being of local businesses and consumers.

Background

The services covered in this chapter operate mainly at county level within a tight regulatory framework and a set of national standards and guidelines. Central government also has a substantial financial interest; though the Fire and Rescue Service is funded through the block grant system, the others are majority funded by the Home Office. In the majority of cases they are additionally subject to annual inspection by the Home Office to ensure that they conform to national standards.

Until recently there has been a close, almost symbiotic relationship between these four services and local government. Service boundaries often align with administrative areas. Operation at a local level is guided by a locally elected authority or committee to ensure that local issues are dealt with and local imperatives met. In many cases one of the most challenging tasks for senior personnel is to strike an equitable and practical balance between the national policy framework and meeting local demands. Despite the fact that each service has been subject in recent years to major reviews involving questions about whether to organise it on a national, regional, subregional or local basis, there continues to be a strong desire for local accountability.

This chapter discusses major relevant developments in each service and some key cross-service issues. It goes on to draw out the implications for future local government structure.

The Police

Historically, the English, Welsh and Scottish police forces developed as local units, rather than as national organisations under central control. The Home Secretary has not been in any sense a minister of police or justice for the whole country. Local chief police officers have enjoyed a considerable autonomy in the direction and control of their forces. The 43 forces in England and Wales vary considerably in size and crime profile. Some are combined forces but most (other than in metropolitan areas) align with county boundaries.

Provision and management of police forces are the combined responsibility of the Home Office, the local Police Authority, and Chief Constables, as follows:

- the Police Authority is required to secure the maintenance of an adequate and efficient police force for its area and, subject to the Home Secretary's approval, determines how many officers of each rank there should be and appoints a Chief Constable;
- the Chief Constable is responsible for the direction and control of the force;
- the Home Office determines the national policy and resources framework (though pay and conditions are the responsibility of the independently chaired Police Negotiating Board), authorises the establishment size for each authority, and through Her Majesty's Inspectorate of Constabulary, monitors efficiency and ensures that local forces conform with national standards and priorities.

The Home Office pays 51 per cent of recurrent expenditure through specific grants, with police authorities contributing the remaining 49 per cent. Two-thirds of the police authority are, by statute, councillors, while the remainder are magistrates, chosen by fellow magistrates in the area.

In recent years the exercise and control of police powers has become increasingly a matter of public concern. The police have been put under pressure by increasing crime and violence in society. Extensive new legislation, notably the Police and Criminal Evidence

Act 1984, has had a profound effect on operational procedures. The police have become more aware of and sensitive to shifts in public attitudes, and to the need to win public support for their approach to enforcement and prevention. The last few years have also seen a growing national and international dimension to many problems faced by the police, particularly drugs, fraud, terrorism, and organised crime.

The ambiguities of current arrangements put a premium upon the development of effective relationships between the police service and police authorities, against an increasingly controversial background of national policy debate. The effectiveness of a police force is not simply a matter of adequate provision of premises and equipment. Effective law enforcement and crime prevention covers a number of policy issues related to the use of resources and the way in which the law is applied. The police authority's responsibilities require at minimum an interest in, and understanding of, operational matters, and an awareness of police performance.

But the doctrine of police independence, whereby the function of the police is to enforce the law and maintain the Queen's peace, not to serve either local or national political interests, is fiercely defended by those who believe it to be a great strength of the British system that the police are both independent of political control and known by the public to have this independence. In Sir Robert Mark's words:

> A police chief in Britain serves five masters. The first, the criminal law which he is sworn to uphold and enforce impartially. The second, his police authority. The third, the men and women he commands, whose interests may not always coincide with those of his police authority, in financial matters, for example. The fourth, the people of the police district under his command, who look to him for security and tranquillity. The fifth — and most important — his conscience. For in Britain, policemen are not merely allowed to have consciences, they are required to have them. Their authority under the law is personal, as is their accountability.

This notably omits mention of central government. There is resistance both to the idea of a national police force (implying stronger central political control) and to the proposition that police authorities should have more control over the operations of their police forces and a statutory responsibility for law enforcement policy. Police accountability therefore remains something of a dilemma, depending less upon legal or constitutional definition than upon effective practice, based upon a relationship of trust and confidence between the Chief Constable and his police authority. The 1982 Scarman Report, quoting the then Home Secretary, William Whitelaw, described this in the following terms:

. . . police authorities should see themselves not just as providers of resources, but as a means whereby the chief constable can give account of his policing policy to the democratically elected representatives of the community, and in turn, they can express to him the views of the community on these matters.

In recent years, and influenced by the Scarman Report's emphasis on the need for consultation and explanation, several new initiatives have emerged to communicate police actions and policies to enlist public support. For example, the Police and Criminal Evidence Act requires that 'arrangements shall be made in each police area for obtaining the views of the people in that area about matters concerning the policing of the area, and for obtaining their cooperation with the police in preventing crime'. There is a new emphasis on visibility of police actions through lay visiting of police stations and the development of more responsive complaints procedures. Increasingly Chief Constables now set annual policy objectives and priorities after public consultation and with the agreement of the police authority. Force structures are increasingly oriented towards giving more responsibility to local police commanders so as to streamline management and tailor the service to the community. There is a growing recognition of mutual dependence between police forces and their communities. This is developing within the existing structure of police authorities, and is essential to effective policing.

Fire and Rescue Service

The provision of fire services is governed by the Fire Services Acts of 1947 and 1959, under which it is the duty of every fire authority to secure:

- *the services of a fire brigade to meet national standards of fire cover;*
- *training for fire brigade officers;*
- *arrangements for dealing with emergency calls;*
- *arrangements for providing fire prevention advice;*
- *assistance to neighbouring authorities in dealing with fires when called upon.*

In addition, an increasing proportion of the work of the Fire and Rescue Service is dealing with a wide range of non-fire emergencies, from cats in trees, to major road, rail and air disasters and spillage of hazardous chemicals.

National standards of fire cover determine the resources and time limit for response to a fire of a given speed and weight of attack. Response times have a significant impact upon the location of fire stations. Responsibility for funding rests with local authorities, to whom the Government makes a contribution through revenue support grant, based upon a central assessment of spending required for an acceptable level of service meeting national standards. Such standards are minima which fire authorities can and do exceed according to local choice. Local decisions on resources, including premises, tenders and other equipment, can have a major impact on effectiveness. Currently, for example, there is debate about updating communication and mobilising computer systems.

The Fire Service was last extensively reviewed in the Holroyd report of 1970. Holroyd was highly critical of small units and argued strongly for larger and more uniform areas under combined, rather than joint, authorities, for both operational and resource management reasons. Current operational circumstances continue to predicate services on a wider area base, whilst resource needs are more readily met by larger rather than smaller authorities.

The Magistrates' Courts Service

The Magistracy is a very old institution which for many centuries was synonymous with local government outside municipal boroughs. JPs lost their administrative functions to elected located authorities in 1888 and 1894, after which their role was purely that of carrying out local justice. Formal courts of summary jurisdiction were created in 1949; these are at the centre of the criminal justice process, dealing with 95 per cent of all criminal proceedings and channelling the remainder through to the Crown Courts.

As well as criminal cases (amounting to 80 per cent of total sitting time) they deal with high volumes of civil cases, particularly domestic issues, licence applications, and debt recovery. There are currently some 28,000 lay magistrates and 63 stipendiaries, appointed to one of 58 areas and assigned to a Bench covering one of 549 Petty Sessional Divisions, which are the catchment areas for court business. Courts in each area are run by Magistrates' Courts Committees, which typically draw heavily upon county council officers for committee support and financial advice. Councils also provide professional and technical support.

The 1949 Justices of the Peace Act introduced central government funding to what had previously been an entirely locally resourced system. Inclusion of the Magistrates Courts within the national criminal justice system was considered in the early 1970s but rejected by the Government. Instead the ratio of funding between local and central government was formalised at 20:80 respectively, and the Home Secretary acquired powers to regulate the running of the Service.

The Service has recently been re-examined in the Le Vay report, which concluded that national and local responsibilities were confused and that resource management arrangements were unsatisfactory. As a result, two models for the management of the service were proposed: a national service, in the form of a Next Steps Executive Agency at 'arms length' from the Home Office; or a set of regional boards, entirely funded by central government, directly managed and inspected by the Home Office.

However, it now seems certain that the Service will remain locally-based, managed through courts' committees of local magistrates, whose role is to be strengthened and clarified. The Government has also said that 'no immediate change is envisaged in the balance between central and local financing of the Service'. Though the present Home Secretary has described this decision as 'a substantial vote of confidence in resilience of local services and their ability to adapt to management demands', it is accompanied by a number of other changes, which, under the guise of modernisation and the achievement of consistent performance, are likely to increase the influence of central government in the management of the service.

Responsibility for the Service will be transferred to the Lord Chancellor's Department from 1 April 1992, bringing together the previously divided central government interest in the administration of the court system. An inspectorate reporting to the Lord Chancellor will be established 'to provide an effective audit of court administration and promote the spread of best practice'. For the first time, a Commons Ministerial post will provide for improved Parliamentary scrutiny of resource management issues and of the achievement of Citizen's Charter performance commitments. Previously the Lord Chancellor has been represented in the Commons by the Law Officers.

The Probation Service

The Probation of Offenders Act 1907 first gave Petty Sessional Divisions the right to appoint probation officers in their courts to supervise offenders within the community. At first the service was small and organised within very local units. Gradually as the practice expanded, arrangements became more formal and the 'friendly interest' of the Home Office developed into regular inspection and, finally, majority funding. Probation Committees today preside over 56 area probation services considerably larger and more complex than those originally envisaged.

The Probation Service has always been concerned with reducing the incidence of crime and related social breakdown, and with enabling offenders to achieve more satisfactory ways of life. The fundamental aim of probation remains to uphold the law and protect society by working with offenders within the community to understand and overcome the circumstances which have led to the offence, and thereby develop within the individual a sense of responsibility which will prevent re-offending.

However, the character of the service, and the volume, scope and variety of its work, have changed dramatically over the last 20 years. The service now has strong operational links with the Police, Social Services, and Education Departments, as well as a wide range of voluntary and statutory agencies, and is also responsible for:

- *providing information and advice to courts;*
- *undertaking the supervision of offenders subject to court orders;*
- *providing through-care to offenders during and after custody;*
- *operating in penal institutions;*
- *providing day care centres and hostels;*
- *running community service schemes.*

Recently the service has become increasingly involved in the community's wider response to offending, for example through participation in schemes providing through housing, education and employment for the diversion of offenders from the courts, in victim support work, and in new opportunities in the fields of preventative work, mediation and reparation. The close links between local authorities and probation committees arise partly because of dealings on individual cases and also because the local authority is the paying agent for the service's funds. In broad terms, expenditure in each area (counties outside metropolitan areas and outer London) is met by a direct grant of 80 per cent of costs from the Home Office and 20 per cent from local authorities.

The Probation Service is currently reaching the end of a period of some uncertainty. Forced amalgamation and a national service have been rejected in the light of an overwhelming response to the Government's Green Paper that what was required was a local service organised on a local basis. The government has decided that the service is to remain locally structured and partly funded by local authorities 'for the time being'. However, it is to operate within a framework of national standards, objectives and tasks. Committees will undergo a number of changes to strengthen policy making and budget management functions. Under the Criminal Justice Act 1991 cash limiting will be introduced and this will, in many cases, see a significant change in both structure and management methods in the 56 services as they adjust controls to meet new budgetary constraints. Now the Service has to manage a period of significant growth as it implements the policy of supervising more non-violent offenders in the community and focuses on 'at risk' groups, with a view to developing a role in crime prevention as well as offender supervision.

Key Issues

Crime prevention

A main finding of a recent Home Office Working Party on Safer Communities stated that 'crime prevention closely interrelates with many aspects of local government and the diverse elements of the criminal justice system'. A significant facet of work in this area has been the increasing adoption of a partnership approach between local government, the Police, Magistrates' Courts, Probation Service, the local business community and many voluntary and community organisations. Effective crime prevention cannot be achieved without the full cooperation of the community. Essential pre-requisites are therefore:

- *effective communication and coordination of activity;*
- *a common philosophy and understanding of community needs;*
- *an agreed approach to issues within the community;*
- *cost-effective service delivery, whether proactive or emergency reactive.*

Home Office work on 'Partnership in Crime Prevention' sets out six components of successful work in crime prevention:

- *A structure able to provide leadership and support, gather information, formulate local plans, and draw together organisations and individuals with the necessary skills.*
- *A leadership role clearly allocated to one individual or agency able to promote common goals, trust, and a cohesive approach.*
- *Accurate and up-to-date information supplied by the community itself.*
- *A special and distinctive identity for the work to which the community can relate and which clearly communicates the objectives of crime prevention and the reduction of fear.*
- *Durability based on community involvement.*
- *Clearly designated resources.*

There are increasing numbers of successful collaborative schemes (for example, the Northamptonshire interdependency group, the Cambridgeshire crime prevention coordinating group, the Northumbria coalition against crime, the Staffordshire Community Enterprise programme and the Gloucestershire crime reduction programme). Crime prevention is not just a matter for the police and central government. Cooperation between local agencies and local people, and a sound knowledge of local circumstances, are essential if the opportunities for crime are to be reduced.

Individual initiatives need to be implemented within a locally appropriate policy framework which takes a strategic view of wider contextual factors influencing crime, including economic and social deprivation and the physical environment. Such a framework needs to be evolved gradually, as relationships develop, and coterminosity between participating agencies undoubtedly helps. Project implementation, meanwhile, needs to be carried out directly in the community. Effective crime prevention thus requires structures compatible both strategically and operationally.

Local justice

There has long been an argument that the most equitable form of justice is local justice. Crime is predominantly a local phenomenon and the local environment clearly impacts upon it, both in terms of the kind of crime committed and the view the community takes of it. Ready access to the criminal justice system argues in favour of a community-based and local court structure. The lay magistracy derives from the locality; the tendency for it to be drawn from 'established' members of the community has led to efforts to make it more representative of the range of social groups. The historic links between the magistracy and local government reflect its local origins, as with those of the probation service. Local government also offers funding, purchasing power and professional and technical expertise.

Decisions in respect of both the Magistrates Courts Service and the Probation Service have recently demonstrated the continuing importance of local links in the delivery of community-based justice. Yet simultaneously they have exhibited the tension between this and the trend towards an overtly nationally directed system, in the name of more effective management and consistent performance. Both services have been shown to require effective strategic management over a wide geographic area, within which services are delivered locally.

In the case of the Probation Service, it has been recognised that there may need to be some area amalgamation, particularly where this would lead to the provision of a fuller range of services, or allow for improved managerial support. Changes to the Magistrates Courts Service may also produce 'a more coherent geographical structure' and larger areas. Were local government structure to move substantially in the opposite direction, this would lead to the break-up of current managerial and practical links, and could serve to shift the balance further towards national systems by providing the opportunity for further change.

Emergency planning

Since the advent of the cold war, local authorities have had a statutory duty to make provision for the possibility of Britain being involved in nuclear or conventional war. The emphasis of emergency planning has now changed towards a broader based approach, reflecting the reduced risk of nuclear and military conflict, and the need for better peacetime planning for civil emergencies.

Central government has recently recognised this shift in a wide-ranging review of current practice. The review found that though there is a considerable amount of planning taking place, its coordination is not guaranteed and quality is variable, leading to a perception that existing contingency planning is not adequate to cover the possible impact of a wider range of potential civil disasters. Particular short-comings have been identified in some metropolitan areas. The focus of civil defence planning is now to ensure that local authorities are able to continue to deliver the services for which they are responsible in peacetime in a wide range of possible civil emergencies. At a sub-cata-strophic level, proper planning is required for environmental damage and naturally occurring hazardous conditions, such as snow or flood.

The predominant characteristic of effective emergency planning and implementation is the securing of effective cooperation and coordina-tion of many agencies: local government, emergency services, the health service, local voluntary organisations, and private suppliers. Major disasters do not respect administrative boundaries, and experi-ence shows that planning and mobilisation are most effective when achieved over wide geographical areas, building on established con-tacts. The new emphasis on flexible and integrated approaches to peacetime emergency planning is an important development which the local government review will need to take into account in considering the requirements to be met by future structure.

Implications for local government structure

The nature of the relationship between local government and these four services might at first suggest that their operation and management could be wholly independent of local government structure. But it is naive to assume that breaking existing local links would not give rise sooner or later to wider questions about the balance between local and national accountability and control in these key areas.

Maintaining effective local relationships in the future will depend upon three things. Firstly, a flexible but consistent approach at the strategic level to resource allocation and policy priorities. Operational planning and management requires a stable policy and resource framework based on a shared understanding of community needs and an agreed response to a complex external environment.

Secondly, close working contacts at operational levels between professional organisations able to focus their effort on building effective relationships within compatible administrative structures and geographical areas. The partnership approach to community protection requires service organisations able jointly to plan strategy and tactics and maintain close links both with one another and with others such as the business community, the voluntary sector, and other public agencies.

Thirdly, cost-effective delivery of specialist support services. Provision of professional and technical support to protective agencies by local government is a longstanding arrangement based on history, legislation and economics. Local government has both enormous purchasing power and a pool of specialist resource which may be called upon as required. As financial responsibility moves from the 'supplier' to the 'customer' there has been more frequent use of formal arrangements, such as through service level agreements and other budgeting devices. Ultimately these services are likely to be provided on a competitive basis.

Future local government structure must be able to provide for this. Effective partnerships rest on common interests and goals, and must be put into practice at both strategic and operational levels. Partly because of their shared inheritance, the present structure of Home Office services and local government enjoy a high degree of conformity at a key decision-making level, which undoubtedly serves to promote and support effective partnership. The local government review creates the possibility that such conformity might not exist in the future. This would present a number of practical problems.

First, where the areas covered by successor local government authorities were smaller than those of protective agencies, joint boards would need to be created to agree the policy and resources framework and provide for local democratic input to decision-making. Though such boards can be made to work, they tend not to be as effective as single authorities as decision-makers. There are inevitably increased possibilities for disagreement and even for competition; smaller areas are less likely to sink their differences when considering issues in the wider public interest. Scope for differences in the application of national standards, specifications and terms and conditions would increase. Disagreement and corresponding discontent could either support a withdrawal of services from local democratic control or, at least, call into question the size and competence of the authorities comprising the joint boards. Neither scenario would amount to the stable policy and budgetary framework required for effective strategic planning.

Second, working contacts at operational levels would be more complex as a function of the larger number of local government representatives involved. The scope for confusion and delay arising from different policy and resource priorities from one authority to another would also be considerable. Once again parochial interests would tend to take precedence over wider considerations. Services protecting the community require a sophisticated and coordinated approach, and, if they are to command local support, must be seen to be effective and appropriate to community needs. Such an approach is undoubtedly facilitated (though not of course guaranteed) when agencies working at a local level have similar formal jurisdiction and understanding of local circumstances.

The consequences of new arrangements for delivery of support services would depend upon whether protective agencies were able to choose between competing authorities and between private and public sector sources of supply. The trend in this area is already towards greater self-sufficiency; structural change would increase this. Were present single-source arrangements to continue linked to joint board arrangements through a 'lead' authority, provision of highly specialised resources could be affected if the authority was unable economically to provide such people itself, or was unable to exert sufficient purchasing power to procure them cost-effectively externally.

Conclusions

There is a delicate balance to be struck between central and local government influence on community protection. The services' relationships with local government are currently close. Facilitated by better communications, the emphasis has moved more and more over the present century towards central policy making, national standards and national funding. Yet there is no overwhelming case for nationalisation. Local accountability remains important constitutionally and in practice, whether in the context of local justice and law enforcement, or in preventative approaches to crime. An awareness of local issues and of community feeling is increasingly important in the sensitive application of national policies, whilst effective local cooperation and coordination is at the heart of successful delivery of protective services on the ground. Equally, local priorities need to be understood and responded to in the context of the wider public interest.

Change in local government structure need not involve change in the internal organisation and management of protective services, though it may reopen, or intensify, the debate in individual areas about the creation of a national service. But it would involve changes in mechanisms for local policy making and resource control, in day-to-day contacts with local government, and in the provision of support services. Current relationships have become sophisticated in achieving a workable balance between the demands of each service, the national policy framework, and local priorities. The problems involved in the achievement of a successful partnership approach should not be under-estimated. Striking the right balance between the local and the national perspective requires authorities able to manage effectively in the context of a high level of complexity and uncertainty.

There is therefore no suggestion, much less evidence, that any new structure would create additional benefits in relation to effective community protection. Indeed, experience suggests that there would be substantial disadvantage in moving away from current relationships to any structure which involves a lack of conformity between protection agencies and local government authorities, and requires successor authorities of substantially different complexion to take on an increasingly demanding task.

Bibliography

Audit Commission 1991 *Going Straight: Developing Good Practice in the Probation Service.*

Day, P. and Klein, R. 1987 *Accountabilities: Five Public Services.*

Home Office Crime Prevention Unit 1990 *Safer Cities Progress Report 1989–1990* HMSO

Marshall, G. 1989 'The Police: independence and accountability' in Jowell, J. and Oliver, D. (eds) *The Changing Constitution.*

Home Office Press Releases:
  Reorganisation of Magistrates' Courts Service December 1991.
  Future of Emergency Planning July 1991.
  Reorganisation of Probation Service April 1991.

12 Protecting and enhancing the physical environment: the new challenge

> We are a part of the earth and it is a part of us. The perfumed flowers are our sisters; the deer, the horse, the great eagle, these are our brothers. The rocky crests, the juices of the meadows, the body heat of the pony, and man — all belong to the same family
>
> (Chief Seattle 1854)

Introduction

Historically, local government has been a major force for environmental protection, originating in the response to the problems of poverty, disease, crime and squalor which developed as industrialisation and urbanisation increased. Because of the way in which environmental issues were perceived, environmental services tended to be local in influence and functional in organisation and delivery.

A century later the consequences of industrial and economic growth continue to require an active and significant response from local government. Concern has developed over the countryside and the urban environment. But more radical still, perceptions of environmental problems have broadened as it has become more clearly understood that what individuals do in one time and place may affect other individuals, and other species, in other times and places. Thus pollution, rainforest destruction, species extinction, global warming, ozone depletion and many other instances of environmental degradation and damage are at once both global and local problems.

In this lies a new challenge, which presents a key issue for the review of local government structure. Winning hearts and minds to protect and enhance the environment requires local action based in the community, and reflecting local needs and local interests. Yet this community action must be galvanised within a full understanding of complex environmental interactions, and within a strategic policy framework that extends well beyond local geographical boundaries.

Technocracy and democracy must be combined to find solutions that will achieve the required environmental benefits and command public support in the localities where they take effect.

This chapter therefore considers the impact of the new environmental imperative upon local government's responsibilities and ways of operating. It develops a set of criteria to be applied in the review of local government structure to determine the geographical dimension and scale at which a response to environmental problems is most likely to be effective and appropriate, across the developing portfolio of local government's responsibilities. It then considers the implications of these criteria for future structure itself.

The environment: the new challenge

Local government has responded to environmental issues over many decades in many ways, reflecting changing needs and public concern. Its role in protecting and improving the environment originated 150 years ago in the public health movement and the response to the problems of the industrial revolution. A succession of Acts in the nineteenth century required and encouraged major public health and environmental improvements in, for example, sewerage, water supply services and housing, adding to historic functions such as weights and measures and rudimentary food standard controls. Such responsibilities have since expanded significantly to include consumer protection, modern food hygiene and safety, waste management, clean air and pollution, health and safety at work, and animal welfare. In addition, the period since the Second World War has seen the emergence of town and country planning as a major local government function, as pressure on land use has steadily increased.

As well as environmental responsibilities defined by statutory duties, local government has adopted over the years many discretionary powers to protect and enhance the more broadly defined environment. These have become increasingly important, reflecting local government's willingness to initiate action in the light of local circumstances and pressures. Often local initiative has led the wider policy debate. The mix of discretionary actions varies by locality, because of the potential for local experimentation, and the need for differences of emphasis, given varying local environmental conditions. The range of discretionary powers is extensive, e.g. conservation and recreation, urban heritage, archaeology, land reclamation and environmental education.

Key issues

Anxiety about changes in the physical environment and concern about the quality of life have taken a steep change in the last half of the

1980s. They have generated a new and more formidable imperative for the twenty-first century. Major man-made disasters have caused some to question the environmental cost of aspirations to continued economic growth, and have shown clearly that disasters do not respect national frontiers. Some examples illustrate the point: in December 1984, methyl isocyanate leaked from a storage plant in Bhopal killing 2,000 people and affecting a further 200,000. An explosion and fire at the Chernobyl nuclear reactor in April 1986 caused 135,000 people to be evacuated and consequent radiation releases were detected in Scandinavia and the UK. In November 1986, thirty tons of toxic pesticide were washed into the Rhine during fire fighting at the Sandoz chemical plant, killing hundreds of thousands of fish.

At the same time a new international policy agenda has been created through action to protect the global environment. In 1987 the Montreal Protocol set the first international limits on the production and consumption of environmentally damaging products, in this case ozone-depleting substances. It has since been ratified by over 60 countries. In 1988 the international community set up the Inter-Governmental Panel on Climate Change to study the science of climate change, to consider its impact upon the world, and to identify appropriate strategies to tackle the problem. There has been a growing appreciation that environmental damage can be insidious, affecting the sustainability of the planet itself in ways which often cannot be anticipated.

Alongside increasing awareness of global issues, there is also growing public awareness and concern about the environmental and quality of life characteristics of both residential and business areas. Changing patterns of development (including settlement patterns) reflect environmental concerns. They also exercise a significant influence on the local and regional environmental issues which local government has to confront. In contrast to the trends of the previous century, residential decentralisation gained momentum during the 1960s and 1970s. It has continued in the 1980s with net population migration from metropolitan to non-metropolitan areas. Some of the key factors influencing this continuing trend have been:

- difficulties in maintaining urban infrastructure to meet the demands placed upon it, with consequent environmental degradation, particularly increased transport-related air pollution;
- increased demand for improved low-density, small-town or rural environments (creating new development pressures in the Green Belt and in some rural areas);
- and new enabling technology allowing economic activity to be conducted in small, relatively dispersed units.

Various studies have aimed to identify the key environmental factors which affect people's assessment of their quality of life. These include air and noise pollution, crime (particularly against the person), urban design, open space and cleanliness, and accessibility to services, particularly cultural and entertainment facilities. A selection of indicators bears out the impression of increasing environmental concern during the last decade. For example:

- complaints about domestic noise (per million population) rose tenfold in the twelve years to March 1988;
- membership of the National Trust, Greenpeace, Friends of Earth and the World Wildlife Fund rose from 1.5 million in 1985 to 2.8 million in 1990;
- over half of the respondents in a 1990 survey were prepared to pay a premium of 13.3p in £1 for 'green' food products;
- nearly 60 per cent of London residents believed that the quality of life in 1990 was worse compared with 5–10 years ago.

As consumers have become more environmentally alert, so too has the business community. The 1990 CBI/PA survey of 250 companies found that fewer than 15 per cent considered the environment to be of only marginal importance. Air pollution was identified as particularly important across all business sectors, exceeding by a considerable margin concern about other environmental issues such as hazardous chemicals, river pollution and solid waste. Four-fifths of the surveyed companies considered that local authorities were an important influence on business corporate behaviour. Other important influences were, in descending order, the local community, national pressure groups, the media, and local pressure groups. These results illustrate not only general environmental awareness, but also the influence that local interests have on businesses, particularly in view of the important role attributed to the local community and local pressure groups as well as to local authorities.

Such changes raise significant questions in relation to the objectives and performance required from many local services. Urban and rural planning, including management of the interface between urban and rural areas, environmental health, waste management, recreation and leisure, housing and transport increasingly require a strategic approach. This is because of the need to respond to growing awareness of environmental degradation, to influence the pace and direction of the continued shift away from urban areas, and to provide for its social and economic consequences.

In all these areas of policy, the impact on the environment is at more than just local levels, and is of growing technical complexity. Some authorities, especially those responsible for inner urban areas, are faced with major problems in the scale and nature of their inherited environmental conditions, from their changing population mix, and as a result of the lack of mechanisms (institutional, procedural and appraisal) for handling severe environmental conditions. More generally, authorities are constrained by the limited human and financial resources available to address these complex problems.

Local government's future environmental role

The consequences of all these developments for local government's future role in protecting and enhancing the physical environment are fourfold. First, the policy focus is at one level increasingly international. The extent and scale of environmental damage is seen to be so great, and the need to avoid 'beggar my neighbour' policies so important, that effective solutions are often seen to depend on actions at supranational level. Key issues of ozone depletion, global warming, acid rain and biological diversity are all being addressed through international negotiations.

As this process gathers momentum, the agenda of environmental issues dealt with at this level is likely to be extended. In the CBI/PA survey, for example, over 50 per cent referred to national government legislation, corporate social responsibility, and European Community legislation as the 'drivers' of environmental performance. The report concluded that 'the survey demonstrates an awareness of the way in which environmental legislation will in future be framed at a European level, implemented nationally, and enforced by local authorities' (CBI/PA 1990).

Secondly, the emergence of new environmental issues at the national and international level is leading to increasing interaction between different areas of policy and between different agencies of government. For example, waste management and recycling, land-use and transport planning must take account of global warming and other environmental effects, and will bring local government into contact with an ever larger network of government and other agencies. In one way, therefore, whilst local problems are increasing in complexity, local policy discretion and autonomy in formulating a response is decreasing.

Yet, thirdly, enhanced environmental awareness has also led to renewed emphasis on local issues. Individuals and business organisations have been alerted both to the global effects of their own actions and to the quality of their immediate working and living environment — the countryside, the urban form, congestion, pollution, litter and noise — and the consequences of individual behaviour for its present and future state. So, in another sense, the policy focus is moving towards the development of local action to bring together individuals and organisations through local community effort.

Fourthly, the sheer complexity of many environmental issues, and the relative lack of experience in what is still a developing policy area, require the location of policy responsibilities in units of government able to command properly qualified resources and able to demonstrate credibility in dealing with difficult problems. Increasing importance is being attached, at both European and national levels, to the need for full environmental appraisal as an integral part of the policy process.

Environmental assessments of individual projects are now enshrined in legislation. Strategic environmental assessments for plans, policies and programmes are the subject of national and European debate. Methods for assessing the environmental impact and for valuing environmental benefits and costs are sophisticated. They require specialist scientific and technical expertise to ensure that environmental effects are fully identified and evaluated. For example, better sewage processing improves river quality, but uses more energy and creates more sludge, which in turn exacerbates landfill problems and increases sources of toxicity. Similarly, determining the value attached to an environmental improvement such as a visual amenity requires complex and potentially costly analysis.

Environmental monitoring after a decision is equally important to ensuring that policy objectives are achieved. This requires systematic collection of scientifically reliable data. Monitoring may also lead to the need to review or change policies. For example, workers in Athens were restricted to using their cars every other day, in order to reduce the city's severe air pollution problems. But monitoring demonstrated that, not only had pollution not improved, it had become worse; workers had evaded the control by buying a second, older car which was therefore less efficient in terms of emissions. An example closer to home is the need, unforeseen a decade ago, to monitor landfill gas build-up and emissions at waste disposal sites.

To summarise, the environmental challenge facing local government is to respond to:

- a steadily widening and increasingly interactive national and international policy debate about global environmental problems;
- much higher awareness of environmental issues and expectations of environmental improvement in local communities amongst both the general public and business organisations;
- an increasingly sophisticated technical requirement for comprehensive and systematic environmental appraisal and monitoring.

Local government's environmental responsibilities

The 'physical environment' covers a wide range of issues and concerns, the boundaries of which are difficult to define precisely. Traditionally and most obviously, it includes land use, transport, the countryside and the built environment. But this is to exclude important local government environmental functions such as pollution prevention and waste management. It also overlooks the wider role of providing advice and information on environmental issues, as well as satisfying the obligations resting upon local authorities, as upon all organisations and individuals, to consider the environmental consequences of their day to day operations. This chapter therefore takes a broad definition of the 'physical environment', from global warming to dogs' excrement.

The developing policy agenda in the UK has recently been embodied in national legislation and regulation, in the Environmental Protection Act 1990 and especially in commitments in the Government's White Paper on the Environment *This Common Inheritance* (Cm 1200). The implications of this national policy framework for local government are shown in the Appendix to this chapter. European Community Regulations and Directives are also becoming increasingly important as the Community's role in environmental policy develops, along with that of supporting institutions.

The allocation of functions and responsibilities between local and central government and other relevant authorities is complex. For simplicity, seven broadly different types of local government activity are distinguishable:

- pollution control, where local government effectively implements the legislation and regulations of the UK Parliament and the EC;
- maintenance of public health and safety and trading standards, where local government is again largely responsible for implementing UK and EC legislation;
- waste regulation and management, where local government operates within an overall framework provided by Parliament and central government;
- strategic land-use and transport planning and control, which are a matter for local discretion within a broad centrally defined framework; and local development control and plans, where there is likewise considerable local discretion within the framework defined centrally and within local strategic plans;
- heritage conservation and promotion;
- operational management of the authority (such as purchasing policy) to minimise its impact on the environment;
- education, information provision, publicity and lobbying to raise awareness of environmental concerns and to promote an appropriate response.

Table 13.1 summarises the current allocation of responsibilities between the different tiers of local government. In most cases, the responsibilities are shared.

Though current responsibilities must be a starting point for consideration of future structure, it is important for the review of local government to recognise that these are likely to alter in nature and scope. What is required is less a preoccupation with the detail of existing responsibilities, than some forward thinking over the longer term about the institutional arrangements needed to develop and deliver successful environmental policies. The key parameters for the review are therefore:

- the degree of discretion enjoyed by local government within the developing policy framework; and
- the geographical incidence of the environmental impact of local government activity.

It would be wrong to assume that local government's scope is entirely constrained within the regulatory framework, despite increasing national and inter-national interest. Authorities can, and do, achieve much to ensure that regulation and legislation can be oriented towards local interests both at the policy formulation stage and subsequently in the practicalities of implementation and enforcement. Notable examples are implementation of pollution control, waste management and land-use planning legislation. In other cases, local government's activities are more discretionary with few, if any, specific constraints on its activities from higher levels of government. Examples are those intended to educate and inform the public about environmental issues, those relating to the operational management of individual authorities, and those concerning heritage and conservation. Innovative action at local levels has frequently proved a spur to national action.

Activity	Counties	Districts
Pollution control		✓
Public health and safety		✓
Trading standards	✓	
Waste regulation and management	✓	
Strategic land-use and transport planning	✓	
Local development control		✓
Heritage conservation and promotion	✓	✓
Operational management	✓	✓
Education, information provision, publicity	✓	✓

Table 13.1: Allocation of local government environmental responsibilities

It is also misleading to assume that local government has only local impact geographically. Activities fall into three broad categories.

Firstly, actions likely to have a direct and localised environmental impact such that cause and effect can be readily identified at the most local level. Pollution control and environmental health and safety services and regulation fall into this category.

Second, actions likely to be more than local in their environmental impact such that cause and effect are not totally confined to the local level and cannot be understood exclusively at this level. Waste regulation (but not collection) falls into this category. So too do land use and transport planning (legislatively specified) and discretionary actions to promote particular types of land use (including heritage, conservation and recreation policies).

Third, actions likely to have wider, national or even global environmental impacts such that cause and effect may be barely discernible at the local level. In this category are operational management actions (purchasing practice, vehicle fleet and building management).

Education, information provision, publicity and lobbying could impact at any level.

As Table 13.2 shows, the majority of local government's activity impacts beyond the immediate locality.

A key issue for the future, and hence for the review, is how far policy initiatives will continue to be taken below national and supranational levels. Functions and responsibilities will inevitably change in the future as environmental policy develops, as will the institutional framework. For example, a new Environmental Protection Agency is proposed by the Government to bring together the pollution control responsibilities of HMIP and the NRA with the waste regulation func-

Degree of local government discretion	Incidence of geographical impact		
	Local ⟶ ⟶ ⟶		Global
	Educational, information provision, lobbying		
High	Heritage conservation		Operational management
	Land-use and transport planning and controls		
	Public health and safety	Waste regulation and management	
Low	Pollution control		

Table 13.2: Categorisation of local government's environmental activities

tions of local government. This would have a significant impact on the nature of the regulatory regime. Some indication of the breadth of response is given by the Government's recent 'First Year Report' on its Environmental Strategy, which reports on 400 measures taken and sets out over 400 commitments for future action, many of which will involve local government both directly and indirectly.

New themes currently emerging from the policy debate to which local government will be expected to make a significant contribution in the near future are:

- the requirement to secure environmentally sustainable economic development;
- the need to achieve closer integration between land-use and transport planning at the strategic level, to influence and reduce the future need for travel;
- the need to achieve a less environmentally damaging balance between private car and public transport and between personal and energy-based movement, especially in urban areas;
- the increasing emphasis on the need to integrate environmental considerations into agriculture and food production, and to encourage the retention of traditional farming practices to maintain species and landscapes;
- the more demanding standards and increasingly sophisticated techniques in waste management, with more emphasis on waste minimisation and realisation of recycling opportunities;
- the development of countryside strategies which address the economic well-being of rural areas, which integrate conservation and recreation needs, and which draw upon private and voluntary, as well as public, effort and resources;
- the need for better understanding at both a specialist and general level of environmental processes and interactions, and of the underlying science.

The trends already identified towards the internationalisation of policy, mobilisation of local action and increasing technical sophistication are likely to continue. The environmental pressures on local government are likely to become more intense as the legislative and regulatory load increases. Yet there is a continuing need to mobilise and develop support for effective action in local communities and beyond. It will not always be appropriate to adopt a uniform or centralised approach. Good practice locally will continue to be an important source of innovation and a continuing influence on wider policy development. But the resources available to local government with which to mount an effective response will be constrained. The next section looks at ways in which local authorities are already developing their structure, processes and style of environmental management in response to these challenges.

Changing approaches to environmental management

Chapter 2 argued that 'enabling' authorities are 'focused above all on meeting the needs of local communities in the most effective way'. This implies serving many diverse interests even within quite small geographical areas. It also emphasises the importance of ensuring that 'local needs are viewed within a wider policy context, and, conversely, that policy-making within other agencies and at other levels of government is fully informed by local experience and local diversity'. The 'enabling' role is likely to become more demanding in the case of environmental protection and enhancement.

Historically, the environmental functions of local government tended to be local in their influence and provided as discrete components of policy. Environmental issues were perceived as primarily local. They were embodied in incremental legislation giving discrete tasks and responsibilities to different parts of local government, and also reflected in discretionary action responsive to local needs and pressures.

Current concerns about the environment require a more broad-based response. Environmental impacts now extend to global survival and across generations. They are the outcome of complex interactions between the man-made and natural environments. Yet, at the same time global problems need local solutions — winning hearts and minds through local community action. There is a strong consensus that local government's enabling role with regard to protection of the environment will need to be corporate, permeating the life of the authority.

The local authority associations pointed out that effective environmental management 'is more an approach than a distinct aspect of local government. It permeates all aspects of local government and because a local authority's environmental consumers or clients are the whole community, a corporate approach is vital (ACC, ADC, AMA 1990).

The Audit Commission (1991) recommended that 'authorities should develop corporate policies for delivery of environmental health services'.

The Association of Metropolitan Authorities (1989) concluded that 'where control and discretion can be exercised, corporate strategies need to be developed within and across authorities so that the impact on improving the quality of life and conserving what is good can be maximised'.

The Local Government Training Board (1990) emphasised that 'environmental issues must permeate the life of the authority so that environmental factors are taken into account in all decision-taking because the issues are genuinely corporate'.

Equally, effective environmental management should permeate the life of the authority in all its enabling modes of operation. Regulatory responsibilities are bound to become more extensive as further legislation is passed at national and European Community levels. The requirements for implementation of legal requirements are also likely to become more exacting as the effectiveness of local authorities is monitored more closely by the public, consumers and pressure groups.

In addition, local authorities are likely to have to work even more with and through others as well as acting through direct service provision to facilitate, stimulate and influence environmental improvement. Many modes of action will be available. As Chapter 2 made clear, actions can include:

- acting in collaboration with other agencies to promote new ventures;
- creating new bodies with others or unilaterally;
- providing grant support or services in kind to other bodies in support of their activities;
- using purchasing power to influence suppliers;
- publicising issues and providing information;
- bringing individuals or groups together to promote community debate and action; and
- influencing other bodies and public opinion through advisory and policy-making groups.

The local authority associations (1990) identified the foundations of good environmental practice to be corporate in nature in that 'they span all service areas; they relate equally to a local authority's influence as a service provider and regulator, as an enabler and as a major user of resources; most importantly, given the interconnected nature of environmental aims, they are of greatest value when developed and applied consistently across an authority'.

Effective environmental management is not simply an additional factor to be bolted on to the delivery of local government's existing mix of policies and allocation of resources. It is more fundamental as a motivator of change. The elevation of environmental protection and enhancement as a local government priority will affect the mix of interests which it serves and is likely to create new political pressures to which it will accordingly have to respond. Specialist environmental groups are likely to become more powerful in the influence they can exert. For example, Friends of the Earth produced 'The Environmental Charter for Local Government — practical recommendations' in 1989. It provided a declaration of commitment for local authorities and contained 193 recommendations for good environmental practice, span-ning all local government functions. Its influence has been significant in the development of environmental policy and management in local government, guiding its approach to environmental audit.

Furthermore, acceptance by an authority of its broader responsibilities will require it to consider action similarly broad in scope, since it is not required by legislation, nor by specifically local environmental priorities, nor even dictated by narrow value for money considerations. A good example of this is the action taken by about 20 per cent of authorities who have schemes to encourage and facilitate the recovery and recycling of CFCs (ozone depleting substances) from domestic refrigerator disposals (Department of Trade and Industry 1990). Of the 39 English County Councils, 29 now have a CFC recovery scheme, according to a Friends of the Earth study (1991).

Internal change

In order to make the most effective use of limited resources and to bring consistency to environmental policies and actions throughout an authority, local government has increasingly turned to environmental audits, charters and strategies/action plans with cross-authority committees, working groups and/or units to coordinate the work. The County Planning Officers' Society has produced two surveys of County Council environmental initiatives — in January 1990 and August 1991. The surveys covered County Councils and two National Parks, the Lake District and the Peak District. The 1991 survey revealed that more Counties have completed (20 per cent) or started (37 per cent) in-house audits than have completed or started external audits (9 per cent and 15 per cent respectively). This result is not surprising. Internal audits are likely to be simpler and more immediately relevant ('putting your own house in order') than external audits. It also showed that, contrary to expectations, an expansion in external audits has not yet materialised 'almost certainly due to the better understanding of both the terminology and the task involved which has developed over the past 18 months'.

To manage the implementation of new environmental initatives, the majority of survey respondents revealed a preference for special inter-departmental arrangements. About half the respondents have established an environmental unit. Nearly 40 per cent propose to recruit new staff in addition to redeploying existing resources. In terms of outputs, the survey revealed that 75 per cent of respondents have either completed or started environmental charters whilst rather fewer (43 per cent) have completed or started environmental strategies or action plans.

The London Research Centre has reviewed the environmental poli-

	County councils %	London boroughs* %
Appraisal		
Internal audit		
• completed	20	} 45
• started	37	
External audit/state of the environment report		
• completed	9	} 12
• started	15	
Practice		
Cross department working party	78	70
Environmental unit	48**	6
Green forum	39	36
Policy		
Environmental charter	57	30
Environmental strategy		
• completed	13	51
• started	30	24

Notes: *The London Research Centre will be producing revised figures in the light of reactions to these published figures.
**The 48 per cent refers to environmental units in existence or proposed.

Sources: County Planning Officers' Society 1991, London Research Centre 1991

Table 13.3: Environmental appraisal, practices and policies: County Councils and London Boroughs

cies and practices of the London Boroughs. The results are compared (where possible) with the findings of the survey of the Counties in Table 13.3. There are clear similarities in the level and nature of the efforts being made by the Counties and the London Boroughs, the former being somewhat further ahead in external auditing, establishing environmental units and setting out environmental charters. There are as yet no similar systematic data on environmental initiatives and their implementation at district level, although a survey is in progress.

External changes

In addition to establishing corporate mechanisms for dealing with environmental issues, local government is having to work with a much greater variety of other agencies than ever before to develop and deliver its environmental strategies and actions. In its report on environmental health services, for example, the Audit Commission (1991) observed that, even for this one aspect of local government action on the environment, there was a 'complex web of public protection'. It identified 11 agencies or groups of agencies with which environmental health officers had to relate within the web or network of public protection. The picture would have been even more complex if the Audit Commission's remit had extended to the wider environment concerns of local government addressed in this paper. Figure 13.1 illustrates the extent of this network. Protection and enhancement of the environment through local government action involves complex and varied relations with other agencies, many of whom have regional or national terms of reference. Increasingly, policy, even in respect of local issues, is being addressed within a national or even international framework.

Implications for future structure

Criteria for an effective environmental response

It will be clear from the above that the environmental pressures to which local government will need to respond are extensive, diverse and onerous. An effective response will depend upon local government being able to devise policies and actions which:

- meet the needs and interests of local communities;
- are technically effective as solutions to environmental problems;
- do not impose undue economic and financial costs;
- are acceptable to all interested parties and command local, and where appropriate, wider support.

In broad terms, therefore, these are the requirements which future local government structure should support. They are explained in more detail below.

Meeting Community needs

Local government firstly must have a clear duty to act. It is already obliged to implement aspects of European Community and UK legislation which are intended to sustain or improve environmental quality. These obligations are likely to become more important in the future for the reasons already identified. However, in fulfilling them, local government will need to ensure that the regulations are drafted in the light of local experience and then implemented effectively and efficiently. It will wish to respond in general to the needs of local communities, and in particular those organisations subject to regu-

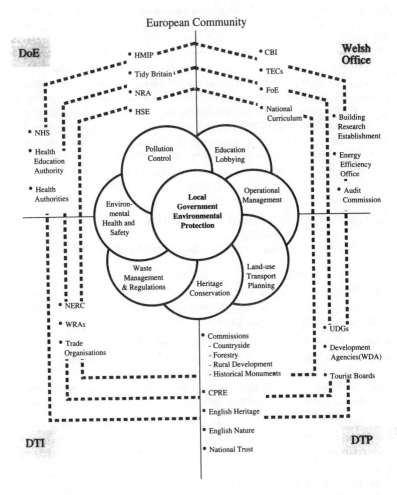

Note: The complex network of environmental protection agencies depicted here is not necessarily complete — e.g. with the exception of the European Community, no other international agencies (such as UNEP) are included; similarly the representation of voluntary agencies is limited (e.g. the Groundwork Trusts are not included).

Figure 12.1: The complex network of environmental protection for local government

lation. Its scope for doing so, however, will depend on how much local discretion it has. For example, within the overall framework for strategic land-use planning, local government presently enjoys considerable discretion as to the appropriate balance between environmental and other considerations. In some other aspects of environmental regulation, such as the implementation of 'BATNEEC', local government has much less discretion. The chosen mode of response to community feelings and preferences will vary accordingly.

Where local government has more discretion to act, a key influence must be local public priorities (customer and consumer led) reflected in political priorities. The perceived balance between the benefits of environmental action and the costs will be an important consideration. The principal factors driving a response will be:

- ability to take effective action to address a particular concern;
- the geographical incidence of the resulting environmental benefits;
- where appropriate, the associated economic costs.

Technical effectiveness

Current experience and practice suggests that the ability to take effective action to protect and improve the quality of the environment depends on the following considerations:

- access to the financial and technical resources needed to:
  — understand the nature of the environmental problem;
  — assess the (potential) environmental impact of particular policies, programmes and projects;
  — monitor compliance with environmental legislation and regulations;
  — respond speedily and effectively to environmental disasters and emergencies;
- ability to identify and adopt technically effective solutions, in part through familiarity with 'best practice';
- the existence of an institutional structure which allows:

  — environmental considerations to be integrated with other policy issues facing local government;
  — coordination between local authorities;
  — effort to be focused on priority issues.

Costs

Technically effective actions need to be weighed against their associated economic costs. Potentially, these will be diverse in nature and include not only those borne directly by local government but also those imposed on the individuals and businesses in the community. They will also include tangible financial costs as well as other costs which are more difficult to identify and value. For example, where appropriate, consideration will need to be given to the impacts on business competitiveness, and to the opportunity cost associated with devoting local government resources to environmental activities.

Acceptability

The acceptability of local government's response to environmental pressures and, in particular, its ability to command the support of interested parties will depend upon several factors:

- whether local government is the policy maker or the implementer of central government or EC policy;
- the extent to which local government's functions and actions either involve meeting nationally recognised standards or reflect local responses to local needs;
- the degree to which the environmental impact is locally confined and significant;
- whether a diversity of interests exists and a range of conflicting concerns must be resolved;
- whether there are potential conflicts of interest within local government because it is both:

  — a practitioner and the regulator;
  — the inspection/enforcement authority and the advisor.

Implications for structure

In relation to environmental issues, the review of local government structure should take a longer term view across a changing and multiple portfolio of possible environmental activities and actions. The relevance of each of the criteria identified above will vary according to the nature of the activity. Equally, the implications of each criterion for the most appropriate spatial level (or levels) at which the actions should be defined and implemented vary across the entire range of possible activities. If current and potential activity is considered in isolation, different spatial levels may emerge as most appropriate for effective protection of each particular aspect of the environment. For this reason, it is more helpful to the review's task to combine activities into more homogenous groupings, reflecting local government's roles in the environmental field more generally:

- regulatory activities, which local government pursues to fulfil its role as the enforcement and planning agency or authority; and
- discretionary activities, where local government is less constrained by either central government or the European Community and where the stimulus to action is the needs of local communities.

However, the distinction between the two groups is not entirely clearcut in practice. Regulatory activities may involve considerable discretion in terms of the approach used. Conversely, local government's discretionary activities, such as education, information provision and publicity across the breadth of environmental issues, initiatives to 'green' an authority's own operations, heritage conservation and promotion, recycling initiatives and the development and implementation of land use and transport policy, may involve operating within a framework defined by another tier of government.

Regulatory activities

Consideration of the criteria set out above suggests that to determine the most appropriate structure of local government for ensuring or enabling the cost-effective and efficient delivery of regulatory services is not straightforward. Simple concern with the (environmental) effectiveness of regulation suggests that it is best undertaken by units which are close to the organisations and/or individuals to be regulated. This is because such closeness:

- encourages greater responsiveness to local needs;
- enables the regulatory authority to develop a better understanding of the potential and/or actual problem areas;
- allows 'better' communication with the regulated organisations so that their requirements can be better understood;
- is more suited to the development of specialist knowledge of particular geographical areas, though not necessarily specific industry sectors or pollution problems;
- permits priority areas and uses to be more readily identified.

Ensuring these benefits can be achieved is a matter for decentralised administration and management; it does not in itself necessarily require devolved government.

On the other hand, there are other factors, partly to do with effectiveness but particularly to do with cost, which suggest that the regulatory activities would be better undertaken by larger units of government. Specifically, larger units of local government would be better placed to:

- establish and make effective use of the specialist skills and equipment needed to implement regulations relating to environmental protection and to handle the diversity of environmental issues and emergencies which arise;

- provide the working conditions and career prospects needed to attract and retain the 'critical skills' needed to undertake the specialist work;
- develop and implement mechanisms for ensuring that environmental considerations can be properly integrated into the other policy issues facing local government;
- ensure that there is effective communication and coordination between local authorities and with central government or the EC, so that regulations are enforced consistently.

Together, these mean that the costs to the authority of providing regulatory services are likely to be minimised. In addition, provided that they are effective in ensuring that regulation is implemented more fairly, consistently and practically, larger units of local government will help to reduce the costs to business and other organisations of complying with environmental regulation.

Where local government enjoys significant amounts of discretion in implementing the regulatory framework, this must be used to balance the needs of the wider community against the local impact on the environment. This raises the issue of the most appropriate level of local government to achieve this, taking into account the incidence of environmental impact.

In the case of land-use and transport planning, for example, larger authorities would be better placed to deal with the political and strategic issues involved, because the impacts often affect large areas. In other cases, most notably perhaps the implementation of trading standards and pollution control legislation, local government's discretion is more limited. Thus, it has little need or scope to balance the diversity of interests which exists. Instead, the structure of local government and the designation of responsibilities need to ensure that there is no (obvious) conflict of interest such that an authority is obligated to regulate itself, for example. This may call into question the justification for it remaining a local government function at all. But, whatever the policy authority, there would still need to be a local organisation responsible for the enforcement procedure, to achieve necessary 'closeness' to the regulated.

Discretionary activities

Local government's discretionary activities can conveniently be split into three groups:

- those where local government develops and implements a series of

projects, programmes and policies intended to provide effective environmental protection and enhancement (e.g. heritage and conservation);
- those where local government informs the local community about environmental issues and, in particular, seeks to influence its response to them (e.g. environmental education); and
- those associated with ensuring that the authority's direct impact on the environment is as benign as it can reasonably be (e.g. through corporate policy on purchasing).

The starting point is to consider local government's possible motivation for pursuing environmental actions. As already noted, a key influence over whether or not an authority pursues an environmental initiative is the perceived balance between the benefits of action and the associated costs, taking account of environmental, economic and social considerations, in the context of public pressure through the political process. Within the framework of political priorities, authorities will tend to respond principally to those environmental pressures where the benefits of taking action accrue within their boundaries, and/or some part of the costs can be transferred outwith their local boundaries.

An implication of this is that small authorities — such as parishes — will tend to focus their efforts on issues where the benefits of environmental action are very specific to the area, such as litter. Larger authorities, however, will tend to contemplate more activities because:

- more of the benefits will be retained within the authority;
- some measure of the costs can be passed on to others outside the authority;
- the unit costs of action will be reduced as economies of scale are realised.

Thus, a larger authority will be more willing to stimulate other actions, such as recycling initiatives, as well as those which a very small authority might undertake, and it will be more likely that environmental issues with a wider spatial impact will be acted upon. This raises the important issue of the level at which local government's response represents effective environmental protection.

Potentially, local government's role as an educator and influencer will also have a pervasive influence on the environment. Already, individual local authorities have launched initiatives aimed at promoting a more effective contribution to environmental managment by the individuals, organisations and business in the local community. The breadth of issues addressed by authorities is extensive and embraces issues where the environmental impact is global as well as those where it is more local.

Local government's willingness to 'green' operational and management procedures will be largely independent of its structure. Potentially, all authorities regardless of their size can improve their purchasing procedures to make them more environmentally friendly. Larger organisations have greater purchasing power and can minimise costs, for example, of 'environmentally friendly' procurement, but such an advantage is relatively small in terms of effective environmental protection.

This analysis suggests that the structure of local government bears directly upon local government's effectiveness in fulfilling discretionary roles. The importance of discretionary action in protecting and enhancing the environment makes it essential that this aspect of local government's functions should be included in the Commission's review. Given limited resources, larger authorities are more likely to deal with issues where the environmental impact is felt over a wider area, whereas smaller authorities will tend to focus on more localised concerns. There are further differences in terms of:

- the likely environmental effectiveness of any action;
- the associated costs — both direct and indirect;
- acceptability to the interested parties.

Table 13.4 summarises the main differences between the three types of discretionary activity against the evaluation criteria set out earlier in the chapter. Inevitably, judgement and generalisation are needed. Nonetheless, the analysis suggests that a structure of local government comprising larger units is likely to be a more effective means of providing environmental protection.

Conclusions

As the world becomes more environmentally intelligent, it is becoming clearer that fewer impacts can be seen as purely local. Even highly localised action can have a global effect. To develop an effective response, and resolve conflicts across wider areas, the system of local government must be capable of acting simultaneously at a broad enough level to take on a wide range of functional responsibilities, and at a narrow enough level to develop familiarity with local conditions and harness local interests and commitment.

Future structure must enable local government to devise environmental policies and actions which:

- meet community needs;
- are technically effective;
- are cost effective;
- command support.

Evaluation Criteria	Discretionary activities		
	Project and policy development (e.g. heritage conservation)	Education, Information provision, lobbying	Operational management (e.g. purchasing)
Responsiveness to community needs	Essentially independent of local government structure		
Effectiveness in protecting the environment:			
— scope for local government action of local government unit	Depends on actions of other tiers of government but increases with the scale		Independent of local government structure
— access to resources	Larger units better able to support specialist resources needed for effective policy	Larger units enjoy better leverage and influence	Slightly favours larger units
— ability to identify and adopt 'best practice'	Favours larger authorities because easier communication	Slightly favours larger units	Favours larger units
— appropriate institutional structure	Larger units likely to have better policy making capability	Slightly favours small number of larger authorities	Independent of structure
Costs of environmental protection:			
— direct	Largely independent of structure	Economics of scale favour larger units	Independent of structure
— indirect	Policies of larger units likely to be more soundly based and less distorting	Independent of structure because all responses are voluntary	Independent of structure
Acceptability:	Larger units more likely to handle issues with wider spatial impact		
— localised environmental impact		Slightly favours larger units of local government	Not relevant
— diversity of interests	Smaller units may respond to specific local concerns	Larger units likely to handle more different and conflicting interests	Not relevant

Table 13.4: Evaluation of discretionary activities

The extent to which local government is wholly free to determine its response will vary in the future, as it does now. As national and international interest and institutions develop in the environmental area, the likelihood of constraint and regulation may increase. Yet it is essential to integrate local needs, interests and actions within wider policies, if they are to be effective.

Whatever the nature of the wider policy framework, purely regulatory functions will be more effective if carried out close to the organisation or individual to be regulated, for the reasons set out above. However, this may not require smaller units of government as long as there are effective devolved management structures within larger units. Skill requirements and communication needs suggest that there are advantages in larger units.

Where the national or international framework assumes higher levels of local discretion, the key issue is to align responsibility with the scale of environmental impact. Larger authorities will increase the likelihood of a response addressing issues with a wider impact; smaller authorities will tend to focus on more localised concerns. Environmental management is more likely to be effective where its organisation is geographically bounded in a way which coincides with the incidence of environmental impact.

The need for balance between a broad-based strategic approach, and effective local action, has influenced the conclusions drawn by many commentators in this field. For example, the Local Government Training Board (1990) observed that:

- a local authority . . . provides a focus for community participation and involvement . . . No environmental programme will succeed unless it is community based.
- a centre of scientific excellence in each county would give the regional support and coordination to the district councils . . . Without (it), environmental data is unlikely to be easily secured in a form that is scientifically competent, reliable and capable for adequately informing public debate at each level of government, at Brussels and in industry.
- local authorities must be prepared to share the environmental concerns of their neighbours and to take supportive action.

The Council for the Protection of Rural England (1991) reached similar conclusions:

- the importance of the strategic tier is becoming increasingly obvious as the environmental imperatives . . . such as transport, agriculture, forestry and the management of energy, water and mineral resources become clearer.

- the promotion of sustainable development requires a local government structure that can think strategically but retain public accountability.
- legislative reforms would . . . be needed to strengthen the role of parish councils and enhance third party rights to offset the loss of accountability and accessibility inherent in a strategic authority.

No single spatial level is optimal for delivery of environmental policy and management across all functions. In the current scenario of reponsibilities, the two-tier system is able to provide for both the purely regulatory role as well as allowing for an approach involving substantial local policy discretion, as long as there is coordination of direction, approach and effort. In the longer term, however, for the reasons set out above, the balance of advantage may lie with larger units. Larger strategic authorities are likely to be most effective in the policy and technical role, would allow for devolved management of regulatory functions requiring close local contact, and would be able to develop a comprehensive 'enabling' framework across all functions.

Appendix

The Environmental Protection Act and The White Paper: Implications for Local Government

Pollution Control

General   - The EPA promotes IPC (Integrated Pollution Control) with shared responsibility between HMIP, Local Authorities and the NRA. The enforcing authorities are Boroughs and District Councils. Their duties include the authorisation of prescribed processes, increased powers of enforcement of BATNEEC and keeping public registers.

Air   - Greater powers to enforce air pollution from certain substances.
- Duty to follow developments in technology and techniques for preventing and reducing such pollution.
- Possible banning of unauthorised fuel sales in smoke control.
- Banning of smoke and stubble burning.
- New Pollution Regulations for incinerators.
- Enforcement of tougher MOT emission tests.
- Increased powers over statutory nuisance including a duty

of inspection, a duty to act on complaints and greater
enforcement powers including abatement, prohibition and
ordering remedial work.

Noise   ● Restatement of authorities' noise control duties.
         ● New noise control levels.
         ● Simplification and extension of abatement powers.

Litter   ● Duty to keep certain land 'clear of litter and refuse . . . so
far as is practicable'.
         ● For Principal Litter Authorities, 'certain land' is land to
which there is public access.
         ● For Local Authorities it is highways.
         ● For Educational Authorities it is controlled land.
         ● Each Litter Authority must maintain a publicly available
register.
         ● Litter Authorities may require businesses and shops to keep
front pavements clear.
         ● Litter Authorities may operate fixed penalty litter schemes.
         ● Individuals may obtain litter abatement orders.

Environmental Health

● Waste Collection Authorities must:

— collect virtually all household waste and, when requested,
commercial waste;
— maintain a public register.

Waste Management

(Note: waste regulation is subject to review following the consultation
paper on the Environment Agency)

● Separation of waste function into the Waste Regulation
Authority (WRA), Waste Disposal Authority (WDA) and
Waste Collection Authority (WCA).
● WRAs will:

— be responsible for waste management licences.
— have a duty to publish disposal plans.
— have a duty to inspect sites and undertake remedial work.
— have a duty to maintain a public register and publish an
annual report.

● Waste Disposal Authorities must:

— dispose of collected waste.
— provide waste disposal facilities for residents.

● Preference for coordinating waste disposal on a regional basis.
● Emphasis on need for regional (as well as national) waste disposal self-sufficiency for most types of waste.
● WRAs and WCAs required to draw up and publish recycling plans.
● Recycling credit scheme whereby savings in waste disposal are passed on from WDAs to WCAs or to voluntary organisations.
● WDAs may recycle waste or use waste for power generation.
● Requirement to consider recycling with regard to new shopping developments.
● Expectation of better recycling of authorities' own material.
● Recycling investment in partnership with private sector.
● Energy recovery from non-recyclable material.
● Kerbside collection and further ways of recycling.

Land-use and Transport Planning

● Counties to produce strategic plans and prepare draft regional planning guidance.
● Counties to produce minerals and waste local plans and to deal with development control.
● Districts to prepare District Local Plans and to exercise most development control.
● Improved relationship between planning and waste pollution control.
● Use of environmental assessment for major or hazardous projects.
● Improved links between land-use and transport.
● Emphasis on environmental improvement, e.g. vitality of town centres, recreation and green spaces, land reclamation and recycling derelict land; countryside.
● Traffic management including powers to introduce 'priority routes'.
● Waste disposers to restore land to safe standards ('aftercare') and possible extension of aftercare to industrial operators.
● Extended controls over agriculture and forestry buildings.

Heritage Conservation

● Extension of powers to tackle dereliction on privately owned sites.

- Protection of trees and hedgerows.
- Programme to bring all rights of way into good order.
- Authorities and Countryside Commission to address management problems in Areas of Outstanding Natural Beauty, Heritage Coasts and countryside.

Operational Management

- Authorities encouraged to 'green' their own operations, e.g. purchasing and building decisions.
- Possible energy savings of £100 million per year available from improved building management.

Education and Information

- Emphasis on environment role in National Curriculum and teacher training.
- Initiatives to examine role of environment in higher and further education.
- Requirement to compile a register of contaminated land.
- Registers of public sector environmental information to be made available to the public.
- Statistics on environment to be published regularly on e.g. waste land.

References

ACC, ADC, AMA (1990) *Environmental Practice in Local Government; a guide prepared by the local authority associations.*

Association of Metropolitan Authorities (1989) *Action for the Future; Priorities for the Environment.*

Audit Commission (1991) *Towards a Healthier Economy; Managing Environmental Health Services* HMSO.

CBI/PA Consulting Group (1990) *Waking up to a Better Environment* March.

Council for the Protection of Rural England (1991) *Shedding Tiers; Local Government Reform and the Environment.*

County Planning Officers' Society (1991) *County Council Environmental Initiatives.*

Department of Trade and Industry (1990) *CFCs and Halons* HMSO.

Friends of the Earth (1991) *Cold Comfort for the Ozone Layer, Local Authorities Recovering and Recycling of CFCs from Domestic Refrigeration Equipment.*

Local Government Training Board (1990) *The Environmental Role of Local Government.*

Bibliography

Association of County Councils 1990 *County Councils and the Environment.*

PAssociation of District Councils 1988 *Pollution: Controlling the Problems.*

Friends of the Earth 1989 *The Environmental Charter for Local Government.*

HMG 1990 *Environmental Protection Act* HMSO.

HMG 1990 *This Common Inheritance; Britain's Environmental Strategy* (Cm. 1200).

London Research Centre 1991 *Greening London: Environmental Policies and Practices of the London Borough.*

13 Local government, planning and transport

God made the country, and man made the town

(William Cowper)

Introduction

The history of human settlement patterns in England is one of a gradual shift from an agricultural to an urban dominance, and subsequently a rise of suburban settlements. It is also a story of increasing government intervention, in order to bring about orderly and consistent development and to regulate investment by public agencies in planning and transportation infrastructure.

One consequence of the long evolution of the present town and country planning process is that many traditional and long standing attitudes remain embodied in arrangements which have to deal with increasingly rapid investment decisions and socio-economic changes. There is a constant tension between the demands of a complex society and the ability of statutory authorities at all levels to respond. Equally, as social and environmental imperatives come to be better understood, there are pressures on the same system to meet an ever-lengthening list of requirements in responding to investment intentions via commercial and other interests.

There are thus many expectations of the planning system which it was not designed to fulfil. Equally a modern society has the right to expect constant adaptation of systems so that they more nearly reflect its aspirations. With the possible advent of local government reorganisation, it is once again opportune to consider what changes may be introduced to present arrangements to maintain the evolution which has been evident to date. Equally, it is important that reorganisation of local government should not prejudice change through imposing structures which inhibit effective land use and transportation planning. Present arrangements of strategic (county) and detailed (district) plan-making permit corporate and political expression of two distinct orientations of thought to exist in an effective relationship. The relationship is not always fully understood, but nonetheless permits these two approaches to complement one another in a way which promotes accountable decision-making.

Increasingly, decisions about land-use and transportation will have to take account of population and commercial migration across ever larger distances. The advent of the single market in Europe will unquestionably alter the pressures on land in this country in coming decades. Competition for inward investment, in which land availability plays a fundamental part, will become more intense. Decisions by planning authorities will be expected to marry the strategic and the local in all aspects, economic, social and environmental, with both rapidity and reliability. Communities in a given area will expect to be both protected from poor investment decisions and supported by beneficial strategies.

Local government reorganisation must enable the community as a whole to look forward to improved planning arrangements. This chapter considers the current planning system, and in particular the need for integration of land-use and transportation planning, taking into account recent changes and future trends. It concludes by examining the implications for local government structure.

The planning system

This chapter reviews the current town and country planning system, the main instrument through which government seeks to influence the pattern of human settlement in England and Wales and associated land use developments. Transport planning and investment are, or should be, an integral set of considerations when discussing land-use planning. Societal innovation invariably leads to changes in modes and patterns of movement. Similarly new investment in transportation infrastructure can itself determine changes in locational behaviour. Strategic thinking must encompass land-use and transportation as twin elements in the debate about local government structure.

To determine the most appropriate arrangements for this function in terms of local government structure, it is necessary to focus on current performance and recent changes, and then to reflect on future influences and pressures for change in institutional arrangements, most notably the advent of the Single European Market. This section of the chapter therefore considers:

- *current roles and responsibilities;*
- *the evolution of roles in response to social and demographic change; and*

- *current effectiveness.*

The basis of contemporary town and country planning legislation, established in the Town and Country Planning Act 1947, now comprises three elements (Nuffield 1986):

- a system of statutory plans providing directions for the future land-use of a given area over a defined period of time;
- a system of controls to ensure that development is carried out in accordance with plans, policies and statutes;
- a system of governmental (central and local) and quasi-governmental agencies to administer the planning and development control functions and to secure development.

Since 1947 the system has undergone significant revision, reflecting changes in central and local government institutional arrangements, but also changing perceptions of the role, scope, objectives and techniques of town and country planning and practice. The following paragraphs set out, in outline, current institutional responsibility for the town and country planning system and the four main tiers of planning activity: central, regional, county and district (there is also a consultative role at parish and town council level, not covered below) (ACC and Coopers and Lybrand Deloitte 1992).

Central government

The Secretary of State for the Environment is charged with 'securing consistency and continuity in the framing and execution of a national policy with respect to the use and development of land' and is responsible within government and through Parliament for:

- *framing new legislation;*
- *making regulations, rules and orders under existing legislation;*
- *clarifying policy and issuing guidance in the form of statements, circulars and decisions;*
- *monitoring policy and enforcing performance;*
- *acting in a judicial role in the context of appeals, non-performance and decision-making.*

Beneath central government, in a semi-hierarchical relationship, there exists a range of development plans, each the responsibility of local government to draw up:

- regional guidance — the responsibility of the Secretary of State for the Environment acting on advice from groupings of local planning authorities;

- structure plans — the responsibility of county councils;
- unitary plans — the responsibility of metropolitan districts and London boroughs;
- local plans — primarily the responsibility of non-metropolitan district councils;
- minerals and waste — the responsibility of county councils in planning terms.

Regional guidance

Existing regional planning arrangements — as advocated by the Government — are that county councils should voluntarily group together to lead regional conferences, generally based on the existing standard regions, which prepare regional advice for the Secretary of State (revised PPG Note 12), who in turn issues regional guidance as an input to the development plan system. This arrangement is based on the approach adopted by the London and South East Regional Planning Conference (SERPLAN).

The new Planning and Compensation Act (1991) requires county councils 'to have regard to regional planning guidance' when preparing structure plans. The Royal Town Planning Institute (RTPI) issued in May 1991 a discussion document entitled *The Regional Planning Process* setting out proposals for the improvement of the regional planning process. The RTPI (1991) considers the main aims of regional planning to be:

- *identification of realistic levels of change;*
- *provision of input to national planning and compatibility on inter-regional issues;*
- *provision of a regional framework for structure plans;*
- *securing of resources to implement regional objectives.*

Regional planning is deemed to be important because it is believed that a number of policies and proposals need to be considered at a spatial scale larger than counties, e.g. transport infrastructure, environmental protection and housing land supply (including the development of new settlements).

Structure plans and local plans

County councils are responsible for preparing structure plans, a type of development plan first introduced by the Town and Country Planning Act of 1968. Until then, the system of development plans and development control set up under the 1947 Act had operated for two decades without significant change. However by the mid-1960s the system was perceived to suffer from a number of defects (Collingworth 1988):

It has proved extremely difficult to keep these plans not only up to date but forward looking and responsive to the demands of change. Over the years the plans have become more and more out of touch with emergent planning problems and policies, and have in many cases become no more than local land-use maps.

Because of these defects, the Planning Advisory Group (PAG) was formed by Government in May 1964 to review the broad structure of the planning system, and in particular development plans. Its report *The Future of Development Plans*, published in 1965, proposed a basic change which distinguished between policy or strategic issues and detailed tactical issues. Only the former would be subject to Ministerial approval; the latter would be for local decisions within the framework of approved policy.

Legislative effect to the PAG proposals was given by the Town and Country Planning Act 1968. However, this system was devised in advance of local government reorganisation and was based on a key assumption that a single authority would be responsible for both structure planning and local planning. The Local Government Act 1972 actually established two main types of local authority and divided the planning functions between them. Thus while county councils were made responsible for planning strategy (structure planning), district councils became responsible for most local planning, including the great majority of development control work (Collingworth 1988).

This division necessitated a series of complex statutory provisions for redefining the respective planning roles and responsibilities of the two types of authority. For example, statutory provision empowered county councils to certify that local plans conformed to an approved structure plan. In addition county councils were required to prepare development plan schemes setting out the allocation of responsibility and the programme for the preparation of local plans. Both of these were often matters of controversy between counties and districts.

During the 1980s the structure plan/local plan system was extensively criticised by a variety of sources, including institutes, special interest groups and academics, prompting the DOE's 1986 review of the system which highlighted the following points:

- *structure plans were often too long and contained irrelevant and over-detailed policies;*
- *the relationship between structure and local plans was unsatisfactory;*
- *the procedures for preparing development plans were too complex;*
- *the preparation and approval or adoption of plans took far too long;*

- *development plans were not kept up to date and relevant to the needs of the areas concerned.*

Interestingly the DOE's review contained no assessment of the extent to which structure and local plans contributed to the implementation of planning policies contained within them. The success (or otherwise) of the structure plan/local plan system was not well explored. This clearly should be a key issue in evaluating the relative merits of different local government structures and how they impact on the effectiveness of statutory town and country planning.

In the early to mid-1980s it was clear that Government viewed the town and country planning system as inhibiting economic restructuring and recovery. A 1980 DOE circular (22/80) asked local planning authorities to use the development control system to facilitate development and always to grant permission 'unless there are sound and clear cut reasons for refusal'. A further circular (14/85) added the notion that 'the development plan is one of a number of material considerations in determining planning applications'.

In the early 1980s the Government again adjusted the balance of planning control between counties and districts. The Local Government Planning and Land Act 1980 made district councils responsible for determining all planning applications formerly classified as county matters except those relating to mineral workings, waste and national parks. Development control was thus largely directed to the district level with arrangements for consultation between the two levels. In addition, an expedited procedure for the adoption of local plans in advance of the approval of a structure plan was introduced.

Clarity on the future of structure plans had to await the publication of *Planning and Local Choice* by the Secretary of State for the Environment in October 1989. This document contained a restated emphasis on the importance of both counties and districts making policies for their areas in structure and local plans, and a reassurance that 'they can do so in the confidence that so long as plans are realistic about the overall level of provision they will carry considerable weight'.

The philosophy contained in *Planning and Local Choice* provided the basis for the Planning and Compensation Act, 1991, which introduced a development plan-led planning system, retaining both structure and local plans. Section 54(a) of the Act makes it mandatory for non-metropolitan district authorities to prepare local plans covering the whole of their territorial area.

The Act, also introduced some important changes in responsibilities, procedures and plan content:

Structure plans will be a statement of general policies, including proposals in respect of development and use of land. At present they are statements of policy and general proposals. (Clearly it is the DOE's intention that structure plans should become more broad brush and less land-use specific.)

To speed up structure plan preparation and adoption, county councils will have powers not only to prepare but also to adopt or replace a structure plan, subject to the provision that they would have regard to regional or strategic planning guidance from the Secretary of State.

Districts need no longer to ask counties for a certificate of conformity with the structure plan. On being sent a copy of the proposals in compliance with the published requirements counties have to send to districts a statement of conformity or non-conformity as appropriate.

A new requirement is added for minerals local plans and waste local plans to be prepared by counties.

Transport planning

Transport is a key factor in influencing land-use patterns, and is also inextricably linked with economic growth. Decentralised and low density forms of development, including out-of-town retailing and office complexes, encourage travel by private vehicle. New roads can and often do stimulate major developments, generating large volumes of traffic, which lead to pressure for further infrastructure investment, and so on. Allowance for this must be made in the design of new highway and transport facilities and in land-use planning decisions. Centralised forms of development, employment and services allow for the more efficient provision of public transport. Land-use policies affect the need for travel and movement, and help shape transport systems. There is an increasing need to reappraise the balance between the need for transport and the needs of the environment, through a more integrated transport strategy serving the needs of both rural and urban situations and including road, rail and where appropriate, airports and canals.

Since the publication of the Buchanan Report in the early 1960s, the idea of integrating transport and land-use development has gained widespread acceptance. The report argued that no amount of road and parking provision could satisfy the prospective unrestrained demand for access by private car. It suggested that the development plans for larger urban areas should be supplemented by transportation plans which would be part of the statutory submission then required to central government.

In the decade following the Buchanan Report several major changes were introduced which facilitated an integrated approach. These included:

● the introduction of the two-tier development plan system referred to earlier with proposals for the management of traffic as part of its statutory remit;

- reform of local government to create county-wide administrative units which broadly corresponded to the main commuting areas;
- allocation to county authorities of responsibilities for strategic planning, highways and public transport coordination;
- reform of the arrangements for central government grants towards local transport expenditure and payment of a single transport supplementary Grant (TSG) towards expenditure approved from integrated transport policies and programmes (TPPs) submitted annually.

Although integration was and is quoted as a policy objective, the town planning responsibilities of the Department of the Environment and the transportation responsibilities of the Department of Transport have never fully combined. The proposals in the Buchanan Report that transportation planning should be incorporated in the statutory development plan system has not generally been reflected in the lower level of local plans, though counties have been able to exploit their role as statutory highway authorities to provide major urban relief roads and rural bypasses within an overall highway and land use strategy. Some counties are developing transport strategies to encompass new rail initiatives, linked to new development (the Ivanhoe Line in Leicestershire and Derbyshire is an example).

In general, however, transport expenditure continues to be assessed in terms of its effect on mobility (travel conditions in isolation) rather than on accessibility (travel as a means of enabling people to reach the facilities they require). Budgetary provision is dominated by road scheme financing. As a result land-use/transport planning is arguably dominated by considerations of more and longer motorised trips (which generate large-scale benefits) rather than exploiting local development and other opportunities which would reduce the need to travel at all.

In the 1980s, the increasing control of public expenditure and reduced role for local authorities and other public agencies led to considerable changes in planning and transport. These included:

- transformation of the TPP system into a single-purpose bid for highway capital funding only;
- abolition of the GLC and metropolitan county councils and the assumption of additional trunk road responsibilities within Greater London by central government;
- county-wide structure plans for metropolitan areas replaced by more limited strategic guidance issued by the Secretary of State;
- deregulation of local bus services, and creation of individual business sectors within British Rail, reducing subsidies and applying quasi-commercial remits.

As a result, the present arrangements for coordinating land-use and transport planning are considered deficient in many respects. Understanding of the impact of particular transport investments on land-use patterns is limited. Changes which alter travel-to-work patterns, for example, are particularly difficult to evaluate.

In metropolitan areas, in particular, the separation of town planning and passenger functions has removed any semblance of unified responsibility for accessibility conditions. As a result, there is much less likelihood of them being measured, and hence of problems being anticipated and addressed. The function of raising and exploring areawide issues previously performed by the structure planning process has largely disappeared (RTPI 1989).

> The arrangements for strategic guidance which are being put in their place (including the expedient of district planning authorities collectively framing their advice to the Secretary of State) are essentially a makeshift remedy for the absence of genuine guidance on national policy on the one hand and the lack of a proper strategic planning framework for local plans and programmes on the other.

The problem of accommodating the long-term growth of traffic, within terms addressed by the Buchanan Report, has still not been solved, while the balance of investment between road, rail and other transport is still a matter on which strategic guidance is non-existent, perhaps accurately reflecting a national policy shortfall.

Along with the availability of skilled manpower and a flexible approach to land-use planning, the key factor in creating the right physical, demographic and regulatory conditions conducive to economic development is the provision of good communications. As travel-to-work areas increase and markets become more dispersed, inward investors looking to set up new or larger enterprises will be attracted by integrated communications networks which provide easy access to a relatively large geographical region. Good communications depend on good transportation planning.

Conclusions

Land-use and transportation planning in this country is undertaken through a complex and sophisticated system administered by central and local government. It has evolved over several generations, the post-war years being seminal in that development.

The role of the planning system is widely accepted as essential in balancing demands for development against the need to protect and conserve, in terms of community interests, physical heritage, and the environment. Criticism of process or policy, often a reflection of changing social perceptions, has not negated this fundamental need to ensure that land is used beneficially. Where development is considered harmful or inappropriate, planning permission is withheld.

Over the past decade, in particular, it has been recognised that a sophisticated economy, with a well-educated and articulate population, makes demands upon a planning system which are hard to satisfy. At the very least, as society changes with growing rapidity, flexibility is essential. In a complex legislative framework this is hard to achieve. In consequence statutory plans have grown less precise, offering instead guidance and locational policy, together with broad land allocations. Thus, within a general framework, individuals and corporate bodies can pursue their development needs.

With the reduction of the prescriptive dimension, however, pressures for change have emerged in other ways. Society's plural nature has gained increasing recognition, measured in both social and economic terms. Perhaps most marked in urban areas, it has become apparent that the planning system is expected to respond to community aspirations which may not be part of a broad consensus. This, together with a growing understanding of the environmental aspects of development, has maintained the debate about the role of land-use planning.

The same dichotomy applies to transportation, in the sense that rapid, long-distance movement requires long-term planning and investment decisions while achieving results that are responsive to changing demands. Again, the individual seeks to exercise rights of choice and must be catered for in this respect, while the demands of environmental protection and conservation must similarly be taken into account. The relationship between land-use planning and transportation is a close one in which private interests and public good must be balanced. The creation of a structure providing for their more effective integration is a key issue for the review.

Implications for future structure

The implications of change in the structure of local government are wide ranging, not least because unitary authorities would clearly require fundamental change to the planning system, which currently reflects two-tier arrangements, and introduces a third tier in the form of regional planning groups.

The key issues for the review are therefore:

● Taking into account future large-scale trends, what structure of planning activity, in terms of land-use and transportation, would most effectively meet the needs of the community in economic, social and environmental matters?

● What role should local government play in the administration of land-use planning and transportation investment, integrating the two effectively?

Future trends

Activity on the land-use planning and transportation investment fronts varies substantially with the rise and fall of the national economy. Planning applications, for example, grew dramatically in number through the 1980s, and are now showing a down-turn as investment is withheld. Currently, while the pressures of economic growth have receded, the same systems have to cope with zero or low growth. Attracting scarce investment and ensuring cost effectiveness is in many ways a harder task than regulating intense demand. Future arrangements must take account of the incidence of economic cycles so that they are not designed simply for one phase, be it growth or decline.

Beyond the cycle of growth and contraction, there are more substantial and longer term trends which have to be taken into account, in particular population mobility and labour movement. Changes in society, both in terms of demography and consumer preference, lead to changes in land-use settlement patterns. Different facilities are demanded, priority is given to different forms of investment, and the resulting obsolescence of physical structures requires their replacement. At the same time, a search for better living environments has prompted urban populations to relocate, often over quite short distances but in very large numbers. These changes must be expected to continue, and probably to accelerate.

Among anticipated macro changes must be the continued restructuring of industry from manufacturing to service sectors and the globalisation of investment. The Single European Market must be expected to accelerate and emphasise these changes. If economic turbulence is one consequence of both the Single Market and the liberalisation of Eastern Europe, at least over the coming decade, it will be important that the local planning capabilities of local government are strengthened. This strengthening must take two forms. The first is an ability to operate in an international arena, which suggests larger authorities with regional horizons achieved either in their own right or through appropriate groupings. The second must be in relation to the ability to intervene selectively, but effectively, in both local economies and local environments to enable social and economic growth to occur, consistent with local aspirations.

Structure and need

Decisions about the development of land for one purpose or another require guidance. Such guidance should be both consistent and comprehensive if a wide variety of material considerations are to be properly taken into account. Demands for greater speed and flexibility are rarely, if ever, accompanied by demands for the dismantling of a system of regulation and control, or fewer opportunities for public consideration.

Such development decisions are made or sought at very different levels in terms of detail. There is thus a continuum of consideration from the large scale and strategic to the small scale and detailed. The former may involve time horizons of at least 5 to 15 years; the latter, no more than months. The planning framework therefore has to cater fully for this continuum. This argues for a highly differentiated system which permits the relevant authorities to propose strategic guidance and specific development approvals in a coherent manner without either unacceptably prejudicing the other.

Satisfying the strategic end of the continuum requires a capacity to look forward over extended time periods, and to analyse substantial quantities of social and economic data often covering large geographical areas and wide ranging interests in the fields of conservation and development. Satisfying detailed demands requires a clear understanding of the needs and preferences of local communities, and the capacity to adjudicate between highly detailed arguments, often with extended local histories.

The future trends described above suggest that the continuum of planning considerations is expanding rather than contracting. Strategic issues are likely to relate in future to larger geographical areas, larger scale investments and longer time periods than at present. Detailed decisions are likely to have to incorporate increasingly precise understanding of micro-economic and environmental impacts, as well as developing consumer expectations of many kinds.

At each point in the continuum from strategic to local, accountability for decision making, procedures and appeals will have to be clear and unambiguous in order to meet growing demands for consumer rights and to fulfil contractual obligations, however framed. Real accountability must be sustained by adequate information. At a strategic level, those accountable must have access to Government, national and transnational agencies and comprehensive information drawn from many different sources. At the local level, accountability must be accompanied by detailed awareness of individual communities, local businesses and the many institutions which have a day-to-day role in the affairs of smaller-scale settlements.

The dividing line between 'strategic' and 'local' will never be precise. In the past, efforts have been made to resolve this dilemma by identifying building blocks of society in terms of cohesive communities. The debate about local government structure has always involved a search for a universally acceptable definition, which has proved an elusive goal. An unduly prescriptive system will invariably be overrun by fast evolving society. Instead, any arrangements put in place should have the capacity to respond effectively to whatever configuration of community is relevant in particular circumstances. Communities present themselves in different configurations according to different circumstances.

Accepting that the boundary between the strategic and the local is inevitably blurred, the former are usually designated county matters and the latter district matters, in the present system. Thus two sets of elected representatives, albeit sometimes overlapping in individual membership, are brought into play, each orientated towards one or other focus. This arrangement effectively establishes one group of elected representatives as a counterpoint to another. While the resulting relationship is not always harmonious, it does demonstrate the need to expose the potential for conflict between wider interests of the community at large, and the local impact of any proposed development.

There can be little disagreement about the dangers of large scale and strategic considerations in land-use planning subsuming or neglecting local concerns. The same applies in reverse in terms of parochial perspectives obscuring larger scale considerations and promoting a narrow view of need. The question of arbitration inevitably arises, and the present system of land-use planning, imperfect though it may be, casts the Secretary of State in the role of the arbiter as well as the source of strategic policy guidance.

Introduction of unitary authorities would merge the two roles into one. Though there are many ways of decentralising services provided by a unitary authority so that they are more locally focused and accountable, the key question remains the extent to which pluralism is well served, and how this is expressed corporately and politically.

Elected members represent particular localities, and in this sense, represent a diversity of minority interests. The issue is how far this creates institutional pressures effective enough to establish different perspectives and argue them through, so that the 'strategic' and the 'local' are fully provided for.

The local authority role

Land-use planning has been a function of local government from its modern day beginnings. While the preparation of plans and the processing of some operational elements may yet be subject to compulsory competitive tendering, the formulation of policy is likely to remain a public role. This is entirely consistent with the fact that planning and transportation decisions have substantial implications for individuals and a close relationship with land values and property prices. A reorganised local government structure must take account of this dimension.

The private sector is increasingly accepted to have an integral role in promoting social and economic well-being, however. Partnership between the private and the public sectors is emphasised in many areas of government activity, not least in urban renewal, rural development and transportation infrastructure, and is recognised by all the main political parties. As land-use planning seeks increasingly to integrate public and private investment, shaping them to a common good, so the capacity of local government to play a full part in this process increases in importance.

This greatly enlarges the range of considerations of which local authorities need to be aware. An understanding of commercial imperatives, business culture and investment appraisal methods is becoming a vital dimension of strategic and local planning. The advent of TECs indicates that intermediary bodies are thought necessary to bridge the perceived gulf between local government and the private sector in the economic sphere. That individual TECs are now working closely with counties and district councils in areas touching upon land-use planning is a sign that local authorities themselves recognise the importance of partnership.

To increase the integration of various interests in land-use development, local authorities are increasingly expected to have the capability to undertake analysis and research of a sophisticated nature. The need to attract the necessary skills to work in an increasingly complex and more international policy environment, and to avoid the diseconomies and inefficiencies of fragmentation, points to larger bodies capable of sustaining the necessary effort and marshalling the necessary resources on a consistent basis. The strategic planning dimension therefore inevitably calls for authorities comparable with existing counties, with both a geographical and a resource base on a commensurate scale.

At local level, the debate is about access as much as capacity. This in turn demands local knowledge so that access is measured not simply in terms of opportunity or physical proximity but also in terms of understanding and reciprocity. The best district councils have established working relationships with their communities, both residential and business, which rely heavily on common perceptions between elected representatives and constituents and a common understanding of very detailed issues. As well as local awareness and orientation, a detailed knowledge of land-use histories is required. Development control is about both beneficial development and precedent, upon which judicial decisions rest when arguments arise, and an understanding of local priorities and precedents requires more than factual data.

Planning brings together a range of activities which include the delivery of services and the balancing of external interests. Distinguishing between these is often difficult since both largely involve land and property in private hands. As a regulatory process, land-use planning arguably cannot be regarded simply as one of local government's service functions. The quasi-judicial role involved in determining planning applications in the light of opposition makes it a unique local authority function. It is an intensely political process undertaken with full and parallel public scrutiny.

For the more service-based aspects of planning, unification of the process under one authority could be contemplated with equanimity. Protecting the environment, conservation and historic buildings work, the providing of routine advice, research and education could be undertaken on a unitary basis, perhaps with decentralised outlets. This could also apply to a substantial proportion of minor day-to-day development control work, involving as it does a predominance of residential applications often subject to officer delegation. Good management practices through appropriate delegation mechanisms could develop local access and knowledge within the strategic policy framework of a large unitary authority, and larger scale authorities would have no difficulty compiling the necessary records and maintaining databanks.

The difficulties would mount as larger and more controversial cases were introduced, bringing into play both the strategic/local dimension and the conflicts of interest these frequently expose.

Conclusions

The land-use and transportation planning systems currently in place in this country have in the past been regarded as a model for other countries. The creation of a codified and comprehensive set of arrangements was something of which the UK could be properly proud. Despite criticisms of the rigidity and slowness of the system, and concerns that it does not deal adequately with certain key dimensions of development, it provides the basis for bringing together a wide variety of supply and demand relationships in land-use terms.

Projecting the nature of society and its consequent land-use demands will remain an important part of the planning process. As unexpected changes occur, planning policies will have to change quickly and sensitively, so that legitimate social developments are helped rather than hindered. At the same time, it is an inherent part of the planning process that control should be exercised over undesirable and unhelpful development pressures so that the wider community can be protected, and less empowered sections can participate fully in decisions in the public domain.

The planning system has largely succeeded in these aims over the past generation. It must remain in the public domain for reasons which are fundamentally important and inherently right: it is a process concerned with public good, not private benefit, compromise not partiality, and openness not secrecy. It will thus remain a key role for local government, in order to preserve the local accountability and awareness which are crucial to its effective function. In that arena, however, there will be increasing pressure to deal with both strategic and local matters in an integrated way, and these pressures are likely to continue to suggest to some that a unitary form of local government would be preferable.

The arguments above suggest that there are inherent dilemmas in all options for the structure of local government in the search for the optimal balance between strategic and local interests. Several decades of rapid social and economic change have seen the complexities of development planning continuously increase, and future trends are likely to accelerate this further. The demand for a pluralistic and responsive approach has intensified along with the need for bodies capable of operating effectively at a strategic level within a national and international policy framework. No arrangements are likely entirely to satisfy all interests — all systems require checks and balances.

A unitary system would have the capacity to increase and promote better coordination, but in doing so would run the risk of obscuring dissenting viewpoints, whether because strategic considerations transcend local concerns, or because too parochial a viewpoint promotes a narrow view of need to the exclusion of the wider public interest. Difficult choices are inherent in the planning function, and whilst a unitary system might offer gains in terms of efficiency and effectiveness, it might also lose something fundamental, namely forms of opposition. A two-tier structure can, in principle, incorporate both viewpoints.

Faced with the Government's presumption of unitary authorities, therefore, this presents the review of local government structure with a difficult issue. Planning is not a service provided by local authorities to consumers in the same way as other services. It is a process administered by local government on behalf of the community at large, using powers derived from Parliament and issuing quasi-judicial decisions on which interest, or balance of interests, should be responded to in any given circumstance. As such, it is not ideally suited to a unitary framework. However, the weight of evidence in other local government service areas may suggest that the balance of advantage lies in general with a unitary system. If such authorities are created, it will be essential to provide for both strategic considerations and local interests in the planning system in some other way than through the separate institutions of a two-tier structure.

A structure based predominantly on smaller scale unitary authorities would need realistically to deal with questions relating to larger geographical areas, larger scale investment, and longer time periods. Such authorities would need to demonstrate a convincing ability to confront the problems likely to be faced in drawing up agreed statements of policy on wider issues. Equally, it would be essential for a structure based on larger scale unitary authorities (as recommended in other chapters) to be accompanied by arrangements which ensured that a local voice was heard and that local interests were fully taken into account, whether through the development of internal, area committee type structures, or through greater involvement of parish and town council representatives in planning decisions.

In either scenario, it is essential for the review to recognise that the future of the planning system and that of local government are intimately bound up, given that local government is the prime agent for administering the system. The choices which lie ahead in the context of the review are therefore of profound importance to the future of the planning system over the next decade and beyond.

References

Association of County Councils and Coopers & Lybrand Deloitte (1992) *Making the Most of Parish and Town Councils.*

Collingworth (1988) *Town and Country Planning in Britain.*

Nuffield (1986) *Town and Country Planning: The Report of a Committee of Inquiry appointed by the Nuffield Foundation.*

RTPI/South West Branch (1991) *The Regional Planning Process.*

RTPI Transport Working Party (1989) *Transport Planning in a New Era* RTPI.

14 Changing the shape of local government: the continuing controversy

> For from the place where he now stood . . . the way was all along set
> so full of snares, traps, gins and nets here, and so full of pits, pitfalls,
> deep holes and shelvings down there, that had it now been dark . . .
> had he had a thousand souls, they had in reason been cast away; . . .
> but the sun was rising
>
> *(The Pilgrim's Progress,* John Bunyan)

Introduction

Over many years of evolution and development, three features in particular have come to distinguish local government from all other
aspects of government. It is:

- democratically founded in local communities, consisting of representatives elected by the members of those communities, whose
  identity is thereby given active expression in a measure of self-government;
- multi-purpose, fulfilling several different roles, providing for a very
  wide range of individual and collective needs, across many different
  services, through many different relationships and modes of operation;
- local, responsible only within a specific spatial area, contiguous
  with the areas of peer authorities.

These essential qualities of local government remain, even though
its institutions, as part of the 'body politic', are inevitably in a state of
continuous change and development. The shape and structure of local
government has been subject to near-continuous examination and proposals for reform. Less than twenty years after the last reorganisation,
further change is proposed.

Chapters 1 and 2 considered the historic development of local government's role as part of the British constitution, and explored local

government's changing style. They argued that the starting point for the review must be the requirement to support a continuing and active constitutional role for local government, reinforced by the further development and achievement of the 'enabling' style.

Equally fundamental to consideration of future change is an understanding of the factors influencing present form. Many of the issues raised in the past about local government structure are with us still. But until now, it has generally been presumed that the pattern of local government (in each country of the United Kingdom) should be at least uniform. The present review, however, may allow for different solutions in different places. The Government has encouraged the prospect of structures matching the particular circumstances of each area, rather than following a blueprint designed in the abstract.

This encouragement of diversity presents the review with a complex and demanding task. Some kind of general framework will be required upon which to approach each area and base specific conclusions. This chapter therefore sets out the context to the review and presents a set of general criteria intended to focus the review upon the issues to be considered in each locality, and against which any proposed structure may be tested.

The development of the present structure

The present structure of local government in England (outside London) and Wales consists of:

- a top tier of 47 county councils (39 in England and 8 in Wales), ranging in population from 116,800 (Powys) to 1,558,400 (Essex);
- in county areas, a middle tier of 333 so-called 'shire' district councils (of which 37 are in Wales), ranging in population from 23,000 (Radnor) to 370,000 (Bristol);
- a third tier of 8,159 parish and town councils in England, the majority of which are very small (40 per cent represent fewer than 500 people) but a small number of which represent communities of over 20,000, and 790 community and town councils in Wales;
- in metropolitan areas (which were until 1986 covered by the six metropolitan counties of Greater Manchester, Merseyside, West Midlands, Tyne and Wear, South Yorkshire and West Yorkshire) a single tier of 36 metropolitan district or borough councils, ranging in population from 152,000 (Knowsley) to 984,900 (Birmingham) (CIPFA 1991–2).

The present structure is of relatively recent origin, being created by the Local Government Act 1972 (operative from 1974). It replaced one largely unchanged (outside London) since the end of the nineteenth century. Though five counties were newly created in 1974 (Avon, Cleveland, Cumbria, Humberside and North Yorkshire), and there were some amalgamations (Hereford with Worcester, Rutland into Leicestershire, and Huntingdonshire into Cambridgeshire), and many boundary changes at a detailed level, the county tier in England exhibits a high degree of continuity and stability as a group of administrative units. Similarly, the majority of parish councils are almost 100 years old, while the parish has been an active administrative entity for over five hundred years.

The main changes have been in the middle tier and in metropolitan areas. The majority of present districts were new creations in 1974, replacing some 1,086 borough, urban and rural district councils, whilst the metropolitan areas have seen many changes to reflect the shifts in population between 'town' and 'country' (discussed in more detail in the next section). In Wales, the 1974 changes affected the top tier also; 8 new county councils replaced 13 counties and 4 county boroughs, through both amalgamation and division.

That the nineteenth century structure had become out of date some 70 or 80 years later is less remarkable than the absence of substantial reform in the meantime, notwithstanding frequent re-examination. Until the 1972/74 changes, local government structure had consisted of:

- a top tier of county councils, based largely on the existing counties and county borough councils, centred around existing boroughs meeting a specified population criterion (originally more than 50,000);
- within counties, a middle tier of urban and rural district councils (UDCs and RDCs), based on consolidated sanitary districts established under the Public Health Act 1872, and non-county borough councils, existing boroughs not meeting the criterion for county borough status;
- within rural districts, a third tier of parish councils.

With hindsight, the problems associated with such a structure as society developed seem inevitable. Pressure for change began to build rapidly almost as soon as it had been put in place. From 1899 to 1925, 21 new county boroughs were created and there were over a hundred county borough boundary changes to reflect the movement of population from country to town (see below). This involved counties in a substantial loss of rateable value (and hence revenue). Eventually the problems were sufficiently acute to lead to a Royal Commission on Local Government 1923–29 'to inquire as to the existing law and procedure relating the extension . . . and creation of . . . county boroughs . . . and the effect . . . on counties . . . non-county boroughs, urban districts and rural districts; to investigate the relations between these several local authorities'.

The Commission did not challenge the principles of the structure, adopting instead an incremental approach. So far as county boroughs were concerned, pressure for change was controlled by raising the population criterion to 75,000. Elsewhere, the Commission found that 'there are at present authorities who cannot efficiently discharge the functions entrusted to them' and recommended that counties should undertake reviews 'in order to see how far ineffective units can be eliminated by reorganisation'. Between 1931–37, many of the smallest districts were merged with their neighbours, so that numbers of UDCs and RDCs reduced from 1606 to 1048.

But conflict was accentuated and exacerbated by shifts of population and industry during the 1939–45 war. The continuing growth of the suburbs suggested that the boundaries of county boroughs should be extended, and led to renewed pressure from non-county boroughs for county borough status. Yet the effect of this was to remove from counties urban areas essential for the generation of adequate resources to sustain services in increasingly thinly populated rural areas.

In 1945 the Government set up a Local Government Boundary Commission, to survey boundaries throughout England and Wales (outside London), to adjust, unite and divide, but not to create or abolish. The Commission, however, felt that their terms of reference were inadequate to deal with what they saw as very considerable need for change, and instead in 1947 proposed more radical reform of the structure. Only the twenty largest county boroughs would remain as single-tier authorities. The rest, together with the larger non-county boroughs, would form a new category of 'most-purpose' authorities within counties. County councils would carry out those functions requiring a larger scale of organisation; larger counties would be divided, the smaller united with their neighbours. Outside the 'most-purpose' authorities, there would be a uniform system of districts, formed from UDCs, RDCs, and small boroughs.

The opportunity for thorough-going reform was not taken, despite, or perhaps because of, the substantial changes going on elsewhere. The proposals met with substantial opposition from most of the affected authorities. Aneurin Bevan, the responsible Minister, was preoccupied with the creation of the National Health Service and was reluctant to become involved in conflict over local government structure. The Commission was abolished, and no action was taken, nor policy announced, by any Government until 1956, notwithstanding extensive discussion in the meantime with the local authority associations about the form any change should take. Declaring that 'there is no convincing case for radically reshaping the existing form of local government in England and Wales', the Government instead established new Boundary Commissions, able to propose changes only in the area and status of county councils and county boroughs, except in five Special Review Areas in the conurbations, where they were given wider scope to change structure and functions.

As a result, some changes were proposed in specific areas, and a few were accepted. Others (such as the abolition of Rutland) created strong opposition. But the English Commission was only half way through the process of review when the Government announced a complete review of local government structure (the Welsh Commission had completed its work, but had itself come to the conclusion that its terms of reference excluded it from putting forward a really sound scheme). The 1966–9 Redcliffe–Maud Royal Commission described its work as the 'first attempt ever to examine government of towns and country-side from top to bottom and plan a radically new start'.

The Redcliffe–Maud Commission

By this time there was a consensus on the need for substantial change. It was widely recognised that the nineteenth century structure was not suited to twentieth century circumstances. The Commission heard evidence from over 2000 witnesses and undertook its own research. Their diagnosis, broadly agreed by most commentators, was that:

- local government areas did not fit modern living and working patterns;
- there was now an artificial separation of big towns from their surrounding hinterlands, through the county borough and county structure, which was impeding sensible planning and leading to an atmosphere of hostility between authorities;
- split responsibilities between counties and county boroughs, and between counties and districts, led to fragmented services;
- there were too many small authorities, short of the staff and equipment they needed to deal with the problems they faced;

and that therefore:

- complex local government machinery seemed impotent and irrelevant;
- central government doubted local government's ability to run local affairs;
- variety in size and type of authorities prevented local government acting effectively as a single body in its dealings with central government.

But, as ever, there was dispute about the proposed remedy. The Commission concluded that most of England should be divided into 58 largely new areas, each having a population between 250,000 and 1,000,000, with a single authority responsible for all functions. In three other metropolitan areas, all densely populated, a single tier was seen as unable to provide effectively for both environmental services (requiring a larger scale) and personal services (requiring a smaller scale) to be in the hands of one authority (which the Commission preferred) and a two-tier structure was recommended. At grass-roots level, local councils were required, to serve as an essential link between the public and the main authority, and to promote and watch over the particular interests of communities in city, town and village. At regional level, eight indirectly elected 'provincial councils' would determine the strategy and planning framework within which the main authorities would operate.

The Redcliffe–Maud proposals exposed a dilemma which proponents of local government reform (and its agents) must still confront. The Commission had set itself four criteria for the future system of local government: efficiency, democracy, the pattern of living, and the existing structure. But they were not necessarily compatible, requiring a difficult balance to be struck between them in any specific proposals. About that balance, both in principle and in application, there was infinite room for disagreement. Critics argued that the proposed unitary authorities 'were government but not local, that local councils were local but not government, while the provincial councils were neither local nor government' (Byrne 1990). Instead, they favoured a two-tier system throughout the country, not just in metropolitan areas. The incoming Conservative Government eventually adopted this approach in the 1972 legislation (HMG 1971):

> Concentrating authority for all services in the hands of one authority in each area has similar advantages (of simplicity and intelligibility) and makes for coherence in administration. But it carries the grave penalty that if such areas are to be large enough for some services they will be too large for others. Furthermore, the theoretical advantages of radical restructuring must be weighed against the advantages of building on the existing well-established organisations and minimising the disorganisation of services during the period of transition.

The present review is in some sense the legacy of nearly fifty years of continuing disagreement about the shape of local government. The existing structure is essentially an evolution from the late nineteenth century system, which was itself an evolution from a system developed for a variety of historical reasons. Inevitably it has both virtues and defects, and suits some areas better than others. Locally, continuing resistance to specific changes introduced in 1974 has been fuelled by old loyalties, which die hard. More widely, issues of settlement and of size and scale continue to provoke argument, to which are added new preoccupations with local identity and a more generalised fear that the value of local democracy has been reduced and obscured by several decades of centralisation, bureaucratisation at all levels, and a gradual lessening of local independence (see Chapter 1).

The next sections of this chapter consider some key themes of the continuing debate, in particular:

- the potential influence of population and settlement trends upon the future shape of local government, and, in particular, the ebb and flow of population between 'town' and 'country';
- developing concepts of 'community' and its implications for local government structure;
- the issue of size of local authorities;
- changing relationships within the wider system of government affecting local government's dual role as agent of central government (and the European Community) and the voice of local communities.

It concludes with a set of key criteria, based on the above discussion, against which proposals for future structures should be evaluated.

Population and settlement trends

The influence of population growth and settlement trends in prompting debate about change in administrative structures and determining the course of local government reform has been clearly marked over the last century and a half. Since the 1970s, however, the size of the UK's population has been almost at a standstill. Current population is estimated at around 57.3 million, and forecasters estimate that it will be no more than 58 million by the year 2000. But significant demographic trends still occur in the distribution and mix of the population, rather than in overall numbers.

The population of the UK today is by no means spread evenly. Structural changes in the economy have been by far the most important driving forces behind the major changes in distribution that have taken place since the first census nearly 200 years ago. For most of the population, where they live has been heavily influenced by the location and accessibility of the factories, shops or offices at which they work, and by the availability of transport. Social change has also been significant in producing a larger number of (on average) smaller households.

When the UK was a predominantly agricultural country, its population was more evenly spread, making use of farming land in plentiful supply in most places. The rapid growth of major cities and towns (apart perhaps from London) really began with the industrial revolution. Resulting demographic change had a profound effect on the political landscape of the nineteenth century, contributing to the pressures for electoral and administrative reform, and to the growth and development of democratic local government.

By the 1930s, however, the 'smokestack' areas of the industrial revolution were already in decline. New industrial regions had emerged in the South East and in the West Midlands. When J. B. Priestley in 1933 was collecting material for his *English Journey*, he found three Englands: the old England of the guidebooks, nineteenth century industrial England, and twentieth century England of bypasses and suburbia. To the drift to the towns was added the drift to the south. Post-war, the larger metropolitan areas, in London, the Midlands, and the North, began to experience a loss of population and employment. This became particularly noticeable in 'inner-city' areas, giving rise to greater concentrations of poorer people and of social disadvantage.

By contrast, suburban areas increased in relative wealth, developed more local employment and enjoyed more social amenities, creating a better quality of life. With improved transport networks and greater wealth, many people were able to live at lower densities further out of city centres, leading to a continued widening of 'travel-to-work' areas. Concern about countryside erosion led to 'green belts' of land, usually several miles wide, around larger cities. Planning restrictions limited the amount of suburban growth that could be added to existing built-up areas. Developers began to look to surrounding rings of settlement, lying within increasing commuting distance of city centres.

The 1981 census showed a substantial decline in the population of Britain's larger cities. Population migration continued away from traditional industrial and inner-city areas, to smaller urban centres, new towns, and coastal retirement areas. Previously remote and rural areas experienced a switch into growth after decades of depopulation. Preliminary results from the 1991 census have confirmed this trend, and continue to show a drift away from the North. Between 1981–91, population fell in all large cities and in many larger towns. The fastest growing regions were East Anglia (up 7.7 per cent), the South West (up 5.5 per cent) and the East Midlands (up 2.5 per cent) — the biggest falls in population were in the North West (down 4.3 per cent) and the North (down 3 per cent).

Major population shifts thus remain a key issue for local government structure. There is concern about what is called in the US the 'doughnut' effect, where an outer ring of people and resources surround an inner centre of urban dereliction and neglect. The better-off move out, leaving behind the elderly, unskilled, and impoverished. Decisions made for the benefit of the periphery will not necessarily benefit the inner core. One area has access to more resources than it might need, the other is without the resources to handle the needs it undoubtedly has. In such a scenario, an overall strategic outlook able to take into account the needs of both areas is likely to be preferable to administrative (and political) separation.

On this aspect, events have vindicated the Redcliffe–Maud Royal Commission, who attached great importance to the need to secure interdependence between town and country, and to the need for each local authority to be responsible for a continuous area forming a coherent social and economic whole, matching the way of life of an increasingly mobile society, and giving the authority the space needed to assess and deal with problems. Twenty years on, however, the picture is more complex still. In the past decade, there has been rapid change in the structure of the economy, in employment patterns and in overall mobility, for example (Gyford 1991):

- *decline in manufacturing and the growth of the service sector;*
- *the growing involvement of women in employment;*
- *the growth of part-time work;*
- *the persistence of under-employment and unemployment;*
- *a shift of employment from large cities to smaller towns and rural areas;*
- *the growth of small firms alongside multi-national corporations;*
- *the increasing role of the informal economy.*

Such changes have increased the country's economic and social diversity. As local labour markets develop and diversify, the balance between cities and their surrounding areas may change so that surrounding areas acquire a life of their own, perhaps even dominating (Steeley 1990):

> The dynamic of the urban periphery will redirect itself, not solely to its own city centre . . . but more to adjoining urban peripheries across the greenbelt seas. The dynamism of these urban shorelines may well generate a new arena in which urban life will evolve.

For economic, environmental, and social reasons, the next century is likely to see a continuing decline in the dominance of large cities and industrial conurbations. The 'post-modernist' English Journey may find a fourth England, of prosperous, small, 'market' towns, new and old, in attractive countryside, housing telecommuters and small firms, and accommodating varied working and leisure patterns. What this may suggest is that settlement patterns across the country are likely to become more diverse, and that there is likely to be rapid change in those patterns as local economies develop and interact.

To this must be added the growing influence of changes in Europe. It has been suggested that 'the Single European Market from January 1993 might open a phase of significant population movements: the drift to southern states by those who retire from work in the UK; and the drift into the UK by those from other European states wanting work' (Lock 1991). The development of a highly efficient trans-European rail network linked to the Channel Tunnel, increasing air traffic, and the lifting of restrictions on cross-border movements between countries, will allow more people to circulate around Europe, including the UK, settling where and when they like. The geography of the UK may therefore gradually change away from the predominantly radial pattern of communications from London to the regions, to a pattern that ties the country to the European mainland from the Midlands across East Anglia.

The complex interaction of these trends would seem to rule out recourse in the review to any single design model (for example, analogous to the 'city-region' of the late sixties) for future local government areas. Instead it will be necessary to understand the specific economic and social factors which in each area influence the interactions between patterns of residence, employment, leisure, shopping and travel — how the 'urban shoreline' is changing and likely to change. A key issue for the review will be the inevitable tension between the rapidly changing demands of post-industrial society, which demonstrates complex and diverse patterns of settlement, and the prevailing pattern of administrative and political organisation, which has tended to exhibit a high degree of conservatism despite major social change.

In some areas, adjustment of existing boundaries, and possibly the creation of new authorities, may be necessary to respond to the policy issues raised as substantially new patterns of development have evolved. In others, existing structures and boundaries may be quite adequate for the foreseeable future. The review will need to consider a range of options appropriate to the circumstances of each area. Ability to respond effectively and flexibly to changing living and working patterns remains an important criterion by which to test proposed local government structures.

Local identity and concepts of community

The concept of 'community' has exercised an increasing influence on public policy in the latter years of the present century, and shows no sign of diminishing. From early beginnings in the health and welfare fields, the word is now everywhere — Business in the Community, community architecture, community development, community arts, community radio, community service, even community charge. The popularity of the term has tended to obscure rather than clarify its meaning. Amongst the confusion, however, there is agreement that 'community' can refer both to the population of a particular geographical area, the 'territorial community', or to people who share in common something other than physical proximity. (The discussion in this section draws heavily upon Willmott 1989.)

In the first usage, the territorial community can be as small as a few streets or as large as a nation (or even several nations, like the European Community). For the second usage, the term 'interest community' has been adopted. What is shared is more than 'interest', in simple terms it is likely to involve characteristics as varied as ethnicity, language, religion, profession, occupation, even sexual propensity, or may involve a common physical or mental condition, or social problem. The two concepts are not mutually exclusive, but they are often not coterminous. A territory may contain several interest communities; and interest communities can also be widely geographically dispersed across territorial boundaries.

Beyond these two dimensions, however, there is a third. People sometimes, but by no means always, feel a sense of identity, of common membership, with others living in the same area, notwithstanding their differences of interest. 'Community' is also used in this sense, to refer to sentiment, or feelings, and to social bonds and patterns of behaviour which create structures of association distinguishing one community from another. This has been called an 'attachment community' — a function of the extent and density of social relationships, and of perceptions, of identity with a place or solidarity with one's neighbours.

By no means all territorial communities, however, are necessarily attachment communities. Indeed the distinction has the important function of drawing attention to the potential problems when 'community' is used indiscriminately to justify a particular initiative or point of view, or to raise emotions for commercial or political ends. For this reason some social research has avoided the term, finding it too vague and emotive a basis for scientific method.

There are also contrasting views about the role of 'community', in this third sense of attachment, in modern societies such as Britain. On the one hand, many social and economic trends have acted to disperse traditional communities. With economic growth and increased educational opportunity, there is greater choice available to individuals about where to live, where to work and with whom to mix. Many people belong to dispersed kinship and friendship networks of great significance which are nonetheless widely geographically dispersed. Modern transport, especially the private car, modern communications, increased leisure time and rising personal wealth have all worked against the locality.

On the other hand, research also suggests that there are factors pointing the other way; some current trends are tending to strengthen local ties. For example, the proportion of older people in the population is increasing, and they are likely to spend more time in their immediate locality than younger people. Among the working population, 'stickiness' in the housing market, coupled with substantial inter-regional price differences, may have reduced mobility, especially when coupled with an increasing number of two-career households, which tend to restrict unilateral moves. Unemployment, early retirement, and the increase in self-employment and small firms have also led to other people of working age tending to emphasise the locality. It has therefore been argued by some commentators that such changes have served to reinforce people's need for local identity and that there is a 'widespread wish to live in a knowable community' (Bagguley *et al.* 1989).

It is a truism that the impact of these changes has varied from area to area. Some places are attachment communities to a greater degree than others. In 1967, when a national survey of this issue was last undertaken, nearly 4 people out of every 5 reported some feeling of attachment to their local area. Subsequent smaller and more localised surveys have mostly produced a similar reponse, except in inner-city areas, where the proportion feeling a sense of local attachment tended to be much lower.

This suggests that local identity remains relevant in today's society, but is not the dominant story of people's lives as it once was. Most people now have much more choice about whether, and how much, they will participate in their community. It is possible in today's society to find 'traditional' communities, displaying long residence, local kinship, and strong local association, alongside 'new' communities, of relatively recent origin, based more upon participation in locally based organisations reflecting shared aims and interests. Reflecting this, the research evidence (Willmott 1989) suggests that places are likely to be strong attachment communities when there is a mix of both 'traditional' and 'new' community features, for example:

- *there has been relative population stability;*
- *kin live in the area;*
- *many people work in a local industry;*
- *many people are alike in social class and income, or share membership of a particular minority group;*
- *there are many locally-based organisations;*
- *a large proportion of people have the skills and inclination to build local relationships and value their importance;*
- *there is some external threat against which people join together;*
- *physical geography encourages meeting among community members and creates a sense of separation from others 'outside';*
- *a place is particularly isolated.*

What then is the significance of 'community' for the future structure of local government? It would be wrong for the review to approach its task with a utopian notion of a Britain consisting of a mosaic of readily identifiable, harmonious local communities, around which new political and administrative entities may be conveniently structured. The pattern of modern living is more complex, and in consequence the pattern of local attachment is too variable. Furthermore, people living in the same place will not always want the same things; rather, different 'interest communities' are more likely to have divergent views of the need and priority. For example, local planning controversies frequently centre upon 'development' versus 'conservation' issues.

In a democratic and pluralistic society, such conflicts are mediated primarily through the political system. Local government structures must enable people within an area, however defined, to articulate and agree upon a 'commonwealth' of interest. In this sense, local government must be able to transcend simple locality. Political processes, however, are undoubtedly facilitated where people are able to feel a sense of attachment to government bodies as the expression of a wider identity, whether at local, national, or even international level.

Particularly where administrative units have been in place for a long time, or where there are strong economic or cultural ties, it is possible to define and reinforce a common identity, beyond the immediate locality, with which people can identify despite differences of opinion and conflicting interests. Where people would otherwise be rather vague about the boundaries of 'their' community, administrative territories may provide ready-made definitions, with their own history and other social and cultural associations. This may be partly why attempts to alter administrative boundaries frequently inspire very strong local opposition.

Against the background of a complex economic, social, and emotional geography, it will be the task of the review to create wherever possible an interdependence of 'community' and locality, through an appropriate local government structure. To do so, the review will need to test whether existing or proposed administrative territories compel attachment from those living within them, in such a way as to develop an active and robust local democracy reinforced by a genuine sense of 'community'. The above discussion suggests that factors reinforcing a strong sense of community are likely to be:

- *continuity of administration;*
- *administrative boundaries closely linked with physical geography;*
- *administrative boundaries closely linked with economic geography;*

- *active social organisation, demonstrating strong patterns of informal and formal association;*
- *physical environment, culture, folklore and myth constituting a shared heritage.*

The review cannot expect comprehensively to draw boundaries which once and for all define cohesive communities. Calling a locality a 'community' does not necessarily make it one. The factors above may not all be present, or may point in different directions. In such circumstances, the system of local government faces the challenge of mobilising 'community' through managerial and political mechanisms such as organisational decentralisation, local consultation, and area enfranchisement and involvement in political decision-making. The development of structures and mechanisms enabling such mobilisation is likewise a key test of local government's ability to respond to diverse and changing configurations of 'community'.

Size, scale and services

During the twentieth century British local authorities have tended to increase in size. Recent years, however, have seen something of a reaction against big organisations, whether in the public or private sectors. Trends in structural fashion are just as influential in determining organisational design as more objective considerations: 'Paris has its salons of haute couture; likewise New York has its offices of haute structure' (Mintzberg 1983). The current fashion is to denigrate large size as 'remote and unresponsive'. Prejudice aside, there are theoretical arguments for both smaller and larger authorities.

Proponents of small scale argue that it:

- facilitates better understanding of political issues and greater familiarity with (and therefore increased control by) elected representatives;
- increases the opportunities for individuals to become involved in the political process;
- makes it easier to reflect the wishes of inhabitants;
- provides a more effective focus on local issues;
- allows a more direct relationship between decisions on expenditure and the revenue required to finance it;
- by increasing the number of local authorities, promotes greater variety in the provision of goods and services, and therefore allows a wider choice for the consumer/elector (assuming his readiness to relocate wherever the packages of taxes and services best suits his preferences).

Proponents of large scale argue that it:

- allows the achievement of economies of scale in service delivery and promotes more effective purchasing where services are provided by outside contract;
- offers responsibility and opportunity more attractive to higher quality elected members and staff;
- allows specialised facilities and resources to be provided economically;
- by reducing the number of local authorities, internalises otherwise complex decisions requiring the balance of competing interests, reduces frictions caused by boundary problems, and thereby reduces costs;
- provides a more effective focus on strategic issues;
- facilitates redistributive policies, whether initiated by local government itself or by central government;
- enables greater financial flexibility and stability in managing fluctuating revenues and costs;
- simplifies and reduces the transaction costs of relationships with central government, business, and other bodies;
- more readily balances the power of central government.

Over the years, however, there has been little conclusive empirical evidence about the advantages of larger or smaller size as such. For example, a review of evidence across Europe, the UK and the USA in 1982 (Newton 1982) concluded first that any conclusion about the relationship between size, effectiveness and democracy must be tentative, because of the lack of hard information; second, that authorities of different sizes, whether urban or rural, do not differ by more than a small amount, if they differ at all, on many measures of functional effectiveness and democracy, and may have advantages in both respects; and third, that size is largely irrelevant in any case to many aspects of functional effectiveness and democracy. Indeed, the preoccupation with the virtues of small size was attributed to over-romanticism and wishful thinking. In practice, therefore, variation in standards and styles of management and service delivery may outweigh the impact of any theoretical differences associated with size as such.

The discussion is also affected by arguments based on the different perspective of particular services, as other chapters in this book make clear. When the Redcliffe–Maud Commission reviewed findings of reports on local government services in relation to the size of unit necessary for effective service delivery, they found that 'the general drift . . . of most reports has been towards larger units . . . (though) the sizes recommended were (not) of the same order' but they also drew attention to the difficulty they had found in determining an optimum size for all services. A similar, but more recent, broadly based review by

INLOGOV (Davey *et al.* 1986) concluded that:

> ... the range of functions that local government performs creates different and conflicting needs on size ... There is obviously a need for authorities to be big and small in their operation at the same time, to enable large area planning and closeness to the community to be maintained simultaneously.

Other chapters in this book consider the issue of size, or scale, in more depth from a policy perspective in relation to the major services for which local government is responsible. But experience suggests that tension across and between the requirements and circumstances of different services is inevitable. Consequently, there is unlikely to be a single easy answer to the question of scale. Theoretical arguments require an ideologically oriented choice between promoting the virtues of equity or stressing the importance of authorities competing with one another to provide services most cheaply. If political issues are avoided, the arguments seem to suggest a dichotomy between the achievement of cost-effectiveness or local responsiveness, yet it is obvious that local government must achieve both. Empirical evidence, meanwhile, is inconclusive.

Progress will only be made if the review avoids the use of a criterion based on a simple statement of size (measured by population) as a principal determinant of structure, and instead takes an open-minded approach, sensitive to the circumstances of different areas and to the different issues raised by different services. In general, issues of style, competence and flexibility to respond in different ways according to need are likely to be more important in practice. Chapter 2 drew attention to the development of a new set of 'enabling' attributes for local authorities:

- the exercise of economic leverage, taking into account the different cost structures of different services, so as to secure the most cost-effective means of service delivery, whether direct or indirect;
- responsiveness to the complexity and diversity of local communities through decentralised management and participative decision-making processes;
- recognition of different types of need, through processes and mechanisms which allow either a localised or a more aggregated approach, depending upon the requirement, and through the grouping together of key political and professional competencies;
- the ability to formulate and implement a credible and effective policy response, based on extensive inter-agency working integrating a strategic view with local circumstances and experience, across the range of policy issues facing local government, whether small or large in scale and impact.

What these attributes require are structures able to demonstrate both a truly strategic and genuinely local capability. They do not dictate a particular pattern in terms of numbers of tiers or size of authority, though they present a demanding test for any proposed structure, including the present one. Though a two tier structure combines both smaller and larger areas, making the most of this combination requires the two tiers to work closely together, and this is not always achievable. In a unitary structure, smaller authorities would need to develop mechanisms for effective joint working on a wide range of strategic issues. Here the difficulty is that joint bodies have a bad reputation (Flynn and Leach 1984). Experience in the metropolitan areas has largely confirmed the difficulties inherent in joint arrangements through lack of accountability.

Larger unitary authorities, on the other hand, would need to develop mechanisms for encouraging active participation at the most local level, as suggested in Chapter 8. The old criterion of size therefore needs to be replaced by a new 'enabling' criterion for structures aiming for the best combination of 'bigness' and 'smallness', and which combine political and economic 'clout' with an effective community-based response, so as to match the particular circumstances of each area.

Changing relationships

The history of local government since the term was first coined has reflected shifting relationships with central government, traced in Chapter 1. Much of the debate about local government structure is still seen predominantly in terms of this relationship, whether in the context of purpose, functions or finance. It would be unrealistic to expect this to change significantly; indeed, the nature of the relationship is of fundamental constitutional importance.

However, the review should recognise that concentrating on relations with central government is a one-dimensional view of local government's place in an increasingly multi-dimensional system of government. First, it reflects a preoccupation with local government's role purely as an agency for decentralised administration of particular tasks. Increasingly, the shift to the enabling style is emphasising that local government also simultaneously acts as the expression of local communities coming together to fulfil commonly perceived purposes and needs.

Second, this dual role — as government agent and community voice — is itself changing. At one end of the spectrum is the growing influence of the European Community and an increasingly complex policy environment in many fields. At the other is a recognition that there is a need to 'empower' local communities, and through them, the individual, through decentralised management structures, a new orientation towards the 'customer', and new relationships with the most local level of authorities at parish, town and community council level.

In the past, the administrative and managerial interests of central government have been seen in terms of reducing the number of agencies with whom it deals locally and creating bodies able to exercise delegated policy and executive authority across a wide range of functions, within a national framework. Organisational theorists have pointed to these arguments as the parallels in the public sector to divisionalisation in the corporate sector (notwithstanding the role of locally elected representatives with independent mandates). Politically, it has also been argued that a proliferation of small authorities would be likely to lead to the removal of significant functions from local government altogether to other special-purpose bodies, or, at minimum, to substantially increased levels of inspection and control to ensure satisfactory standards of performance were achieved.

The range of functions for which local government is responsible, and the policy framework which determines the nature of those responsibilities, is perpetually changing, as other chapters in this book indicate. The division of labour between different levels of government at any one time and in any one area is the result of many complex factors, which the present review will have to balance against each other, as its predecessors had to do. Increasingly, however, there is a recognition that the relationship between 'higher' and 'lower' authorities in a system of government, or between the core and the periphery of an organisation, should be guided in general by the principle of 'subsidiarity', which is concerned with the devolution of power to the most appropriate lower level, and lays down that the requirement for depriving a lower level of power must be the proof that it is not capable of meeting any need in question. The principle also presumes that it is in the general interest for higher levels to support lower levels to enable them to fulfil their responsibility.

Subsidiarity is often used at national levels within the European Community to protect national sovereignty against the extension of Community competence. But it applies equally to the relationship between central and local government. Greater emphasis in Europe upon the role of sub-national government in the Community's counsels and as a key policy agent in evening up the economic 'playing field' will create a new counterpoise to the old debate about central–local relations, and require new competencies from local government to demonstrate capability in meeting new needs (see Chapter 7).

Local government's role is expanding and becoming more complex. It requires a high degree of political, economic and professional leverage, and an increasing portfolio of skills. Local authorities are no longer self-sufficient. They work in partnerships with many different bodies, varying widely in size and style. Above all they must increasingly be capable of flexible response: strategic issues require a strategic approach, highly localised issues require a local approach, many issues require both. The principle of subsidiarity sets a demanding test for proposed structures. Responsibility to act must be aligned with competence to perform, across the full range of needs for which local government provides, and across the full spectrum of relationships. It will be essential for the review to consider what structures will best be able to deliver an effective service to the many bodies with whom local government has to work — other public agencies, the private sector, voluntary groups, local communities — and central government itself. Weak, ineffectual and moribund local authorities are in no-one's real interests.

Conclusion

This chapter has reviewed the background of previous attempts at local government reform and has singled out some key themes which remain highly relevant to the debate today. Based on this discussion, the following represent a set of key criteria, as part of a general framework for the forthcoming review, against which proposed structures may be evaluated:

Changing living and working patterns

- Does the proposed structure satisfactorily provide for a strategic response to areas forming a well-established and coherent social and economic whole?
- Does it equally provide for areas already exhibiting, or likely to undergo, rapid change in settlement patterns?

Sense of community identity

- Do proposed administrative units and boundaries provide a clear identity able to reinforce a sense of 'community', through the influence of any or all of the following?

  — continuity of administration;
  — administrative boundaries closely linked with physical geography;
  — administrative boundaries closely linked with economic geography;
  — active social organisation, demonstrating strong patterns of informal and formal association;

— physical environment, culture, folklore and myth constituting a shared heritage.

● Where sense of 'community' is weak or under-developed, do proposed structures enable the future development of community feeling and a sense of attachment, through decentralised management, local consultation and local area enfranchisement?

Style, competence and relationships

● Do proposals allow for the achievement of both 'bigness' and 'smallness' through the development of enabling attributes so as to demonstrate both a truly strategic and genuinely local capability?
● Do proposals conform with the principle of subsidiarity, and align responsibility to act with competence to perform across the full range of needs for which local government provides, and across the full spectrum of relationships?

This review is the latest in a long line to address the question of local government reform. Views on structure are as divided as ever, whilst the tasks local government has to carry out have become increasingly complex. For the first time, however, there is no presumption of uniformity, notwithstanding the Government's stated preference for the unitary model. There need be no search for a single right answer. Instead there is the potential for building a diverse and flexible structure which can accommodate change where it is needed, simultaneously strengthening the system of local government as a whole. It is essential that the review takes an independent approach, viewing the circumstances of each area of the country without prejudice to others. Only then can the resulting structure have the potential to match the needs of the people it is designed to serve.

References

Bagguley, P. *et al.* (1989) in Cooke, P. (ed.) *Localities: The Changing Face of Urban Britain* quoted in Gyford, 1991.

Byrne, T. (1990) *Local Government in Britain*, 5th Edition.

CIPFA (1992) *Finance and General Statistics 1991–92*.

Davey, K. *et al.* (1986) *The Future Role and Organisation of Local Government* INLOGOV.

Flynn, N. and Leach, S. (1984) *Joint Boards and Joint Committees: an Evaluation* INLOGOV.

Gyford, J. (1991) *Does Place Matter? Locality and Local Democracy* Belgrave Papers No 3.

HMG (1971) *Local Government in England, Government Proposals for Reorganisation*, Command 4584, HMSO.

Lock, D. (1991) 'Future Definitive', RTPI Conference.

Mintzberg, H. (1983) *Structure in Fives: Designing Effective Organisations* Prentice-Hall International.

Newton, K. (1982) 'Is small really so beautiful? Is big really so ugly? Size, effectiveness and democracy' *Local Government, Political Studies* **XXX**, No 2.

Steeley, G. (1990) 'Aegean Cities' *Town & Country Planning*.

Willmott, P. (1989) *Community Initiatives: Patterns and Prospects*, Policy Studies Institute.

15   Conclusion: consent upon a sure foundation. The future structure of local government

When we mean to build,
We first survey the plot, then draw the model,
And, when we see the figure of the house,
Then must we rate the cost of the erection;
Which, if we find outweighs ability,
What do we then,but draw anew the model
In fewer offices, or, at least, desist
To build at all? Much more, in this great work
(Which is, almost, to pluck a kingdom down,
And set another up) should we survey
The plot of situation, and the model;
Consent upon a sure foundation;
Question surveyors, know our own estate,
How able such a work to undergo . . .

(Henry IV, Part II, Shakespeare)

Introduction

Previous chapters in this book have examined the key issues of public policy which provide the background to the review of local government structure and have identified the factors most relevant to determining future structure. It remains to draw the threads together and present some conclusions about the form future structure should take.

The Government has promised a far-reaching review, 'the most radical this century', to simplify structure, assess functions, increase accountability, improve efficiency, reform finance, and 'give local government back to local people' (Hansard 1991). Specifically, it has been asserted that the present structure in some areas is not accepted by local communities, and more generally, that a two tier system causes confusion about which authority is responsible for which service, or for expenditure, and hinders effective coordination of related services (DoE 1991).

Some outcomes of the Government's review are already evident.

The finance system is to be reformed by replacing the Community Charge with the Council Tax. Further improvements to local government's efficiency are to be encouraged by the extension of compulsory competitive tendering. The key outstanding issues for the review are what can be done to improve the accountability of, and increase empathy with, local government.

The review is proceeding on the basis that structural reform, specifically a move to unitary authorities, may provide the answer. The Local Government Act 1992 s.13(5) requires the Local Government Commission for England to review the structure, electoral arrangements and boundaries of local government having regard to the needs to reflect the identities and interests of local communities and to secure effective and convenient local government. In Wales, the Secretary of State is conducting his own review without the benefit of a Commission. But the British system of local government has been constantly thought to be in need of change, although disagreement about the nature of such change has been equally constant. No organisational structure is likely to be problem-free or to command unanimous support. The key to successful organisation structures is to fit form to function. Hence, the case for change rests upon whether any proposed change will secure sufficiently worthwhile improvements for local communities and the services they receive to justify the inevitable costs and disruption. The need to justify structural change rigorously is especially important given that local government already faces considerable pressures to develop new working practices and to establish relationships with new partners.

But the limited agenda set by the review process should not be allowed to go by default. Local government need not be merely a passive recipient of a prescribed future. Its vision of its role, and of the systems best suited to enable that role to be fulfilled, is as legitimate as that handed down by central government. From the perspective of local government, the review has not yet shown signs of integrating consideration of local government's purpose, functions, financing, internal management, political character, and structure. A clear statement is needed by central government accepting the contemporary democratic validity of the local mandate and recognising the need for tolerance of political difference at national and local levels. The UK government should confirm the position of local government, for example by endorsing the European Charter of Local Self-Government. Local government's record of innovation, for example in such developments as local management of schools, customer charters, and contracting out service delivery, where the best local authorities pioneered the way well before central government appropriated the ideas and approaches, deserves to be better known.

These considerations matter because unless such fundamental points are considered, the review will not only fail to live up to its advance billing of being 'the most radical this century', but will run the risk that its conclusions will be as narrow and limited as its premises. Structural form, function, and finance are interactive and interdependent: to consider any one of these in isolation will lead to a partial and distorted view of the whole. More fundamentally still, it is difficult to design an organisation without deciding first what objectives and purposes it should aim to achieve.

This chapter, therefore, ranges widely in examining key issues of public policy. It considers not only the tasks that local government will be called upon to perform but also the wider issues which it will have to confront. The analyses of the requirements local government must meet now and in the future lead to new parameters for the type of local authority most likely to fulfil effectively the future role of local government, and to suggestions as to the structure best suited to meeting these needs.

Responding to change

The 'enabling' authority

The challenges facing local government are causing local authorities themselves to question traditional assumptions underlying the way they have operated in the past, and to initiate significant changes in style, structures, and methods of management. Discussion of these changes has been dominated by the concept of the 'enabling' authority. What characterises 'enabling' is not any particular political orthodoxy, but the development of more flexible ways of operating to meet the needs of local communities in the most effective and efficient way (Chapter 2). Some consistent signs of this changing style are merging as good practice:

- a strategic approach to key policy issues and changing needs of local communities;
- a focus on determining the most effective response to those needs, whether directly or through external providers;
- an emphasis on clear objectives and standards, and on monitoring performance against them;
- investment in building long-term relationships with other agencies and organisations;
- an innovative approach to influencing, interpreting and implementing the regulatory framework in the interests of local communities;
- closer links with the public which encourage improved access to facilities, and greater involvement in all levels of decision-making.

'Enabling' is not an answer to structure, but an input. It implies authorities with a new set of attributes:

- the ability to exercise economic leverage to secure the most cost-effective means of service delivery, whether direct or indirect;
- the flexibility to respond to the complexity and diversity of local communities through decentralised management and participative decision-making processes;
- the recognition of different types of needs through a varied range of processes and mechanisms, and by grouping together key political and professional competencies;
- the formulation and implementation of policy responses based on extensive inter-agency working across the range of issues facing local government.

Responsiveness has gained a new significance with the emergence of the 'Charter' movement. The Citizen's Charter will establish a quasi-contractual relationship between the individual and the local authority. Individuals will effectively be guaranteed certain rights of service with strengthened complaints procedures and compensation mechanisms.

'Enabling' also typically means a good deal of change internally in working relationships between members and officers, in departmental structures and systems, and in skills and working style. The role will facilitate more strategic political management and encourage authorities to adopt styles of management which focus on policy making and performance monitoring. It is essential that the future structure fully facilitates the enabling style, and further encourages local authorities in the changes they are already making.

The final dimension

As the Government has recognised, structural reform is only one aspect of equipping local government to respond to the challenges it faces. Structure, function and finance are interdependent. Given that one of the reasons for the current review of local government was the failure of the Community Charge to gain public acceptance, the review needs to give full consideration to the links between local finance and local authority area and structure. If these links are not recognised, there are three potential dangers.

First, authorities covering limited areas would show wide variations in resource base and spending need, and so would be likely to have widely varying levels of local tax. Authorities covering wider areas are likely to be more homogeneous in resource base, spending need and local tax rate. Although the central government grant system is intended to compensate for inequalities in resource base and spending need, it has proved difficult in practice for it to operate in a way which commands general acceptance. Its insensitivity contributes to financial volatility, and the impact is more marked in smaller authorities, which can be faced with major problems as a consequence of grant loss.

Second, the smaller the authority, and the lower its budget, the greater is the likely impact of even marginal year-on-year fluctuations in its grant level or in its spending, and the more marked the variation in its local tax rate. Conversely, the larger the authority and its budget, the more robust its financial base and the greater the likelihood that it will be able to smooth out its tax rate year-on-year.

The third danger arises where two tiers of government share the same locally determined tax instrument, currently the Community Charge but, in due course, the Council Tax. In such circumstances, local taxpayers find it difficult to relate the services received to their local tax payments. This weakens accountability and implies that, so long as local government has access to only one tax instrument, a unitary system of local government would be better suited to promoting accountability. An alternative is to introduce a system of billing which distinguishes clearly the cost to the taxpayer of the different tiers of government.

The issue of finance is, therefore, of great significance in indicating the scale of any new authorities. Differences between local authorities' resource base and spending need depend to a considerable extent on the area they cover. A robust and workable system of local government finance, without extreme and unacceptable variations in local tax rates between areas and year-on-year, requires larger rather than smaller authorities.

Here the review needs to take into consideration two wider issues. First, the successful introduction of the Council Tax should not be jeopardised by a review undertaken in isolation from the issues of scale and structure outlined above. And second, the longer-term interests of local government are in securing a locally-determined revenue source which is both acceptable to the public and sufficient to give authorities true accountability. The financial perspective is, therefore, vital to the success of the review in creating a dynamic system of local government for the future.

Towards a new model

It is the prerogative of each generation to see the problems it faces as unique, of unparalleled importance and unprecedented complexity. In 1969, the Redcliffe–Maud Commission found that (HMG 1969):

> Scientific discovery and industrial progress are reshaping the life and work of the people of England faster and more fundamentally than in any previous period of our history. The material on which local gov-

ernment has to work, the situations that confront it, the patterns of settlement in town and country, have never stood still; but in recent years and in the years ahead they have altered and will alter in a quite new way.

A generation later, the rate of change has not lessened. Local government, like any other organisation, must be structured with a view to managing for the future.

Local government faces major challenges. It must work to create a new consensus about its value in an active democracy. It must respond to an increasingly multi-dimensional system of government and, at the same time, to the need to 'empower' local communities and safeguard the rights of the individual to a good quality of service. It must bind together community and locality against a background of diverse and rapidly changing settlement patterns, and a varying sense of local identity. It must address major policy issues, significant internal changes in several key functions, and new modes of operation.

At a more detailed level, all local government activities display specific issues and problems to be addressed and overcome. But there are some common themes. Local authorities of the future will have to manage increasing complexity, in the policy issues themselves, the operational approaches required to respond, and the institutional framework of implementation. This will require them to:

- consult regularly and effectively with local communities and with individuals about their needs and preferences;
- participate effectively in the development of policy and the regulatory framework, both nationally and in the EC, especially in the areas of environmental protection and economic development;
- develop integrated policies and strategies across traditional service and functional boundaries, especially in the economic and environmental fields, but also increasingly in social policy;
- mediate between and, where possible, integrate the strategic view and local interests, in a way which is transparent and provides accountability to the different interests involved;
- make difficult choices between competing priorities so as to target limited resources in a way which improves efficiency and value for money;
- work in partnership with other public, private and voluntary organisations to determine priorities, to decide on the approach to implementation, and to establish a contractual relationship for services supplied, where appropriate;
- integrate specialist capabilities, in diverse technical and professional fields, within a multi-disciplinary and multi-agency working environment;

- monitor service performance to ensure satisfactory quality.

Responding to these challenges will require local government to adopt new styles and approaches.

The review will need to consider whether local government's performance in meeting these challenges would be improved by a new structure. The Local Government Commission for England must 'weigh the costs of change, including transitional costs, against the benefits of its proposals' (DoE 1992b). The case for change from the present structure, therefore, requires a demonstration that the expected benefits exceed the likely costs. The principal question, therefore, is whether the case for a change in local government structure has been made. It can be considered in three parts:

- Are unitary authorities generally to be preferred to the present two-tier structure of counties and districts?
- If so, what are the desirable characteristics of future unitary authorities?
- Would there be advantage in allowing for different structural solutions in different places?

Unitary authorities

Proponents of unitary authorities argue that:

- they enable a comprehensive assessment of the needs and problems of the local community as a whole, and so can better identify and respond to local needs;
- they make for clearer accountability for decisions and spending;
- they are better able to develop a coordinated strategic framework and inter-service coordination;
- they simplify partnerships with other organisations;
- they are more credible to higher levels of government because they can speak with one voice about their area;
- they have greater flexibility to switch resources between competing priorities;
- they reduce the costs of local government by removing duplication.

There would be advantages from a unitary structure in some areas of local government activity, especially:

- to develop a comprehensive response to environmental issues;
- to assist coordination and integration of policy and operations in relation to community care and housing, and to enable a more strategic approach to be taken to housing demand;
- to improve coordination, communication, and consistency of regulation of business;

- to facilitate the achievement of critical mass across all functions in order to improve economic leverage.

Against the prevailing orthodoxy of unitaryism, advocates of multi-tier systems argue that:

- separate authorities provide democratic pluralism and 'checks and balances', especially in matters such as planning;
- separate authorities with a clear scale difference are an effective way of meeting needs, providing services and articulating views at a very local level, and of determining strategy and representing communities at a broader level;
- evidence of popular dissatisfaction with the structure of local government (as opposed to the names of councils and their territorial areas) is limited;
- separate authorities reflect the twin communities which most people identify with: first their village, town or neighbourhood, and second their county, major city or sub-regional area;
- 'unitary' is a misnomer because smaller 'unitary' authorities would require joint arrangements for major services and strategic functions, while larger 'unitary' authorities generally implement devolved administrative arrangements to increase local responsiveness, so any 'unitary' system is actually a disguised two-tier one;
- in most countries which have some form of local government, there is more than one tier: it is not clear that Britain is a special case.

There is thus a case to consider for both 'unitary' and 'multi-tier' structures. This is hardly surprising given the complexity of the issues set out in this paper. It will be for the Commission to consider whether, in any area, the benefits of a move to a unitary structure outweigh the costs and disruption created by change. In many cases, a unitary structure would appear to offer significant advantages over the existing structure of local government, particularly in terms of greater cost-effectiveness. A key issue, therefore, is the characteristics of the unitary authorities most likely to realise such benefits.

Desirable characteristics

It has recently been observed that (Drucker 1992):

> Corporate size will by the end of the coming decade have become a strategic decision. Neither 'big is better' nor 'small is beautiful' makes much sense. Neither elephant nor mouse nor butterfly is, in itself, 'better' or 'more beautiful'. Size follows function.

In this review, function is reflected in the requirement for structure to produce 'effective and convenient local government'. This means authorities which combine strategic capability with being close to local communities. Strategic capability will be secured by authorities which:

- have substantial policy and decision-making scope and the ability to integrate distinct services and functions;
- realise economies of scale in skills, information, and facilities, whether through purchasing or direct provision;
- identify and exploit opportunities for partnerships and joint ventures with other organisations in the public, private and voluntary sectors;
- have a resource base large enough to allow flexibility in resource deployment in response to changing needs and to sustain specialist skills in an economic way;
- maintain a policy dialogue credibly with other local, national and international agencies.

These characteristics are most likely to occur in larger authorities.

Closeness to local communities, and reflection of their identities and interests, will follow from:

- an awareness of individual and community needs, sustained by regular communication with local communities and a high degree of local presence;
- a detailed understanding of local economic and environmental circumstances;
- decentralised management and political structures and processes;
- community involvement in policy decisions and service delivery.

Larger authorities would have considerable scope and a direct interest in working with parish and town councils or developing area structures to provide very local services and representation.

From the point of view of local authority services, structure should be based on authorities of sufficient scale (Chapter 9):

- to sustain an active 'enabling' role in education and to maximise added value and cost-effectiveness;
- to bring together disparate interests into a coherent strategy for economic development in a highly competitive environment;
- to create new opportunities to work with housing providers and central government to respond to the emerging need for growth in social housing;
- to maintain effective local relationships at strategic and operational levels with the providers of protective services;
- to ensure that local government is capable of working effectively with national and EC institutions;
- to ensure consistent and effective implementation of new social services legislation;
- to develop strategic solutions to environmental problems;

- to achieve the most cost-effective structure in the regulatory field;
- to realise the management and administrative economies available, in particular by exploiting IT effectively.

Larger authorities would also avoid the problems of joint arrangements of any kind. Joint arrangements are not as effective or as accountable as individual authorities. Any structure which relies on joint arrangements must be held to have failed the basic test of clarifying accountability for spending and services.

Overall, therefore, larger unitary authorities would be best placed to provide effective local government and to reflect the identities and interests of local communities.

Uniformity

An important issue is whether the review needs to create a uniform structure. The history of local government reform suggests that no universal blueprint for change will work. The Guidance to the Local Government Commission recognises this and recommends in-depth analysis of local situations and needs so that solutions which meet local circumstances and command a high degree of local consent are identified.

Such an approach has the advantage of enabling different areas to have unitary or multi-tier structures depending on what factors are seen to be most important locally. Furthermore, such a system ought to retain the capacity to evolve to meet changing local circumstances. Creating a self-adjusting mechanism of this kind would help to break away from the artificial rigidities of choice between one national structure and another which have bedevilled debate about local government for nearly fifty years.

The retention of a two-tier structure of local government will depend on no clear benefits being demonstrable for a change to a unitary system, in the terms of the twin criteria for the review. Any local case for the retention of the two-tier system will be strengthened if it can demonstrate:

- *a majority of popular support;*
- *a large degree of inter-authority agreement;*
- *the ability to adapt to meet likely future demands.*

The two-tier system stands as the benchmark against which options for change should be tested.

Conclusion

What structure is most likely to present a 'sure foundation' for local government in the future?

The history of local government reform suggests that there is no universally applicable structural blueprint which will work across all times and areas. If local government is to respond to dynamic circumstances, it will require a dynamic and flexible structure which can evolve to meet changing needs. The case for a universal and uniform pattern of unitary authorities is, therefore, not compelling.

The current debate is dominated by the choice between the rigidities of only two structural systems, the introduction of unitary authorities or the retention of the present multi-tier system. Neither is likely to be universally satisfactory, but allowing different areas to have either a unitary or a multi-tier system, depending on local factors and the costs of change, offers some valuable flexibility. Greater flexibility to adjust local government form and area to circumstances as they change locally, rather than waiting upon a national review when action may be needed in only limited areas, would be a substantial advance.

The Guidance to the Local Government Commission places the burden of proof of the merits of change on its proponents. In addition to demonstrating that the benefits of change will outweigh the costs, advocates of unitary authorities in any area will need to show that such authorities will be stable yet flexible, robust but responsive, strategic in competence but local in identity. Equally, those who favour the retention or modification of the present two-tier structure will need to show that concerns about clarity of accountability and cost-effectiveness can be answered.

The most advantageous combination of strategic capability and closeness to the community is likely to be achieved where unitary authorities are established, providing they are of sufficient scale to achieve strategic competence, if they embrace a commitment to the 'enabling' concept, and if they devolve managerial, service delivery and representational responsibilities in the spirit of subsidiarity and in partnership with other local bodies.

But it should not be overlooked that, whatever its structure, if local government is to preserve true vitality and engage local loyalties, it must be based on authorities with the qualities outlined above: stability combined with flexibility, robustness and responsiveness, strategic competence and local identity. The prospects for change would be most favourable if any new structure is based on a further evolution from the counties, which have historically shown the capacity to adapt flexibly to new circumstances while providing a stable base and constant local identity.

Local government's future vitality and effectiveness ultimately depend upon more than its structural framework. They require a climate of trust, commitment, and an underlying sense of purpose, deriving from a recognition of the legitimacy of political difference between central and local government, and the accommodation within national objectives of local diversity. Local government has a key role in the future in defining and creating a better system of government as a whole, for the balance between integration and diversity, a key issue in contemporary European politics, has to be struck afresh in every gener ation.

References

DoE (1991) *Local Government Review: The Structure of Local Government in England*, A Consultation Paper, HMSO.
DoE (1992a) *Parish and Town Councils in England: A Survey*, Public Sector Management Research Centre, Aston Business School, HMSO.
DoE (1992b) *Policy Guidance to the Local Government Commission for England* HMSO.
Drucker, P. F. (1992) *Managing for the Future* Butterworth-Heinemann.
HMG (1969) *Local Government Reform* Short Version of the Report of the Royal Commission on Local Government in England, Cmnd 4039, HMSO.
The Prime Minister (1991) *Hansard* 27 March 1991, Col. 973.